Truth Without Reconciliation

PENNSYLVANIA STUDIES IN HUMAN RIGHTS

Bert B. Lockwood, Jr., Series Editor

A complete list of books in the series
is available from the publisher.

Truth Without Reconciliation

A Human Rights History
of Ghana

Abena Ampofoa Asare

PENN

UNIVERSITY OF PENNSYLVANIA PRESS

PHILADELPHIA

Published by
University of Pennsylvania Press
Philadelphia, Pennsylvania 19104-4112
www.upenn.edu/pennpress

Printed in the United States of America on acid-free paper
1 3 5 7 9 10 8 6 4 2

Library of Congress Cataloging-in-Publication Data

Names: Asare, Abena Ampofoa, author.
Title: Truth without reconciliation: a human rights history of Ghana / Abena Ampofoa Asare.
Other titles: Pennsylvania studies in human rights.
Description: 1st edition. | Philadelphia: University of Pennsylvania Press, [2018] | Series:
    Pennsylvania studies in human rights | Includes bibliographical references and index.
Identifiers: LCCN 2017058290 | ISBN 9780812250398 (hardcover: alk. paper)
Subjects: LCSH: Human rights—Ghana—History. | Truth commissions—Ghana—History. |
    Reconciliation—Political aspects—Ghana. | Ghana—Politics and government—1979–2001.
Classification: LCC DT512.32 .A68 2018 | DDC 323.09667—dc23
LC record available at https://lccn.loc.gov/2017058290

For my family, especially my parents

CONTENTS

In 2007, when I located the records of Ghana's National Reconciliation Commission (NRC) at the University of Ghana's Balme Library, my access was limited and closely monitored. Although I could read these records and take notes, the library staff did not allow photocopies or digital reproductions; they kept a close eye on my progress. I wended my way somewhat haphazardly through the overstuffed boxes of files, stopping at times to close the folders and catch my breath. In those days, I would leave the Balme Library feeling disoriented. As I passed by the James Fort Prison, I would no longer look at the sea. Instead, I would stare at the building's small windows and imagine what it would be like to be detained there indefinitely. While shopping for cloth at Makola Market, a vision of the market aflame would flash before my eyes. When I rode the government transport bus, a sheen of sweat would cling to my back: What would I do if army men boarded the bus? What would I say? Reading the NRC stories day in, day out changed the geography and landscape of my Accra; the past seemed separated from the present by only the thinnest of cotton.

As part of the Ghanaian diaspora, I am no stranger to the country's political history. My own family's story of transatlantic migration in the 1980s is tied to the turbulent history of Ghana's birth and growing pains. However, the library documents described violence of a different magnitude and scope. Although I had heard stories of politicians detained behind prison walls, disappeared high court judges and public executions of former heads of state, I did not know about the taxi drivers, market traders, and security guards who entered and exited Nsawam Prison or Ussher Fort Prison without the fanfare or public regret bestowed on their better-known counterparts. The documents at Balme Library suggested that the trouble in Ghanaian history was both more devastating and more mundane than fixed flashpoints of egregious physical loss. Here, the road to destruction was broad. Violence did not begin with a single soldier named Jerry John Rawlings, but instead with years of grinding economic scarcity and obdurate government. The inability to pay school fees, joblessness, watching a child suffer because of lack of health care—Ghanaians also counted these as grievous wrongs that produced exile, family dissolution, and even death. Moreover, Jerry John Rawlings was only one of many national leaders who presided over the suffering of citizens. No political regime or leader emerged unscathed—not the visionary anti-colonialist Kwame Nkrumah, or the liberal jurist Kofi Abrefa Busia, or even then president John Agyekum Kufuor.

I assumed that the impact of these stories—the way they changed the ground on which I walked—was a factor of my distance, youth, and ignorance. As I began to talk with Ghanaian colleagues and family members about the contents of the NRC files, however, my own beginning assumptions were echoed back to me. "No one who was minding his own business was affected." "Only during the Rawlings years did people suffer like that." "As a peace-loving people, Ghanaians just allowed the soldiers to run roughshod over them." There was a disjuncture between the contents of the NRC folders and the public discussions about national political violence. This difference, the space between these representations of Ghana's past, emboldened me to write this book.

When I began, the library staff's concern about who might access the NRC files seemed out of place. After all, Ghanaians furnished these documents within a public history project. Why should the public then be kept away? Exposure was not an unexpected eventuality; it was central to the purpose of the NRC records. Looking back now, I understand much better the Balme Library staff's protectiveness, their desire to guard against the unknown futures of these documents. These are stories that should not be uncoupled from the logic of their production. Ghanaians entrusted their words and narratives to the commission as an act of hope. Individuals brought their bodies and voices to the NRC, sometimes borrowing money for transportation, standing in long lines, and defying illness, old age, and cynicism, because they believed this experiment would create something positive. Participating in the NRC was a means to an end. Some citizens came to set the story straight, to seek the government's help in sorting a land claim, or to request specific monetary remuneration and aid. Amid this diversity of purpose, the common ground is that the NRC participants willingly offered up versions of the past with the expectation that their lives might somehow be transformed.

Back in 2007, I tried to explain to the Balme Library staff that my intention was not to appropriate these documents, but to learn from them. In the years since, I have come to see the NRC records as an image, albeit imperfect, of the expanded political agora made possible when diverse individuals and communities speak—and someone is there to listen. I take the NRC documents seriously because within them, members of the Ghanaian community who rarely have a public platform insert their insights, complaints, and hopes into the historical record. The language, images, and logic of the NRC participants were central to my research process and analysis and I have, accordingly, made them central in the text. As truth and reconciliation commissions make their way around the world, they also generate new archives worthy of sustained study. I have benefited from the insight and courage reflected in these documents and I would encourage future researchers to seek out these sources. There is much more story to be told.

I am grateful to the library staff who allowed me to do this research without knowing exactly what the outcome would be and to the participants in Ghana's truth and reconciliation process who dreamed of a better future and dared to speak of the past.

Introduction

I happened to be in Accra in June 2005, not long after Ghana's National Reconciliation Commission (NRC) concluded its public hearings. I watched, mesmerized, as Ghana (colloquially called the Black Star nation because of its pioneering role in African independence) publicly reckoned with its passage through a violent twentieth century. I was initially skeptical of Ghana's decision to embrace a truth and reconciliation commission (TRC). As "official, temporary, non-judicial fact-finding bodies" built on the premise that communities can escape history's undertow by investigating, revealing, mourning and redressing past violence, TRCs are stunning in their political optimism.[1] They are also complex instruments that consistently evade the expectations of historical revelation and political change embedded in their very name.[2] With Ghana facing a substantial national debt burden and government policies that pursue "growth without economic transformation," what could a toothless truth commission produce for Ghanaian people?[3]

The decision to join the growing community of African nations using TRCs to wade into the past was part of the competition between the country's two major political parties: the New Patriotic Party (NPP) and the National Democratic Congress (NDC). For the newly elected NPP, calling for a truth and reconciliation process christened its recent electoral success a moral victory on the order of the end of apartheid in South Africa or the defeat of Chile's Augusto Pinochet dictatorship. For the outgoing NDC, a Ghanaian truth commission was an attack on the person of Jerry John Rawlings, the dictator-cum-democrat whose authoritarian leadership (1979–2000) is, for better or worse, central to the story of Ghana's reconfiguration as one of Africa's hardiest electoral democracies.[4] In this arena, truth and reconciliation appeared to be political theater as usual. The NRC was expected to rattle the national skeletons again before laying them to rest; however, the past was not so easily buried.

In the transition from campaign promise to national reality the NRC became an unprecedented review of Ghanaian political history. In order to avoid allegations of partisan bias, Ghana's Parliament was compelled to broaden and extend the NRC mandate. Eventually, the commission was charged with recommending "appropriate redress for persons who have suffered any injury, hurt, damage, grievance, or who have in any other manner been adversely affected by violations and abuses of their human rights arising from activities or inactivities of public institutions or persons holding public office."[5] Moreover, the vast majority of the national history—the years from independence in 1957 to the democratic transition of 1992—was placed under investigation.

Although Ghana today is the quintessential African success story, political violence pockmarks the country's past. Civilian governments have left political dissidents to die behind bars, expelled thousands of migrants, purged the civil service, and jailed journalists. Military leaders have paraded disgraced politicians in cages through the capital, publicly executed former heads of state, and unleashed marauding soldiers on vulnerable citizens. On at least five separate occasions since independence, the Ghanaian army has intruded into the country's politics, each time declaring the utter brokenness of the political system. All of this fell under the NRC's expansive mandate and victim's stories were the guide through this turbulent past.

In 2005, while listening to portions of the NRC public hearings rebroadcast on the national news, the voices of the Ghanaian people stopped me in my tracks. To my ear, Ghana's history emerged as a vast field populated by thousands of individuals, each with her own troubles and desired futures. This was a version of Ghanaian history that I had yet to hear. The self-described victims included market women assaulted by soldiers, army men whose missing pensions rendered them unable to provide for their elderly relatives, and children left behind when a father crossed borders because of fear, hunger, or both. Human rights abuse included the brutality meted out to inmates by prison guards, the devastating pairing of high school fees that were too costly and jobs that were too scarce, and the lack of appropriate medical care at government hospitals. These stories were not easily corralled into a triumphalist transitional-justice narrative of violence vanquished and conflict overcome. They also did not fit easily into the framework of discretely separated perpetrators and victims. Soldiers were also casualties of state violence; prison guards reported the violence of the country's carceral institutions. These representations of political violence display the "contradictions and complexity of victim identity" and elude party lines.[6] What was the "appropriate redress" that the NRC would recommend in response to this multifarious and complex truth? What might these narratives of the suffering awaken in twenty-first-century Ghana?

Ghana's truth and reconciliation experiment involved a sequence of structured interactions between citizens, the government-appointed commission, and the state. Citizen complaints, articulated in written petitions and public testimony, would allow the NRC staff, led by nine esteemed commissioners, to recommend a course of action; subsequently, the government would respond. When I returned to Accra in August 2007 the NRC was decidedly over. Almost three years had passed since the end of public hearings and the submission of the National Reconciliation Commission Report (hereafter final report), and the government had made provisions for limited reparations payments. To the degree that the NRC still garnered public comment, the focus was on Rawlings's bombastic public testimony, or on whether the appointed commissioners acted objectively. The lasting image of the NRC was as a site of partisan contest, not citizen testimony. Even locating the thousands of pages of NRC petitions and supporting documents was difficult; the headquarters were closed and the records moved to an unknown location.[7]

The brief afterlife of a national TRC originally billed as a catalyst for individual, social, and national transformation seemed to confirm my earlier skepticism. Moreover, I began to doubt my own memory of the NRC. These stories had struck my ear as novel because they featured everyday Ghanaians—not the politicians, military men, traditional rulers, and elites of public record—as the agents, subjects, and objects of the national history. How had these kaleidoscopic narratives of Ghanaian people been overshadowed by a single story reducing national reconciliation to another site of partisan striving by political elites?

Still and all, I could not forget the vibrancy of the voices of Ghana's survivors. When I found the commission's documents stored at the University of Ghana's Balme Library, I immersed myself in the 4,240 petitions that Ghanaians brought to the NRC, eventually processing approximately 1,020 of these files. I also listened to digital recordings of the public hearings held in the Balme Library and in the Human Rights Archive at Duke University's David M. Rubenstein Rare Book and Manuscript Library. In the decade since beginning this research, I have come to believe that the stories called into being, preserved, and organized by the truth and reconciliation imperative are simultaneously the most valuable and the most frequently overlooked product of Ghana's NRC.

This national truth commission did not produce unimpeachable truths. Nor did it fix the country's politics. But it did lead to an unprecedented public accounting of Ghana's past, by Ghanaian people, at the turn of the twenty-first century. Although more than a decade has passed since the NRC began its work, the stories remain as glimpses of Ghanaians' political and historical consciousness. The testimonies and petitions banished to the stacks are more than partisan wrangling, more than sentimental catharsis, and more than the jockeying of citizens for scarce goods. Each of these assumptions—that the Ghana NRC was simply a place to cry, to lie, or to play politics—masks the richness of the stories therein. When the tour guides into the past are the self-described victims of the state's machinations, they fix the spotlight squarely on Ghana's people, the approximately twenty million human beings who survived the tumult of the first fifty years of postcolonial independence.

It has been said that until the lion writes history, tales of the hunt will always glorify the hunter. This study amends the proverb—until the gazelles, the weaver birds, the baobab trees, and even the tsetse flies write history, the story of the savannah will always be a tale of the hunt. The NRC stories teach us that when historical production is democratized, there is a fundamental shift in the subject and content of political history. In *Truth Without Reconciliation,* I hold the NRC records up to the light, turn them this way and that, and consider what was created and what was undone by Ghana's encounter with the TRC. In this public human rights review, participants shared stories about the moments that shattered their intimately held aspirations for self, family, and nation. Entering Ghanaian political history in this way, as a matter of particular moments, people, and places, ushers us past "big men" and political parties toward a meditation on the relationship between citizen and state in Ghana. How did diverse people experience the turbulence of the past half century? How did they survive? The NRC records create a people-centered narrative; Ghanaians locate national political turmoil within individual, family, and local histories of suffering. Against a backdrop where politicians, traditional rulers, and wealthy families have usually been at the center of the national politics, these citizen stories of harm across scales mark a shift in Ghana's public record.[8]

Beyond Ghanaian borders, these records also suggest new possibilities for the language and practices of international human rights that are utilized, domesticated, and transformed in local soil. Here, human rights victims are more than objects of pity or rescue, they are experts whose voices illuminate the dilemmas of poverty, inequality, violence, and injustice in Ghana. Critics, especially those sympathetic to the inequalities of the international political and economic order, challenge the moral solidity of human rights initiatives that reflect the imperatives, priorities, and epistemologies of powerful global actors.[9] Truth commissions that amplify and preserve citizen voices complicate this picture. This study asserts that the potential of human rights is not contained in a parade of sterile documents delineating abstract ideals but, instead, is hidden in the mouths of everyday people gripping tightly to human rights as a sturdy platform from which to narrate their past, present, and futures. Only as local communities breathe life into the hollowness of human rights—claiming it as a method of organizing people, a means to combat marginalization, and a language with which to debate the premises and content of political justice—does "rights talk" find roots and wings.[10] Below, I use concepts of archive, cacophony, and democracy to sketch the contours of Ghana's encounter with the truth and reconciliation commission.

The TRC Phenomenon

This is the conundrum from which this study began: How could a truth commission that drew out thousands of statements and petitions have such limited political impact? How could this remarkable public review so swiftly and effectively disappear? A sense of intertwined possibility and deficiency extends beyond the Ghana case and troubles the TRC phenomenon at large. In the past twenty-five years, thirteen (and counting) of Africa's fifty-four countries have used these quasi-judicial instruments to confront diverse experiences of historical violence.[11] The TRC has become "all but obligatory" in the effort to enshrine peace, democracy, and stability in the aftermath of conflict.[12] The United Nations, regional organizations like the African Union, and institutional donors champion and support these commissions as a matter of global policy.[13] Truth and reconciliation commissions are rooted in an ascendant international human rights framework and the part displays the contradictions of the whole.

TRCs capture the world's imagination by suggesting that alignment of the political and moral order is possible. If the Nuremberg trials anchored the principle of global accountability for atrocity, South Africa's TRC promised that the evils of modernity might yet be made whole.[14] It was, in the words of Archbishop Desmond Tutu, a "beacon of hope" for a "tired, disillusioned, cynical world hurting so frequently and so grievously."[15] By publicly condemning the devastation of apartheid and simultaneously safeguarding political stability, a "barbaric society" might "become minimally decent."[16] An element of magical thinking has always shadowed the TRC dream of formulaically substituting a ghastly past for a bright future. With the proliferation of commissions around the world, the gap between rhetoric and reality has begun to first yawn and then gape. A palpable whiff of disappointment has come to surround the truth commission ideal of extracting forgiveness, remorse, and political progress from the ashes of historical violence.

In the last years of the twentieth century, Michael Ignatieff quipped that the sum of a truth commission's power was simply to reduce the number of lies that circulate unchallenged in public. At the time, this notion was a corrective to the starry-eyed optimism holding that TRCs would battle impunity, knit together deeply divided political communities, heal and relieve victims, and establish definitive accounts of historical violence.[17] Two decades later, scholars and victims challenge even this minimalist vision of what TRCs may accomplish in South Africa and beyond.[18]

The supposed catharsis that victims of violence gain from TRC public testimony has proven elusive.[19] The Khulumani Support Group, a community of South African survivors of apartheid violence, perhaps put it best: "At the end of so much digging for the truth in the TRC so many people found themselves still bleeding from open wounds."[20] A number of empirical studies also challenge the assumption that TRCs always expand the public record; by commissioning truth, transitional justice instruments may actually construct silences.[21] Even the premise that TRCs guard against political impunity by levying a cost on leaders who oversee atrocity now seems naïve. The scenario in Liberia, where political elites condemned and dismissed a freshly-released TRC report, appears much more likely.[22] Freed from the deluge of a priori and optimistic praise, the TRC is a form both politically and analytically contingent, with uncertain futures and complicated outcomes. From this vantage point, the disappearance of Ghana's NRC is less of a mystery; a government that is invested in creating a truth commission may also be decidedly uninterested in that commission's conclusions. Still, there are the voices. In Ghana, the thousands of stories gathered up by the national reconciliation experiment are the remnant that is more valuable than the whole.

On the TRC as an Archive

If "people study history in order to participate in contemporary politics," they write history for much the same reasons.[23] We gather up, represent, and inscribe the past in order to carve out new futures for our family, community, and nation. In TRCs, diverse individuals enter into this history work. By describing the NRC documents as an archive, I highlight the historical relevance of the records; this designation also illuminates the complex mechanisms of "inclusion, exclusion, forgetting, remembering, construction and reconstruction" that shape how Ghanaians parsed the past in public.[24] Speaking of archives requires that we attend to the power relations that shape how history is organized, preserved, and interpreted.[25] Kirsten Weld uses the language of archive profitably in her analysis of Guatemalan secret police records. Dating from the 1970s, these documents were originally weapons of state "surveillance, social control and ideological management" used to terrorize the Guatemalan activists and citizens. Later, these same documents were recovered and used within historical justice initiatives toward very different ends. Considering that the same documents may be used for variable, shifting, even conflicting political agendas requires, in Weld's estimation, "archival thinking:" interrogating how and why documents exist as an assemblage. In this way we may discern the "archival logics"—the organizing principles, reasons for being—that exist beyond a document's material substance.[26]

Multiple and varied political imperatives fueled and shaped the contours of the NRC's review of Ghana's human rights history. The NPP first proposed a truth and reconciliation process as part of its party manifesto for the national elections in the year 2000.[27] Accordingly, the rival NDC party insisted that the NRC was actually a "Nail Rawlings Commission," designed to besmirch and delegitimize the legacy of the party's founder.[28] Veering away from this partisan context, sponsoring Ghanaian president John Agyekum Kufuor described the NRC as a step forward in the country's battle against poverty, its "greatest enemy." Kufuor's insistence that at truth commission would generate positive goods like economic development, unity, and political progress for Ghana, reflects what Pierre Hazan calls transitional justice's "ambitious gamble": the idea that delving into the past supposedly creates a desired future.[29] Although Ghanaian participants shared this sense of optimism about the NRC's impact on the future, their ambitions were often slightly different. For many Ghanaians reconciliation was not about achieving neoliberally defined, broad, national concepts (read: democracy, progress, development) but about achieving distinctively local goals: land reallocation, educational welfare, small-business seed capital, and the like. Consider the words of Edward Yeboah Abrokwah, a farmer and former police corporal who came to "plead with the commission . . . to ensure that I am either reinstated into the police or I receive my pension to be able to make ends meet." In the NRC records such entreaties abound. For Abrokwah, his forced unemployment in 1980 was both an injustice (he had not committed any offense) and an act of violence (two of his ten children had died as a result).[30] While President Kufuor justified the NRC as the first step in a journey that would lead from TRC to national unity to political will and thus to economic growth, Abrokwah's stated aims—a pension or a job—were entirely more local. Although both men looked to the NRC for economic transformation, their dreams were positioned at very different scales. The multiple archival logics of the NRC records reflect the complexity of state initiatives that are also havens for citizen political consciousness.

On the Value of Cacophony

In the NRC records, the self-appointed victims of violence spoke and the result was a remarkable cacophony, a conflicted and disorienting clamor of narratives. The acts of aggression, neglect, and omission that Ghanaians marked as state violence range from land alienation to torture at the hands of border guards, inaccessible health care, and even public execution. Dueling petitions and testimonies exist; there are stories that directly contradict one another. Some self-described victims wrote one thing in their petition and then publicly testified to something different. Others refused to testify at all, submitting a petition and then taking themselves out of the public review. On its face, this openly riotous record is a shortcoming, another marker of failure for a commission charged with producing reconciliation rather than division. What, and where, is the truth among these contested and contradictory stories? How do we come to know the past, Urvashi Butalia asks, apart from the ways it is handed down to us?[31] There is value in national history that is handed down as cacophony; the pursuit of truth that does not produce reconciliation is, perhaps, the beginning of justice in postindependence Africa.

After all, homogenization and exclusion are the violent undercarriage of modern nationalism. "Cleansing the sacred space of the nation," Gyanendra

Pandey explains, requires containing or disciplining difference, which is perceived as an "impure element."[32] History writing is often complicit in these nationalist purification rites. By marking particular communities as "minorities" and rationalizing borders, nationalist historiography often imagines a past in alignment with a mythically-cohesive contemporary nation.[33] The TRC, this government-directed public-history project garbed in a vivid moralism, appears at first glance, to be nation-building as usual. However, the cacophony of citizen testimony complicates the nationalist narrative. These dissonant voices are not evidence of failure but a glimpse of the ways truth commissions may allow citizens to push against the imperatives of nationalism's cleansed and streamlined histories.

The variety and complexity of the records produced by Ghana's NRC give rise to this productive cacophony. Aligned with Annelies Verdoolaege's expansive description of the material components of the South African TRC archive, I describe a Ghanaian NRC archive that is not limited to the citizen petitions and testimonies and also includes the documents produced about the commission, including media reportage, staff reports, investigations, correspondence, commentary and speeches.[34] Betwixt and between these different documents, an archive emerges—and it is the site of passionate debate about the past, present, and future of Ghanaian politics. The citizen petitions and testimonies alone make it plain that Ghanaian citizenship has never been a unitary experience. Political violence has been mediated by identity. Geographic and social location—profession, wealth, gender, family names, social networks—shape how people have experienced and survived the political transformations of Ghana's twentieth century. These records illuminate the fault lines crisscrossing the body politic; there are multiple histories of state violence and diverse experiences of any particular regime or leader. Although the NRC archive is limited, it gestures toward the innumerable narratives that exist beyond its relatively small cohort of participants by displaying the yoke between identity and political experience.

Cacophony, then, is the hallmark of what I call the NRC's democratized historiography. A complicated, riotous archive is evidence of the ways Ghanaians used the TRC to present, revise, and interpret their country's political history for diverse ends. Here, then, is the assertion at the center of this study: the NRC participants as history writers, and their stories as artful representations of the past. Claiming these stories as carefully articulated histories, as I do, is a step away from the barren preoccupation with whether these narratives are objectively true. Inevitably, they are not—or rather, they cannot all be, according to the evidentiary standards that prevail in most courts of law. In the NRC, Ghanaians sought to display versions of the past that might better serve them in the present. Their narratives were influenced by failures of memory and courage, as well as by the intertwined imperatives of economic scarcity, emotional suffering, and political optimism. Whether as contested truths or complicated lies, these stories are analytically valuable. In them, Ghanaians reflect on the series of moments or the sequence of days that ruptured the relationship between citizen and state.

On History and Democracy

My description of the Ghanaian NRC as a public history project that evades the disciplining of nationalist historiography veers away from the assessment of many historians who have been suspicious of TRCs as attempts to paper over the vulgarities of nation building with the moralistic language of human rights and truth seeking.[35] In a 2009 issue of the *American Historical Review,* Elazar Barkan exhorted his fellow historians to engage with transitional justice instruments despite the clear tension between academic history and government-sponsored commissions seeking a presumably incontestable "truth" about the past.[36] When historians steer clear of this emerging field, Barkan warned, they risk ceding critical public-history sites to ideologues and raw nationalists. Accordingly, historians have usually played a corrective role by illuminating the crevices (and chasms) between TRC truth and historical understanding.

Greg Grandin and Thomas Klubock, looking primarily at South America's transitional justice experience, place truth commissions squarely among the "myths and rituals of nationalism [that] sacramentalize violence into a useful creation myth."[37] Mahmood Mamdani has roundly criticized the groundbreaking South African TRC for pursuing truths that obfuscate the history of apartheid's violence. By focusing on individual victims and perpetrators, Mamdani claims, the South Africa TRC masked the structural violence of apartheid by writing this history as a matter of individuals who were kidnapped, imprisoned, or murdered.[38] Substituting this moral tale of good and evil may have cleared the path for a relatively smooth transition beyond the apartheid state and garnered Nobel Peace Prizes along the way, but it did not serve as a sufficiently robust historical analysis of the ways apartheid devastated South African lives.[39] By pursuing versions of the past that are "inseparable from a humanist project," TRCs inevitably limit their interpretive outcomes.[40] What of the voices, narratives, and interpretations of apartheid that are not amenable to the Rainbow Nation's reconciliation project? "Profound obstacles to the production of historical truth" arise when the past becomes a means to a particular social or political end.[41]

Nevertheless, the Ghana NRC archive cannot be reduced to the nationalist striving for a collective identity nor the humanistic reconciliation imperative. Although the NRC final report and the sponsoring government's public rhetoric did hew to a patently reconciling narrative, these are portions of a broader, more complicated archive. Citizen petitions, in particular, resist the neat, moralistic fable of past violence, present reconciliation, and future prosperity. The NRC archive is shaped both by the sponsoring government's mandate and by citizens who presented stories in voices that did not always conform to the official agenda. This productive cacophony is evident only when different parts of this capacious NRC archive—the petitions, commentary, media reports, and public statements—are juxtaposed against one another. Observers and scholars who attend only to the public hearings may easily misread the Ghanaian truth commission (and most other TRCs) as sites where the "elite control and manipulation" of state power prevails.[42] Madeleine Fullard and Nicky Rousseau similarly urge scholars of the South African TRC to look beyond the highly publicized public hearings in order to see the limits of the much-touted Rainbow Nation-building narrative of forgiveness.[43] Even in South Africa, some citizens openly rejected the forgiveness imperative embodied by Archbishop Desmond Tutu.

Describing the expansive and conflicted NRC archive as democratized historiography depends on establishing that Ghana's truth commission was first, a site for the expression of the public will (democracy) and second, a site in which the past was curated, preserved, and written (history). Can TRCs be counted among the "new democratic spaces" where new visions of citizenship are forged?[44] After all, diverse and sometimes unexpected political outcomes follow on the heels of truth and reconciliation. When Morocco's King Mohammed VI created the Instance Equité et Réconciliation (Equity and Reconciliation Commission) it was not a sign that the Moroccan monarchy was crumbling before the forces of democracy. If anything, Morocco's commission signaled the opposite—the monarchy's ability to adapt to the new international climate of human rights and state accountability.[45] Indeed, the Equity and Reconciliation Commission may have further legitimized the Moroccan monarchy by allowing a new king to disassociate himself from the excesses of prior monarchs and thus, restore trust in the system.[46] Even when TRCs do not anchor liberal democracy, there is the matter of the records they generate and preserve.

The archive produced by Ghana's NRC must be counted among the new, heterogeneous, democratic spaces that Andrea Cornwall and Vera Coelho locate on the border of state and society.[47] Truth commissions are part of a new and expanding "participatory sphere" where governments, civil society organizations, and international donors invite people (often marginalized communities) to lend their voices as witnesses to social, political, and economic dilemmas. Coelho and Cornwall astutely ask whether this expansion in democratic expression actually shifts power relations or translates into public policy.[48] *Truth Without Reconciliation* approaches this question of outcomes slightly aslant: I describe the production of new histories as the locus of the NRC's power.

History writing is powerful. Both "that which happened" and "that which is said to have happened," constrain the political imagination.[49] As states wield history as a weapon, marginalized populations have learned to also approach the task of representing the past as a battlefield. These days, national governments openly acknowledge the partiality and oversight of the official record and so may call for a truth commission to gather up the voices of the discontented. There is a risk, as Grandin, Klubock, and many others warn, that this apparent opening will ultimately reinforce the state's power over historical representation and political imagination. However, there is also possibility when TRCs dictate that the self-described victims of the past—unemployed pensioners, dispossessed and frail citizens without wealth or standing, petty traders, and uneducated youth— possess historical insight to which the nation must attend.

The NRC archive differs from academic investigations into the past. Participation in the NRC was profoundly shaped by desire. Citizens raised their voices in pursuit of economic gain, social rehabilitation, and an elusive national progress. Likewise, the government sponsored the commission as part of its political agenda. The stories at the center of this study are instrumental; truth commission testimony is a currency that can be exchanged for political, economic, or social goods. However, academic history also does not spill from the pen clean of self-interest and bias.[50] Relinquishing the myth of objectivity in history allows a reconsideration of the relationship between truth-commission testimony and the historical record. Can "people's stories, notwithstanding all their problems . . . somehow expand, stretch the definitions and boundaries of history and find a place in it"?[51] In authoring, editing, and revising stories of political violence that might better serve them, Ghanaian citizens created an archive in which everyday people are, at once, historical actors and history writers determined to influence how their country's past is known and remembered.

Revising National History:
Beyond Big Men and Partisanship

For much of the twentieth and twenty-first centuries, Ghanaian politics has been shackled by a fierce partisanship that dates to the days of decolonization. Ghana's two main political parties, the NPP and the NDC, situate themselves as the descendants of competing political traditions established in the closing years of the Gold Coast colony.[52] Above, I described a Ghana NRC archive that often spilled beyond the constraints imposed by the official, state-appointed architects of national reconciliation. Challenging this tradition of partisan politics is one of the ways that this citizen-curated public-history project exceeded its context. As citizens made their experiences central in the national human rights review, they created an eclectic archive that pushes past leaders and legacies and recovers a modern history in which torture, incarceration, and intolerance of dissent have been weapons of choice for multiple regimes and in various time periods. This ecumenical vision of political violence is significant because it is so rare.

The NRC stories, rooted in the soil of individual experience and local history, veer *away* from the elite figures that dominate public narrations of Ghanaian politics. These are not the "big man" versions of the national past that continue to dominate Ghanaian textbooks and public political consciousness.[53] In the NRC, Ghanaians placed themselves and their families at the center of the national story. By thrusting their local experiences onto the national platform, Ghanaians shifted the terrain on which Ghana's politics is known and discussed.

Despite the supposedly stabilizing force of partisanship in Ghanaian democracy, a divided politics also hamstrings political transformation. Consider the critique of Ghana's partisan politics articulated by political cartoonist Selorm Dogoe, a.k.a. Vinnietoonist.

The image is entitled "The Secret of Ghana's Peace." Two men representing the NPP and NDC are locked in conflict. Each has one hand wrapped around his adversary's throat; in the other hand he gingerly holds a single

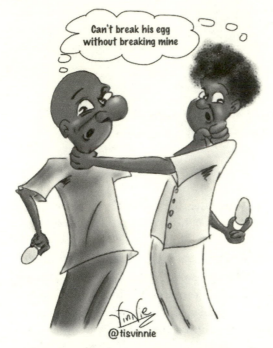

Figure 1. The Secret of Ghana's Peace. Cartoon courtesy of Selorm Dogoe, 2017.

egg. A shared thought bubble hovers above their heads: "Can't break his egg without breaking mine." Ghana's much-lauded peace, the cartoon suggests, is not based on the absence of conflict but on the constant antagonism of two parties locked in perpetual contest. There is equilibrium, but there is also a maddening stagnancy.

Portions of the NRC archive echo this critique of stultifying and combative partisanship. Consider the petition of Patrick Gyimah Danso, who reported that his cousin Kofi Gyamena was killed by soldiers in 1996 for political reasons. "The truth of the matter" was that Gyamena was an NPP activist, but he joined the NDC in 1996 because the party was ascendant, and party affiliation was the metric by which public sector (and often private sector) work was distributed. By joining the NDC, Gyamena obtained a license to work at the Takoradi Harbor as an exporter of finished timber products and yet he continued to make "huge contributions" to the NPP. On August 16, 1996, a soldier arrived at his residence and shot and killed Gyamena and his two children. "I am convinced," Danso wrote, "that it was because of his involvement in both parties."[54] Partisanship, Danso insists, has casualties and takes victims from among the people. For Gyamena, the soldier who ended his brother's life was guilty, but so too was the policy that distributes employment and other necessary goods along party lines. Moreover, partisan analysis—believing that political violence is the domain of only one party or tradition—masks the suffering that Ghanaians have endured throughout and despite the rapid-fire transitions in political regimes. The violence that runs through the citizen petitions make it plain that the critical question for tracing human rights abuses in Ghana is not which regime was guilty (read: all of them), but which communities were targeted at any given moment. In displaying how partisan analysis obfuscates the accumulated and abundant suffering of Ghanaian people, particularly those who are poor or otherwise marginalized, the national reconciliation experiment extended beyond the expectations of the sponsoring NPP government.

There is a growing literature describing transitional justice mechanisms as readily "hijacked," in the words of Jelena Subotic, by international and domestic interests. Truth commissions in the Balkans, Subotic shows, were handily repurposed by elites to perpetuate the nationalist mythologies that spurred violence in the first place.[55] Similarly, Rosalind Shaw and Lars Waldorf, in an excellent collection on transitional justice, describe transitional justice mechanisms as increasingly "evaded, critiqued, reshaped and driven in unexpected directions" by the people they are supposed to serve.[56] Unlike those studies, which lament that TRCs are corrupted in the transition from rhetoric to practice, *Truth Without Reconciliation* suggests that local manipulation of transitional justice instruments is not a fatal flaw but a saving grace. When Ghanaians seized the framework of truth and reconciliation for their own ends, they challenged the narrowness of a transitional justice agenda and the elitism of Ghanaian political analysis.

The following chapters display how the NRC's review of Ghanaian history deftly sidesteps nationalist heroes and party legacies in order to expose a national past that has yet to be reckoned with. This multivocal accounting of Ghana's politics memorializes the voices, sufferings, and desires of a broad cross section of citizens and challenges the exclusions of African political history rendered as a procession of "big men" vying to construct the nation through charismatic presence, speeches, and development programs. The revelation of Ghana's dance with the TRC form extends beyond national borders and into the global arena.

Domesticating a Global Discourse:
Localizing Human Rights

International human rights has been pilloried as an aspirational rhetoric for a world in desperate need of practical solutions.[57] Faced with the wreckage of the late twentieth century, Kenneth Cmiel famously asks, "What good did the expanded human rights agenda do for Afghani women under the Taliban, for the unemployed of Argentina, for the mentally ill now incarcerated in the American jails, for the Kurds in Iraq or Turkey?"[58] Casting an eye across the African continent, the situation appears equally grave. The existence of the Universal Declaration of Human Rights (UDHR) and its progeny of progressively hopeful conventions, declarations, and resolutions have not been able to stamp out hunger, to abolish or even contain civil wars, or to render human life protected or sacred. Whither the UDHR's "right to work" when general unemployment in Zimbabwe exceeds 80 percent? How does the Convention on the Elimination of Discrimination Against Women apply to the victims of the Congo War's sexual violence epidemic? Do the Rights of the Child apply to the Chibok schoolgirls kidnapped by Boko Haram?

And yet international human rights, with its multiple manifestations as law, rhetoric, and practice, is fecund and stunningly diverse; it continues to evade those who would entomb its political potential. First of all, there are those in the academic and activist community who vigorously resist the narrative that human rights law and practice have not produced positive outcomes. Kathryn Sikkink is among these champions of human rights, claiming that the prosecution of powerful world leaders constitutes the beginning of a "justice cascade" which may prevent future violence. Sikkink gives credit to a battery of organizations working under the banner of human rights for improving life expectancy, infant mortality, and other conditions worldwide.[59]

But critics, particularly those looking toward Africa, insist that tracing the impact of international human rights requires looking beyond the mouths fed, schools opened, dictators dragged to The Hague, or elections held. Human rights consists of a "contradictory welter of instruments, documents, statements, cases, and treaties, covering a vast array of subjects," and yet troubling patterns exist regarding how Africa is represented and ultimately, served by human right organizations.[60] International human rights' third rail is the problem of African political agency, or more specifically, the tendency for human rights practice and theory to promote policies and practices that constrain the self-determination, autonomy, and power of African nation-states and peoples. African intellectuals who excoriate the perpetuation of the blighted Africa narrative have not successfully altered the practices of the human rights community which still plies images and narratives that tread well-worn ground by suggesting that Africa is exceptionally broken and its people primarily needy. Chinua Achebe reminds the international development community that "Africa is people," and Chimamanda Ngozi Adichie warns against the danger of a single story about Africa.[61] Teju Cole exposes the "White-Savior Industrial Complex," and Binyavanga Wainaina satirizes the "children of the human rights age," to whom Africa consists of "many small flares of wonderfulness and many small flares of utter horribleness that occasionally rise in a flat and benign world."[62]

The deleterious consequences of this narrative of suffering Africa date back at least to the days when Rudyard Kipling described colonization as a heaven-sent burden for white men, and the British imperialist Frederick Lugard insisted that colonialism would save Africa from itself, namely "the awful misery of the slave trade and inter-tribal war, to human sacrifice and the ordeals of the witch-doctor."[63] The images of Africa that often proliferate in human rights campaigns appear to be a renewal of Joseph Conrad's obsession with the continent as the heart of darkness.

Moving beyond discourse and imagery, other scholars register their critique of human rights' relationship to Africa as a matter of self-determination and democracy. Here, human rights' Africa problem is not a matter of Western origins or cultural imperialism but, instead, is found in the limited role assigned to Africa's people in the interventions and development initiatives grouped under the human rights banner.[64] For Adam Branch, human rights, in its interventionist idiom, is an engine of dependency. Branch describes human rights as a sort of false consciousness that "embeds itself in the political imagination, transforming people's understanding of their social and political worlds" and leads them to seek rescue by the hands of an intervention from beyond.[65] Ironically, the language and practice of human rights, manifest in the humanitarian intervention imperative and in the proliferation of civil society organizations with scant local accountability, may actually undermine the practice of democracy in Africa. Is it reasonable to expect that Africa's freedom and progress will be plotted, imagined, and ultimately won by technocratic experts procured by the United States Agency for International Development, the Gates Foundation, and the UK Department for International Development?

The net consequence of human rights discourse in Africa, Michael Neocosmos warns, may be a narrowing of the space of political freedom. "External forms of intervention—whatever their intentions—rather than turning Africans into subjects of their own history, have over the years frustrated their agency . . . In the long run they have systematically transformed most Africans into victims whose main feature has been passivity, not agency."[66]

Nevertheless, human rights practice, media, theory, and law have never been and are not yet a monolith. As "flexible, ambiguous, and often contradictory" concepts, human rights "can be drawn on to construct a wide array of different discourses" and "can mobilize, legitimate or constitute radically different modes of political practice."[67] There is innovation occurring under the human rights banner.[68] Ghana's NRC is a glimpse of the alternative futures that are possible when international human rights is domesticated and transformed by marginalized communities on the African continent. If international human rights can be redeemed in Africa—that is, if it will assist in the work of unspooling the imbricated violence of repressive national leaders and a rapacious international economic order—the hope is found in the moments when African people commandeer, repurpose, and transform rights talk in order to challenge the known world and imagine new futures.

Dialectical notions of global and local inadequately represent the work of human rights work in the world.[69] Conceiving of two separate, discrete spheres misunderstands the multiple forms of connection across scales—theoretical, philosophical, financial—that create the practice of human rights. "The global and the local are always present in human rights—*always in tension yet mutually constitutive*."[70] This entanglement is particularly evident within TRCs. Yes, Ghanaian citizens made their cultural frameworks, languages, preoccupations, and bodies central in the national reconciliation exercise. The commission was also a creature of the international community: it was partially funded by the Open Society Initiative for West Africa, and experts from the United States and South Africa trained the NRC staff utilizing examples from Sri Lanka, Peru, and El Salvador. Following Mark Goodale's theorization, I describe the NRC as a *locale*: a site where the interaction between global and local unveils new possibilities for a mutable human rights regime.

Over the past two decades, the human rights community's enthusiastic embrace of "localization" has not succeeded in altering the hierarchies of leadership and decision-making that enable international experts—so designated by formal education, passport, language, and multiple axes of power—to organize and interpret human rights practice.[71] The vaunted local participation "may be hollowed out and amount only to an invitation to conform to norms imagined by experts or to fill an assigned role."[72] In her discussion of the "vernacularization" of human rights, Sally Engle Merry describes a world where "indigenous people, ethnic minorities, and women" are "using human rights languages and techniques" in ways that exceed the "Western" foundations of rights ideology. And yet, she notes, they are often dependent on intermediaries, persons who "translate ideas from the global arena down and from local arenas up," and thus play a powerful role in shaping the practice of human rights.[73]

Part of the innovation of the NRC, I claim, is that diverse Ghanaian citizens stepped into this interstitial role, simultaneously asserting victimhood, citizenship, and expertise as they marshaled the language of human rights. At the NRC's Accra public hearings, for example, the former policeman Joseph Kwadwo Nuer was not content to play the role to which he was assigned. After hearing Nuer's story of torture at the hands of soldiers during the 1979 Armed Forces Revolutionary Council uprising, Commissioner Sylvia Boye requested proof of his story. Where were the hospital documents about the harms he had suffered? Where was the official letter granting him leave to recover from the abuse? Nuer's deft response challenged the basic premise of her question: "My Lord, in the course of time, I thought I was never going to have the opportunity for redress and my economic situation was not the best so I used that letter and other documents as toilet papers."[74] As the audience at the Old Parliament House erupted into laughter, Nuer's point was clear. Who has time to preserve important documents when struggling to meet his basic needs? Why would a person jealously protect documents attesting to a victimization that was common and widespread in those times? Where do external expectations of evidentiary and legal truth fall short when assessing Ghana's history of violence? The public hearings were marked by moments like these, times when Ghanaians subtly or explicitly challenged the intimations or questions of the commissioners in order to more firmly control their testimony. Citizens did not only display flayed flesh or gaping need. By interpreting, explaining, and analyzing Ghanaian political history, they went beyond the role of informant and acted as experts.

In the NRC archive, Ghanaian victims reveal themselves as citizen experts who are a bridge between the past's troubles and a desired future. In their own voices, they reflect on many of the continent's most confounding dilemmas. What is the impact of state violence? What should be done for those who have suffered unjustly? What is the way forward for individuals and communities still bearing the wounds of the violent twentieth century? These foundational questions have been and continue to be vigorously debated by technocrats, development experts, scholars, public intellectuals, and politi-cians. In these discussions, however, the voices of African people are often included only in refracted and mediated form. The NRC is the rare locale in which the Ghanaian people, most of whom do not have the world's ear, speak for themselves about the country's political past, present, and future. In so doing, they do not only bear witness to pain, they dissect the limitations and possibility of Ghana's national politics. The NRC archive's lively historical and political critiques display human rights victims as experts in their own right whose stories are worthy of being heard, wrestled with, organized around, and ultimately remembered.

In this role, Ghanaian shared stories that collectively resist the narrative of exceptional African suffering. Those who come to this study expecting only a woeful tale of atrocities visited upon black bodies will find themselves sorely disappointed. Ghanaians marked as human rights abuse not only the spec-tacular atrocities that so often populate the international rhetoric but also the mundane economic and social deprivations that produce banally atrocious outcomes—the varied events that unjustly and irrevocably limited a person's destiny. Instead of the sensationalist images of African suffering, Ghanaians highlight the diverse conditions that devastated lives. Although commission-ers and Ghanaian media often trained their attention on stories of arresting physical violence, the archive is dominated by narratives such as that penned by an unemployed citizen whose complaint was devastatingly simple: "I need a job. That's all."[75] Ghanaians testified eloquently about the violence of eco-nomic injustice, a suffering that is rooted in both the international economic order and national failures.

In the 1980s, Godfred Odame Kissi's father died. "As a result of my father's death I have not been able to attend school and this is what hurts me the most. I don't mind about the assets. I don't have any good occupation due to inade-quate education."[76] Consumed by grief, Kissi plotted murder against the per-son he blamed most for his lot. "At that time I was so hurt that I planned with my friend to kill Rawlings' children who were then at Achimota School. . . . We didn't succeed because he took them to London," he quickly noted.[77] In Kissi's petition, the presence and absence of education is, quite simply a mat-ter of life and death. He joined a number of petitioners who connected their inability to consistently attend school to the policies of J. J. Rawlings. In the 1980s, under the tutelage of the World Bank and the International Monetary Fund, Rawlings oversaw austerity measures that sought to "devolve national public responsibility for the financing of education" and ultimately ended up limiting Ghanaian youth's access to school.[78] Nowadays, even the global lending institutions express regret for these stringent loan policies that closed classroom doors for scores of African children. "In hindsight," a 2009 World Bank report muses, "insufficient attention was given to the impact of these fees and related costs on family budgets, on the spending choices of the poor, and on children's right to education."[79] Testimonies like Kissi's publicly revisit the violence of structural adjustment at a time when Ghana is still gingerly navigating its course through globalization's economic imperatives. In these types of petitions, Ghanaians utilize an internationalist discourse to publicly reconsider a past which "is not even passed."[80] They mark out a history which might yet be a touchstone for the future.

Conclusion

Above I have sketched the political dimensions of an archive, which in its cacophony and democratized historiography constitutes an excess, a prodigal extension beyond the conventions of transitional justice, beyond the tropes of nationalist renderings of Ghanaian history, and beyond the limitations of the human rights "Africa problem." *Truth Without Reconciliation* insists that TRCs may be more than they seem. And yet, are they enough? Even the most cursory glance at Ghana's twenty-first-century politics reveals that the NRC did not transform the country's political or economic structures. What, then, is the value of this citizen-curated public political history? To begin, the assumption that the NRC's value is tied to immediately quantifiable and measurable outcomes misunderstands the relationship between history writing and political change. In the conclusion, I consider the astigmatism of assessing global TRC outcomes as a matter of participant satisfaction, the expansion of legal codes, positive government rhetoric or any other discrete factors that do not take into account the long and winding road between historical consciousness and political change. Better that we recognize, as Moses Chrispus Okello, Chris Dolan, and others suggest, the "ongoing labor" that "unfolds slowly over time and space, needing the healing and repair work of several generations."[81] Nevertheless the question of consequences is unavoidable; after all, the disappearance of the NRC from public view is the conundrum that began this study.

Political movements wrestling with the ideological violence of colonialism and neocolonialism affirm that historical consciousness is central in forging new African futures.[82] "The settler makes history and is conscious of making it," Fanon wrote. Decolonization, then, requires that a marginalized people thrust themselves under the "grandiose glare of history's floodlights," and recognize their struggle as epic. More recently, Michael Neocosmos has suggested that pursuing freedom in Africa requires first, thinking freedom. And this, he warns, is a skill in short supply.[83] Hemmed in by disappointing national leadership, by multinational companies whose trumpeted corporate social responsibility programs will not bring back the fish or the richness of the soil, and by climate change and brain drain, the horizon of political progress is reduced to individual accumulation and more efficient global consumption. However, for "the excluded themselves . . . the issue of freedom remains on the agenda."[84] It is those who are suffering the most—like the urban shack dwellers in South Africa, or the Ghanaians who traveled miles to stand in line and lodge a petition at an NRC office—who are pursuing, headlong, political justice. Neocosmos points to South Africa's Abahlali BaseMjondolo, the Shack Dwellers' Movement, as an example of how marginalized groups, not the middle classes or academic elites, form the vanguard of freedom-oriented political action and theory in contemporary Africa. It is the shack dwellers who dream beyond acquiring a greater share of the liberal democratic dispensation, whose vision turns away from a limited progress and toward emancipation.[85]

The stories of the NRC must be added to this ongoing accounting of African peoples who seize the rhetoric and rituals of political progress as an opportunity to publicly remind their nation (and the world) of both their presence and their suffering. The NRC's accounting is vital as a site where Ghanaian peoples' historical and political thought is gathered; but like all archives, its material consequence depends on how it is used. The potential of the NRC is tied to whether anyone—fellow Ghanaians, diaspora Africans, transitional justice scholars—bothers to listen to the stories that were shared. There are many ways to listen; I am speaking here of taking seriously the critiques raised by the country's citizen experts. If this has not yet happened, perhaps it will in the future. This is, after all, an archive; the documents are preserved, their full audience has not yet been born.

In any case, we must step away from the misplaced hope that TRCs will be a salve for broken societies. Dwelling with these stories is profoundly unsettling; this is as it should be. The violence described is not quarantined to the past; the fault lines that have before flared into atrocity remain active. Human dignity is still rationed by whether your family can pay school fees, whether your mother has the opportunity to receive proper maternal care, or whether you might be able to acquire a job. As a public meditation on the continuing obstacles to justice, freedom, and progress in Ghana, perhaps it is no wonder that the NRC archive has been so efficiently ignored.

Embracing this cacophony is more than a guide into Ghana's history, it is also central to the country's political future. The variety in Ghanaian people's perspectives is neither a failure nor a weakness but instead an impetus to build a politics that recognizes the stratification of the Ghanaian nation and acknowledges the voices of the many. From the communities in Old Fadama to the elites gathered at Ridge Church to the petty traders in Tamale Market, all are part of Ghana and all must be included in the dream for Ghana's future. Against a backdrop where the road to a brighter future in Ghana is described as a matter of clearing slums, privatizing education, and restricting the movement of poor people, the voices of Ghana's diverse constituencies in the NRC create an opportunity to consider a political agenda that does not depend on erasing or ignoring difference. Although unity is central to national political progress, this study argues that cacophony, too, creates a road forward.

Truth Without Reconciliation delves into this rich NRC archive, using citizen petitions and testimonies as historical examples, guides for analysis, allegories, and sites of comparison. Following this introduction, Chapter 1, "Making the NRC Archive," discusses the genesis and trajectory of the National Reconciliation Commission from its beginnings as a campaign promise in the 2000 electoral season, through the rancorous partisan parliamentary debates that established the National Reconciliation Act (2002), the submission of the final report to the government in 2004, and the disbursement of a reparations program in 2007. Defining a capacious NRC archive and interrogating its competing logics, this chapter considers the extent to which Ghanaians were able to seize national reconciliation as a site for democratic expression.

Chapter 2, "Human Rights and Ghanaian History," traces the course of twentieth-century Ghanaian political history from the waning days of British colonialism through the 2000 presidential elections. By weaving the NRC narratives into the historical review, this chapter uses citizen stories to disrupt the elitism, patriarchy, and other exclusions common within Ghanaian nationalist historiography.

The next two chapters consider patterns in how the self-described victims of Ghanaian politics utilized the NRC to represent the national past. Chapter 3, "*Kalabule* Women," interrogates the notion of the "human rights victim" by focusing on a collection of petitions by Ghanaian market women about the intersection of gender violence and political violence. At the NRC, market women thrust their broken bodies before the nation, exposing the violence that occurred at the intersection of sex and social identity. In so doing, their stories brush against the abundant images of African women's suffering that freely circulate within global media representation of international human rights abuse. This chapter considers the national and global consequences of the NRC as a site where Ghanaians stepped into the public identity of the "human rights victim"—to ambivalent ends.

Chapter 4, "Family Histories of Political Violence," explores the narratives of estrangement, divorce and separation, unhappy homes, and broken promises that animate the NRC archive. Here, I consider the consequences when NRC participants describe human rights abuse as that which withered Ghanaian families. By counting the costs of national political violence through the loss of intimate and filial ties, Ghanaians illuminate the domestic, private sphere as a site of political violence. Both chapters confront the risks (both personal and political) of publicly donning the mantle of victimhood in a TRC and place gender at the center of Ghana's history of political violence.

Chapter 5, "The Suffering of Being Developed," focuses on two collections of citizen narratives, both officially deemed nonjurisdictional and placed outside the mandate of Ghana's NRC. The first collection consists of individuals and communities who were displaced and resettled as part of the construction of the Volta River Project's Akosombo Dam. The other collection focuses on the violence that accompanied the privatization of salt production on the Songor Salt Flats. In both, Ghanaians scrutinized development initiatives that displaced and impoverished rural communities. The costs of both nationalist and corporate development approaches are immortalized in stories about how marginalized citizens were brought low by initiatives ostensibly meant to build the country up.

Chapter 6, "Soldier, Victim, Hero, Citizen," interrogates both the ubiquity of suffering and the images of resistance present in the NRC documents. Instead of coming forward to request absolution, most Ghanaian soldiers came to the NRC to insist that they, too, were victims. Similarly, the archive is marked by stories of ambivalent heroes and inadequate acts of courage that result in imprisonment, exile, assault and other ills. Together, these stories undermine a moralistic understanding of African political violence as a matter of clearly demarcated categories of victims, perpetrators, heroes and evildoers and invite a reconsideration of the contours and consequences of resistance to political violence. This complexity, I argue, is productive; it propels us past moral dichotomies and toward a vision of historical justice that recognizes the breadth, depth, and diversity in how human beings suffer, survive, and resist violence.

The importance of nonjurisdictional petitions is also evident in Chapter 7, "Time of Suffering / Time for Justice." Here, Ghanaians describe the continuing impact of colonial violence in today's Ghana and challenge the notion that democratic elections marked the end of state human-rights abuse. Political violence, in citizens' reflections, was cyclical and compounded. The days that caused destruction in the past also set a course for risk in the future. By refusing to consign state violence safely to the past, Ghanaian reject analyses of contemporary African politics that ignore the colonial past and assume the innocence of neoliberal democratic present. These temporally transgressive petitions and testimonies highlight the analytical rigor of an NRC archive rooted in citizen experiences and perspectives.

The conclusion, "The Brief Afterlife of Ghana's Truth Commission," returns to the question of consequences by criticizing the language of success and failure as a constraint on our comprehension of Africa's TRC phenomenon. Truth commissions are neither inherently politically moribund nor implicitly liberating; they are vessels that can be exploited for diverse ends. If the "political consciousness and imagination of African societies" is the fertile ground on which justice struggles must be built, processes that do not immediately result in explicit gains but which *do* change minds, shift allegiances, expose state hypocrisy, and frighten us out of exhaustion and complacency should not be overlooked.[86]

CHAPTER 1

Making the NRC Archive

Truth and reconciliation commissions (TRCs) may not immediately extract justice, peace, or reconciliation from the brokenness of the past, but they always and everywhere produce records of human suffering. Narratives of human rights violation are being gathered all over the world—from Canada to Liberia to East Timor—but after the tears have been shed and the speeches made, what becomes of the stories that have been amassed? Ghana's National Reconciliation Commission (NRC) functioned as a public history-writing project. A diverse cross section of the national population presented, analyzed, and interpreted Ghana's history of political violence in full earshot of the world. The consequent archive is a revelation, but this does not make it an uncomplicated, transparent, or free site where all Ghanaians had their say. The contentious birth of the NRC in the first years of the twenty-first century is the firmest foundation from which to understand the complexity of the stories that Ghanaians shared. The tensions that marked the NRC's genesis and functioning are echoed in its archive.

When I began reading the NRC file folders at the University of Ghana's Balme Library, the contents were immediately arresting. In these stories, marked by colloquialism, analogy, and innuendo, Ghanaian people held forth. At first, I read these documents as rich primary sources in which Africans were "speaking for themselves" about the past.[1] Six months later, after reading one-third of the NRC's 4,240 petitions, I had come to a slightly different conclusion. These records were more profitably read as histories: complex, deliberate, and artful representations of Ghana's past. These citizen stories are not mirrors to the past; they are fabrications reflecting the hand of the authors, forged within a particular season and deliberately crafted to illuminate particular aspects of Ghana's march through the twentieth century. The term "fabrication," as used here, is not a slight on the veracity or accuracy of the archive's contents. Its Latin root, *faber,* gestures toward artisans and describes the work of constructing with one's own hands—utilizing sweat and skill to create. Citizen participation in the NRC occurred on these terms; Ghanaians were making histories, deliberately crafting versions of the past that might serve.

For a process that was supposed to locate the truth about political violence in Ghana, the NRC archive's most striking revelation is the impossibility of establishing a unitary narrative about the past's turbulence. Between the citizen petitions, public hearings, NRC staff legal opinions, and news media reports, there are different images and understanding of human rights abuse in Ghanaian history. What happened to particular populations during different political regimes and under diverse leaders? When did state violence rise to the level of human rights abuse? How might we assess and compare the human impact of different policies? In responding to these questions, Ghanaians produced a multitude of accounts that, when juxtaposed, make it plain that the country's political journey must be written as a history of difference.

The contents of the NRC archive include letters, photographs, land-use maps, funeral programs, dismissal letters, and other information that petitioners submitted as corroborating evidence. Witnesses to violence, who were often neighbors, family or friends, also offered supporting statements. Each file also includes documents created by the NRC staff (legal opinions, investigation reports, etc.) pertinent to the case file. There are video and audio records of the public hearings as well as considerable national media coverage. In reading all these documents together, my goal was not to ascertain the veracity or fallacy of any of these accounts, but instead to place them into a dialogue with each other and with other narratives and ways of knowing Ghana's past. To this end, I spoke with a limited number of NRC employees, including commissioners, the executive secretary, and the head of the psychological unit. I spoke with members of the sponsoring government and Ghanaian politicians, as well as with nongovernmental organizations. I compared the content within the NRC stories with documents about political violence stored in the Ghanaian National Archives in Accra and Cape Coast.

Describing the NRC's diverse petitions, testimonies, videos, reportage, investigations, and reports as an archive speaks to the complexity of the commission's relationship to Ghanaian history. Recording the past is only part of the TRC mission. These commissions endeavor to *work with* the past: to smooth out the rough edges, perform resolution, and create a platform for a future of peace, stability, and prosperity. Recognizing that these commissions pursue both the past and the future, Annelies Verdoolaege describes the South Africa "TRC Archive" in the Foucaultian sense—as a site where power is expressed. Both remembering and forgetting are part of the TRC's work, these documents seek to establish the truth (i.e. "what can and cannot be said") about historical violence.[2] Similarly, the Ghana NRC archive is a site imbricated within state power. The sponsoring Ghanaian government shaped both the NRC's practice and its records. How human rights abuse was defined and classified, which stories were publicly shared, how these documents were preserved and publicized—all of these were shaped by the government-appointed NRC bureaucracy. And yet, Ghanaian citizens themselves also shaped this archive. Their stories were strategic, intentional and often pushed beyond the limits set by the NRC officials. In substance and contour, the NRC archive reflects this bureaucratic web. The voices of the self-proclaimed survivors of history emerge opaquely, in a mediated form. Reading these documents together reveals multiple points of disagreement and rupture; the tensions among individual accountings, and between Ghana's citizen stories and the NRC bureaucracy, are apparent. Inasmuch as the NRC archive reflects state power, it is also a site of citizen struggle and must be navigated as such. In telling the story of Ghana's national reconciliation experiment and its accompanying archive, this chapter reveals the nuance and contingency of both state power and citizen voice in postindependence Africa.

Creation Story

The story of the Ghana NRC begins during the historic 2000 campaign season, when the New Patriotic Party (NPP; one of Ghana's two dominant political parties) calls for a truth and reconciliation commission. The NPP manifesto, "Agenda for Positive Change," described national reconciliation as a way to secure Ghana's political progress. "The festering sores within the body politic must be healed. This is necessary so that the nation can look confidently and boldly into the future." As described in this manifesto, the national reconciliation exercise would "consider all surviving cases of human rights abuse and award appropriate compensation for the victims." Seized properties would be restored, Ghanaians living in exile would be granted unconditional amnesty to return and tell their stories, and persons imprisoned for "politically-related offenses" would be released.[3]

When the NPP triumphed at the ballot box in 2000, the dream of a Ghanaian TRC became a reality. The newly elected president, John Agyekum Kufuor, publicly championed a Ghanaian truth commission as an antidote to the "culture of silence" that had been created when "people were killed, properties were confiscated . . . some destroyed . . . and people were denied their say."[4] This would be, ultimately, a collective renewal project. Meeting with the Western Regional House of Chiefs, Kufuor described the commission as an "exercise to recapture the country's lost soul," and a way for the country to regain the "spirit of showmanship and wealth," tarnished by the violence of the past.[5] Missing in this government rhetoric about the NRC as a site of healing was any recognition that this process might exacerbate, not alleviate political tension in Ghana.

After all, Ghana's successful transition from military rule to electoral democracy had occurred almost a decade prior (1992). The newly-elected government's call for the NRC was itself an assertion that the earlier democratic transition engineered by the rival National Democratic Congress (NDC) had been inadequate. J. J. Rawlings, the military leader who had twice seized control of the state apparatus, exercised authoritarian leadership for more than a decade, and then—under international and domestic pressure—transformed himself into a democrat, had overseen Ghana's return to constitutional rule. The constitution which returned Ghana to democracy also included an indemnity clause that prohibited the prosecution of persons who participated in the past decade's military government at all levels. Nobody in Ghana could be "held liable either jointly or severally, for any act or omission during the [previous] administration."[6] The excesses of the period of military rule could only be addressed informally and voluntarily. Although Rawlings himself had proffered apologies, these previous mea culpas were of "dubious validity and international acceptance,"[7] and generally, "low key . . . opaque, piecemeal and selective."[8]

Given this context, it was not surprising that former president Rawlings and his National Democratic Congress (NDC) party cried foul when the NRC bill arrived in Parliament.[9] The NRC, they claimed, was a "Nail Rawlings Commission" designed to attack the legacy of former president Rawlings, and the legitimacy and prospects of his party.[10] However, the TRC format was well suited for Ghana's context both because of what it promised and what it could not possibly deliver. The NPP's call for a truth commission—a form utilized in response to atrocities like South African apartheid and Guatemalan civil war—was a bold assertion that atrocities occurred on Ghanaian soil and that justice had not yet been done. At the same time, the NPP's call was pragmatic. The accountability that the NRC could provide was limited. No one would be sent to jail because of the NRC or even forced to part with money or property. Reconciliation was the central imperative; truth would be pursued only to the extent that it supported this agenda. President Kufuor made the outcomes clear: persons found to be perpetrators would not face material consequences; they would just have to live with their consciences.[11] And so Ghana's reconciliation experiment remained within the boundaries of the country's fragile political equilibrium.

In the public's perception, the NRC could not step out of the shadow of its partisan beginnings.[12] This was partially because the terms of the 1992 transition made it politically taboo to publicly confront the violence of the Rawlings years, but other aspects of the commission's genesis also fueled the sense that national reconciliation could only be a partisan project. The NPP claimed the NRC as a way to burnish its party legacy. "The NPP solemnly promised the people of Ghana that it would undertake a soul-searching investigation of those human rights violations and abuses if granted the privilege of leading the nation," piously intoned the government's white paper in response to the NRC. "This pledge is not surprising, since the NPP is committed to the promotion of the Rule of Law, respect for human rights, and eradication of the culture of impunity."[13] If national reconciliation was evidence of the NPP's human rights credibility, how could a politically polarized nation rally around it?

Moreover, the version of the NRC bill that President Kufuor presented to the Ghanaian Parliament was based on the premise that human rights violations occurred only under military regimes, so only military regimes would be scrutinized. A more expansive time frame would have been more "in keeping with the spirit of the commission's goal" and have rendered the bill "more conciliatory and inclusive."[14] Immediately, the NDC parliamentarians grumbled that their leadership and political tradition were being unfairly targeted. This temporal restriction made it appear that the NRC was just vulgar politics in a more virtuous form, and the NDC ministers walked out en masse when asked to vote on this version of the NRC bill.[15] Ghanaian democracy building and human rights organizations saved the day by officially requesting an expanded temporal mandate. "The credibility of the Commission to a large extent depends on public perception of its independence," they explained.[16] If the NRC was to transcend accusations of partisan bias, it could not, from the outset, proclaim that only particular regimes were guilty of violence. The final version of the National Reconciliation Commission Act (Act 611) included a broad temporal mandate that reviewed the majority of the national history from independence in 1957 through the reestablishment of political democracy in 1993.[17]

Ghanaian civil-society organizations also challenged President Kufuor's proposal to appoint all the commissioners himself. The parliamentary committee proposed that both the Council of the State and the Parliament should have a hand in appointing commissioners. This advice was ignored; President Kufuor himself appointed all nine commissioners. The people chosen as National Reconciliation commissioners represented the legal community, academia, traditional leaders, religious leaders, trade unions, and the military.[18] Three of the nine were women. While the commissioners held diverse regional and ethnic affiliations, their unilateral appointment suggested that the much-ballyhooed transparency and accountability of the NRC went only so far.[19]

One of the central arguments of this study is that Ghana's NRC generated a breathtaking collection of citizen testimonies about the national past, present, and future. What should be clear from the above section is that before the NRC was a haven for citizen voice, it was a catalyst for partisan political wrangling. This context, in which reviewing historical violence was also a matter of partisan competition, influenced all that followed—from how citizen stories were composed and shared to the commissioners' reactions and recommendations.

Similarly, the nuts and bolts of the NRC's institutional practice, what I call the NRC bureaucracy, also influenced the expression and transmission of citizen voices. The choice of who was hired as a statement taker, how the room was arranged for the public hearings, which stories were valorized and called for hearings and which were dismissed as irrelevant—all of these shape the contents of this archive. Layers of translation, transmission, and transcription mediate the space between petitioners and their audiences. The NRC bureaucracy was a web that constrained and colored the stories that Ghanaians shared. And yet, the voices of the Ghanaian people shone through. With deliberation and intention, the so-called victims of Ghanaian history came forward with stories about the distressing past and the expected future. The NRC bureaucracy publicized the existence and purpose of the NRC, but ultimately individual citizens had to come forward and join in the "healing process."[20] This was no easy task.

Bringing one's voice and body to the NRC inevitably involves a calculation of risk and benefit. What good (personal, familial, moral, national, political) can this initiative create, and how does this compare to the possible negative consequences? Following this assessment, Ghanaians then had to travel to one of five zonal offices spread throughout the country to lodge a petition. Mobility, however, was not equally accessible among the self-described victims of human rights abuse. When Benjamin Amin submitted his petition to the zonal office, he specifically asked not to be called to Accra for the public hearings. "Old age and ill-health" made full participation a barrier for this former soldier. "I am now 69 years, very weak and sick that it would not be easy to travel from Boadua near Akwatia to Accra. . . . I would have to urinate about 8 times before I reach Accra [which] I believe no . . . commercial driver would tolerate."[21] This pitiful description is a sharp reminder of the economic and physical barriers that many Ghanaians had to overcome to answer the NRC's call. Other NRC records illuminate how fear itself was a critical obstacle. After lodging his petition about the military government's repression of religious organizations during the 1980s, a pastor associated with the Nyamesompa Healing Church wrote "to inform the NRC that, due to numerous threatening telephone calls that I have received about my life . . . I have voluntarily decided not to give any evidence at the Commission."[22] The callers warned him that "after the 2004 election NDC will come back to power and [he] will be arrested and killed." His letter, included in the NRC file, was dated April 9, 2003: "This is my personal decision and obligation, which I expect the commission to accept."[23]

Official NRC statistics report that women lodged only 19 percent of the total petitions.[24] Commissioner Henrietta Mensa-Bonsu described the pains that the NRC took to make itself more accessible to Ghanaian women, who, because of higher rates of illiteracy and "intimidation," were less likely to "come before official processes."[25] However, women's limited participation in the petition making, public hearings, and follow-up surveys is best understood in the context of a broader societal restriction on women's lives. The expectation that scores of Ghanaian women would participate in a public, government-backed forum with uncertain material outcomes may have been overly optimistic.[26] Some women lodged petitions but then refused to appear at public hearings, citing the disgrace that would come to their families.[27] Others, like a number of women in Tamale, deliberately missed their hearing dates because they feared their public testimony could be held against them in the event of another regime change. It took a reassuring radio announcement from the NRC chairman before the women of Tamale came forward.[28] The risk-benefit calculation was different for women, who occupy a generally more precarious social, economic, and political position within Ghana.[29] Individual participation in the NRC was fundamentally an act of optimism; good might yet come from engaging with the government's initiative. The good that citizen participants hoped for, however, varied. One witness entirely eschewed the idea of monetary compensation, claiming that he came before the commission to "set the record straight" and to relieve his psychological burden. Another would bring a detailed chart requesting thousands of US dollars as reparations for harms done and damage sustained. The various hopes that led Ghanaians to risk health, comfort, and public esteem in order to tell their stories, are recorded in the petitions they submitted.

In September 2002, the five zonal NRC offices began accepting petitions and statements. The Bolgatanga office served the Upper East and Upper West Regions, Ho served the Volta and Greater Accra Regions, Kumasi served the Eastern and Ashanti Regions, Sekondi-Takoradi served the Western and Central Regions, and Tamale served the Brong-Ahafo and Northern Regions.[30] Beginning in January 2003, for a period of twenty-two months NRC public hearings were held in Accra, Tamale, Kumasi, Takoradi, and Koforidua. By June 2004, a total of 4,240 statements had been submitted to the NRC. About 50 percent of the collected petitions were listed for public hearings.[31] It was in the petition-taking offices and the public hearings that Ghanaians transformed the NRC from a partisan contest into a space for citizen voices.

Petitions and Public Hearings

On the morning of September 3, 2002, a queue had already formed in front of the NRC's temporary headquarters in Accra's Independence Square. This was the first day that Ghanaians could lodge statements with the NRC, and by 5 a.m., more than sixty petitioners were waiting; the first had arrived as early as 3 a.m.[32] Upon arrival at a zonal office, an individual was met by a trained statement taker, who first gathered a battery of demographic data including age, ethnicity, language spoken, religion, and profession. The demographic data form also included a yes/no question about whether the petition maker believed that the harm they suffered was political in nature. The statement taker would also transcribe the citizen's story, in English, onto a text form. Translation was frequently a part of this process, as statement takers would listen to a story told in Twi, Gaa, Hausa, Fante, Wala, Ewe, Dagaari, Sisali, FraFra, or any of the other Ghanaian languages and write it down in English,

asking clarifying questions when necessary.[33] Statement takers were directed
to read the petition back to the petitioner to ensure the individual's satisfaction with the contents. If satisfied, Ghanaians signed their name or left
their mark on the petition. Sometimes, alongside or instead of a statement
taken at the NRC office, Ghanaians brought prepared petitions with them.
Handwritten or typed out in advance, sometimes with the help of a lawyer or
family friend, these petitions were often lengthier and more formal than the
statements taken on the spot.

The interaction between statement taker and petitioner undoubtedly influenced how the story was recorded and read. From spelling and punctuation
to emphasis and inflection, these statement takers shaped the contents of the
NRC archive. As parts of the NRC bureaucracy, these statement takers also
added notations and postscripts about their own perceptions of the veracity,
emotional distress, and clarity of the participating citizens and influenced how
the citizen statements would be henceforth understood. These marginalia are
also intimate glimpses of the NRC bureaucracy at work, interpreting, judging,
and shaping citizen presentations of the past. Clifford Marko's statement at
the Accra office was a harrowing account of his hospitalization in a Ghanaian psychiatric facility. Marko submitted a crowded handwritten document
that complained of "spiritual surveillance hired to climb up spiritually to fight
and follow to bar my way in everything I do."[34] Marko described involuntary
hospitalization and imprisonment as one and the same. His petition focused
on the judge's ruling, the handcuffs clapped on this body, and most of all, the
use of force: "The only question I ask was . . . am I a criminal?" Marko's petition also described the stigma associated with mental illness in Ghana. "I have
been treated unfairly and also my image had been tarnish [*sic*]. . . . I am now
known as a lunatic and a criminal in the country . . . just for the simple reason that I have been sent to the Psychiatric Hospital."[35] Marko's depiction of
mental illness as a criminalized status, marked by unjust social dislocation,
was judged by the statement taker as irrelevant to the NRC's work of reconciling the past. Marko, according to the statement taker, was "incoherent and
evidenc[ing] signs of psychiatric distress." Thus, Marko's story, an illuminating
look at psychological disability and its aftermath in Ghanaian history, was not
recommended for the public hearings.

Similarly, the NRC public hearings were also sites for both the expression of citizen voices and the display of NRC bureaucracy. These hearings
were the means by which most Ghanaians encountered the NRC and were
covered regularly by the news media. They were open to the public and were

well attended, particularly at the beginning of the process.[36] The nine commissioners, the listening audience, the witness, a translator when necessary,
and sometimes the accused perpetrator and his/her legal team were all part
of these hearings. Together, they created the versions of the national past that
ultimately emerged. The hearings were multilingual, with alleged victims,
accused perpetrators, and the commissioners using the most common Ghanaian languages, including English, throughout. In this setting, some of the
petitioners were brought forward to tell their stories in the hearing of the
nation. One of the defining moments in the public hearings was the death of
Joseph Kwadwo Ampah, a barrister-at-law living in London who traveled to
Ghana expressly to participate in the NRC.[37] On June 5, 2003, while beginning his public testimony in Accra, Ampah collapsed and died. This event
shocked the nation and changed the commission's practice. Instead of a simple wooden chair, witnesses now used a "restful cushioned chair." Counselors
were positioned next to the testifying witness to provide comfort during the
testimony. Ambulances were also stationed outside the venue, ready to rush
people to the hospital if necessary.[38] Joseph Kwadwo Ampah's death was a
corporeal reminder of the uncertainty and risk associated with the NRC's
work. Inasmuch as delving into the past could create restoration and renewal,
it might also reap disorder and even destruction.

The nine commissioners were guides and arbiters in these public hearings. They questioned witnesses, urging calm when anger threatened to erupt,
scolded the audience, and offered their sympathies and words of wisdom.[39]
Faced with a sobbing witness, a commissioner might advise counseling and
urge that he "forget the past, forge ahead and build a bright future, instead of
dwelling on the pain."[40] Confronted with a recalcitrant witness who would
not answer the NRC summons, the commissioners could levy a fine.[41] Since
Kufuor had personally appointed all the commissioners, criticism of their
comportment or objectivity was laid at the feet of the president.[42] A *Ghana
Review* article described a scene during the Accra hearings when the commissioners "descended heavily" and "expressed their disgust" at the actions of
an ex-military man accused of brutally beating a market woman.[43] There were
moments when the commissioners' tone and comments drew disapproval
from some quarters; eventually the NDC party officially filed a complaint
stating that supporters of their party were rushed, humiliated, and generally
treated poorly during the NRC hearings.[44]

Beyond this partisan critique, civil-society organizations also expressed
concerns that the public hearings "inappropriately resembled courtroom

proceedings."[45] The nine commissioners sat on a raised dais peering down at witnesses, who transported the conventions of the Ghanaian courts to the NRC and addressed the commissioners formally as "my lord." Lawyers could participate in the proceedings, and high-profile and affluent witnesses, accused persons, and victims often retained an attorney. Individuals who had been named or implicated in a prior presentation were given the right to cross-examine witnesses. As such, accused perpetrators were given the right to publicly question alleged victims. This, according to the commissioners, ensured that those Ghanaians who were skeptical or hostile to the NRC's work would trust in the fairness of the process. However, when the accused perpetrator was a military men or business owners with wealth and standing, a well-heeled lawyer might publicly harangue nervous victims armed only with their words and convictions.[46] This was what befell Aku Sabi, a petitioner who described suffering a miscarriage due to the brutality of hired soldiers paid to enforce a company's privatization of disputed land. At the NRC, the company lawyer publicly cross-examined Sabi, at one point blaming her for the miscarriage and saying that "she did not take good care of [the pregnancy]."[47] Although the psychological and social consequences of subjecting alleged victims to this manner of public cross-examination has not yet been reckoned with in Ghana, there is a growing recognition that TRC practices may reproduce and reinscribe trauma.[48]

By cottoning to this veneer of legalism, the NRC seemed to imply that the truth it pursued was similar to that utilized in Ghanaian courts.[49] In reality, accessing the past's violence through individual human rights testimony is inevitably a journey into the vagaries of memory and representation. People's recollections and stories are based on the life they are currently living. Their perspectives on the past are shaped by the present's desires, secrets, and hopes. In valorizing victim testimony as a way of knowing the past, truth and reconciliation commissions cannot also adhere to the strict evidentiary standards that prevail in courts of law. And yet, because legal scholars and practitioners have been central to the global TRC phenomenon, the pretense that TRC truths are or should be objective continues to stand. Truth commissions should stick to "facts, which can be proved," says José Zalaquett, a lawyer and member of the Chilean truth commission; "this is not the place for an historical analysis of class struggles." "Let historians take over later" is how Susan Slyomovics reads Zalaquett's legal positivism, "and let them talk to each other."[50] The problem with this approach, of course, is that the historians are already involved. In Ghana, everyday people were acting as historians, interpreting and analyzing the past as they lodged petitions and presented testimony.

In the introduction we met Joseph Kwadwo Nuer, the former soldier who subverted the commissioners' demands for evidentiary truth by cheekily explaining that Ghana's grinding poverty had destroyed material evidence that would corroborate his story. Given Ghana's economic situation, Nuer explained, most of his documents had long been used as toilet paper.[51] The message is clear: attempting to fit the NRC archive into the mold of evidentiary fact and public proofs is a misstep. Knee-deep in this capacious NRC archive, the deceptively simple mandate to find out the truth about past human rights violations and abuse becomes a riddle.[52] What is the single knowable truth amid the multiple and divergent stories about the past? If anything, this archive telescopes just how difficult it is to find consensus about what happened to whom, and why, in the Ghanaian past.[53]

Oral-history theory is a way to navigate the NRC archive without falling prey to the sterile debates about the veracity of individual stories. Antjie Krog's dizzying observation that the truth is closest at the moment when the lie rears its head is a guide for reading these newly proliferating human rights archives.[54] Historians, Luise White insists, should approach secrets and lies as opportunities to observe how information is constructed, valorized, and marshaled within a particular social imaginary.[55] If "the invented account is at least as good as the accurate one," the unruliness of TRC records need not be reframed as legal evidence in order to be read or respected.[56] As Alessandro Portelli reminds us, the importance of oral testimony "may lie not in its adherence to fact, but rather in its departure from it, as imagination, symbolism, and desire emerge. Therefore, there is no 'false' oral source."[57] After all, the past is always being reconstructed and reframed according to the changing social and psychological needs of individuals and communities.[58] At the intersection of human rights and history, these scholars challenge the premise that narratives produced from within the belly of conflict must be objective to be useful.

Civil society and legal practitioners have been slower to step away from the vision of TRC history as a corrective to propaganda, error, and erasure. Zalaquett's legal positivism echoes Michael Ignatieff's quip that truth commissions may, at least, reduce the number of lies that are able to circulate unchallenged in public.[59] However attractive this vision of setting the historical record straight may be, in reality, TRCs around the world have been unable to banish the lies that power tells. The minimalist, facts-only approach

ignores the reality that in the house where conflict lives, consensus is out of
the question. No bare rendition of evidence, no profusion of tears, can convince some of us of histories that we cannot emotionally assimilate or psychologically bear. Even now there are those in South Africa who cannot accept
the weight of the TRC testimony about the violence of apartheid. Still they
insist "we didn't know, we didn't intend."[60] For these skeptics, individual testimony can be only partial, emotionally manipulative, calculated, exaggerated,
or myopic. Oral history's methodology directs us to the truths that emerge
within this lack of consensus: we are urged to ask who is rejecting stories of
apartheid suffering, on what grounds, and why? The stories offered in the
NRC archive elide, skirt, and flit in the spaces between fact, memory, rumor,
and lie. They contradict one another, sometimes directly and vehemently.
Nevertheless, the archive's narrative is still "true" as a mapping of the versions of the Ghanaian past deemed useful by citizens at a particular moment.
Instead of seeking to adjudicate between conflicting petitions, approaching
the NRC archive as the work of many authors pursuing diverse goals renders
the disputes comprehensible and legible.

On February 12, 2004, J. J. Rawlings appeared at the Old Parliament
House to testify before the NRC. The whole of Accra seemed to stand still.
In the streets, pedestrians, hawkers, and shopkeepers clustered around their
nearest television screen to watch the former president's questioning by the
commission. Undoubtedly, this was one of the NRC's most dramatic days.
The period of Rawlings's rule covered by the NRC mandate (1979–1992)
included heinous crimes of torture, assault, and murder. Twice, Ghanaian
families came to the NRC begging for help to locate and exhume the remains
of their relatives lost during these years. Rawlings, as a name and an icon,
animated many of the NRC petitions; some petitioners wondered whether
Rawlings himself was aware of all the atrocities that had taken place under
his leadership.[61] Others remembered begging Rawlings for clemency when
some of his soldiers committed brutalities.[62] Others told stories blaming the
chairman for the era's violence.

For all these reasons, the country waited on tenterhooks when Rawlings
was called as a witness to the NRC's investigation of the high-profile kidnapping and murder of three high court judges and an army officer in 1982. Rawlings's role in this particular crime had already been the subject of speculation
within the NRC.[63] The former president strode into the Old Parliament House
amid clapping, hooting, and raucous cheering. Justice Amua-Sakyi warned
the crowd to "comport themselves" appropriately or risk being ejected from

the proceedings. This was only the beginning. The commissioners' encounter with Rawlings was stilted: an awkward dance including timid questions from the NRC about the whereabouts of videotape recordings and the bravado of the former president, who blustered and lectured his way toward admitting that he could neither produce nor locate the tapes in question. Abruptly, the commissioners dismissed Rawlings, saying that their questions were finished and they were satisfied with his responses. Amid cheers and laughter, Rawlings made his way out of the chambers, joined the crowds of supporters thronging around the Old Parliament House, and marched peacefully back to his central Accra residence.[64]

The limited exchange between Rawlings and the commissioners was anticlimactic, to say the least. As one reporter stated, "It took longer for him to come and go than to answer their questions."[65] The factual truth of his testimony was almost beside the point. In the détente between Rawlings and the NRC, the former president's determination to control the story represented a sharp public rebuke to all who presumed that a national human-rights review could bend Rawlings to its will. In the words of one US State Department analyst, "The Commission's focus on carefully structured proceedings may, this day, have missed the mark."[66] Hardly anyone who observed the February 12, 2004, hearings would conclude that the truth of Rawlings's role in past political violence had been determined. Oral-history methodology, however, urges us to consider that silence, stilted speech, avoidance, and rumor often speak eloquently. There is a richer transcript of the détente between former president Rawlings and the commissioners at the NRC.

First, the palpable silences in this exchange speak volumes. The commissioners' laser focus on the whereabouts of certain tapes is a determined evasion of the numerous other questions that could have been put to Rawlings about human rights abuse. Indeed, as described above, some NRC petitioners directly accused Rawlings and/or his wife, Nana Agyeman Konadu Rawlings, of culpability for heinous crimes. Numerous other petitions and testimonies insisted that the order created by Rawlings's rule was toxic, a breeding ground for soldier violence. Despite citizen stories about the role of the Rawlings family, the commission focused exclusively on the whereabouts of tapes recording soldier confessions about a few high-profile acts of violence and rigorously avoided much of the controversy produced by decades of Rawlings' rule. At moments, it appeared that the only one willing to approach the violence of the past was J. J. Rawlings himself. Sitting before the NRC, he hinted at the limitations of the NRC's shallow questions.

NRC: Is there any other information at all on these video tapes, being
    referred to now, that you'd like to give to the Commission?
RAWLINGS: [*Pause*] Lots of them. But um . . .
NRC: Please go ahead.
RAWLINGS: No, if you have specific questions, I'll deal with them.[67]

Similarly, when the NRC Chairperson, Justice Amua-Sakyi, abruptly dismissed the former president, Rawlings opened his eyes wide in surprise and
quipped, "Oh, Sir, why? . . . Is that all?[68] The insinuation was that the commissioners had not yet completed their work, that they had ended the interview too
early and had not yet managed to confront Rawlings on anything of substance.

The silence of the commissioners when presented with the opportunity to
publicly question Rawlings was deafening. In the NRC final report, the commissioners were bolder, going so far as to blame "the highest Executive authority in the land" for igniting the violence that suffused Ghanaian public life;[69]
however, at the public hearings, the commissioners deliberately treated Rawlings with kid gloves. Wise or not, this choice wordlessly revealed the ongoing
power of Ghana's former president as a volatile force in national politics.

From the moment he set foot in the Old Parliament House surrounded
by jubilating crowds, the NRC's dilemma was apparent. Ignoring Rawlings
completely by never seeking his participation would have undermined the
entire initiative; however, delving too deeply into Rawlings's past was also
risky. A rigorous engagement with Rawlings might confirm the skepticism
of those who insisted that the NRC was a partisan enterprise or a threat to
the country's equilibrium. If the only purpose of the hearing was to ask a
few questions about a tape, presumably, Rawlings could have submitted his
responses in writing. However, a decision to never call the former president
into hearings would also have damaged the NRC's reputation. The encounter
gave the commission the appearance, if not the substance, of political authority. The image of Rawlings, in his signature dark glasses, sitting before the
high table, answering questions about human rights abuse, was visually powerful. Indeed, he had been *compelled* to appear. Having successfully created
this illustration of accountability, the NRC quickly extracted itself from this
encounter, careful not to tread on the tail of a tiger.

Indeed, the "truth" revealed by this moment was Rawlings' enduring
power and the limitations of the commission's desire to pursue rigorous historical accountability. In Ghana, all those watching this exchange would have

received the message loud and clear: the violence of the past could not reliably be contained by the present. Digging too deeply was still risky business. Rawlings's day at the NRC displayed the constraints of historical justice in twenty-first-century Ghana. Indeed, Rawlings himself scolded the commissioners like schoolchildren, insisting that they must take the context of revolution into account when assessing the Ghanaian past. "You've got to appreciate the degree of tension that was existing then. . . . It's a complex thing . . . when you're talking about a revolt, the thing erupts from the bottom, and it takes time to restore command and control. And it can be very devastating. And that's what we presided upon. This is a different subject. If you people are interested, we can deal with that later, ok? For now, let's deal with some of your pertinent allegations."[70]

Within the NRC archive, victims of violence rejected this solipsism where "revolution" is description, explanation, and justification of the violence that ordinary Ghanaians faced during these years. The stories of Ghanaians illuminate the scores of men, women, and children injured, stunted, and damaged by agendas and policies that they did not choose and which did not benefit them. "Revolution" does not adequately explain the brief life of Seidu Nombre, shot in the head at Kokompe for answering back to soldiers during the December 31 coup, nor does it contain the grief of his father, Salifu, who testified at the NRC.[71] Revolution does not assuage the anguish of the family of Yaw Fosu Munufie, whose two-year-old niece died in a ditch when soldiers shot her father for breaking curfew.[72] Revolution cannot erase the words of ex-sergeant Abraham Kwaku Botchwey, who suffered torture and begged his captors to fire one bullet and end his life.[73] The narratives of citizen suffering challenge this claim that the ends justify the means in Ghanaian politics.

At the intersection of human rights testimony and life history, Kay Schaffer and Sidonie Smith see an opportunity for the creation of insurgent narratives. "Through acts of remembering," they claim, "individuals and communities narrate alternative or counter-histories coming from the margins, voiced by other kinds of subjects—the tortured, the displaced and overlooked, the silenced and unacknowledged."[74] Ghanaians thrust forward troubling versions of the truth that did not easily align with the government's hope to use the truth commission as an instrument of closure. Nonetheless, this democratized historiography was delivered in jars of clay. The NRC bureaucracy, which questioned just how much truth telling Ghana could bear and survive, actively contained these insurgent narratives.

Conclusion

The NRC was created in response to Ghana's polarized politics, but it became more than a referendum on the nation's parties and leaders. It was created to bring "healing" to a nation wrestling with postcolonial violence, but its archive maps the economic, political, and social fault lines that persist within Ghana. The NRC was supposed to unearth, finally, the truth about the national history, but its cacophonous archive resists any effort to distill a unified or singular narrative. The truth that emerges most clearly is about the salience and politics of difference within Ghana. Why, and how, does the Ghana's NRC archive so persistently transgress the boundaries of its creation? Answering this question requires consideration of the volatility of individual testimony as a tool of public history.

The TRC format—in South Africa, in Canada, even in Greensboro, North Carolina—is based on the assertion that the voices of ordinary people have been overlooked and are necessary when pursuing the past. However, no one knows what people will actually say. In valorizing individual testimony by seeking out, publicizing, and preserving people's voices, Ghana created a complex and contradictory archive marked both by citizen desire and government power. Of course, as described above, neither the petition-making process nor the public hearings allowed for the unconstrained expression of citizen voices. Structural constraints, from economic need to gendered fears, limited citizen participation. Statement takers transmitted and translated citizen stories, often marking (sometimes physically) the documents that the NRC preserved. In the hearings, citizen stories were judged, disbelieved, and sometimes dismissed. Nevertheless, the power of people's voices within Ghana's public history-writing project cannot be overlooked. As people ventured forth to tell these stories despite all manner of risk, oral history's rejection of the truth/lie dichotomy in favor of considering all the ways citizen testimonies speak volumes is a guiding thread.

CHAPTER 2

Human Rights and Ghanaian History

[Ghana's history] has been chequered with little
improvement in the welfare of the ordinary people
who have borne the brunt of maladministration and
incompetence of their successive leaders, leaders who
promised heavens but found it difficult to make even the
earth a comfortable place to live in.

—Lord Cephas Mawuko-Yevugah
"Who's Playing Politics with National Reconciliation"
December 3, 2001

On March 6, 1957, when Gold Coast threw off the cloak of British colonialism, the country was both harbinger and hope of what the "winds of change"
sweeping across Africa might wreak.[1] Far beyond its own borders, the West
African nation's political independence was both a triumph and talisman.
"Ghana tells us that the forces of the universe are on the side of justice," thundered Martin Luther King Jr. "It symbolizes . . . that an old order is passing
away and a new order is coming into being."[2] In South Africa, antiapartheid
activists looked to the newly independent country as a source of succor, both
existential and material.[3] If Ghana's birth "demonstrate[d] . . . the ability of
people born and bred in Africa and native to her ancient soil to govern themselves with efficiency and the dignity of democracy," what should be made the
country's post-colonial political troubles?[4] In its turbulent passage through
the twentieth century Ghana has been a "particularly poignant" emblem of
both the hope and disillusionment of African independence.[5]

This chapter briefly sketches the contours of Ghana's national history.
Unlike other accountings, I place the question of human rights abuse and

Table 1. Governments of Ghana after Independence

Dates	Leader(s)	Party
March 6, 1957– February 24, 1966	Kwame Nkrumah	Convention People's Party (CPP)
February 24, 1966– October 1, 1969	Akwasi Afrifa Joseph Ankrah J. W. K. Harlley Emmanuel Kotoka B. A. Yakubu Albert Ocran Anthony K. Deku J. E. O. Nunoo	National Liberation Council (NLC)
October 1, 1969– January 13, 1972	Kofi Busia	Progress Party (PP)

January 13, 1972–
October 9, 1975
October 9, 1975–
July 5, 1978
July 5, 1978–
June 4, 1979
	Ignatius Kutu
	   Acheampong
	Ignatius Kutu
	   Acheampong
	Fred Akuffo
		National Redemption Council (NRC)
		Supreme Military Council
		Supreme Military Council

June 4, 1979– September 24, 1979	Jerry John Rawlings	Armed Forces Revolutionary Council
September 24, 1979– December 31, 1981	Hilla Liman	People's National Party (PNP)
December 31, 1981– January 7, 1993	Jerry John Rawlings	Provisional National Defence Council (PNDC)
January 7, 1993– January 7, 2001	Jerry John Rawlings	National Democratic Congress (NDC)
January 7, 2001– January 7, 2009	John Agyekum Kufuor	New Patriotic Party (NPP)
January 7, 2009– July 24, 2012	John Atta Mills	National Democratic Congress (NDC)
July 24, 2012– January 7, 2017	John Dramani Mahama	National Democratic Congress (NDC)
January 7, 2017–	Nana Addo Dankwa Akufo-Addo	New Patriotic Party (NPP)

the stories gathered by Ghana's National Reconciliation Commission (NRC) at the center of this narration. Approaching Ghana's story in this way seems to fly in the face of the country's contemporary image as a place of peace and stability. As in the past, Ghana continues to be a potent political symbol—but the prevailing narrative is no longer about Pan-African liberation but about the possibility of African "success" in the global neoliberal economic order. From the *New York Times*'s declaration of Ghana as "a good kid in a bad neighborhood" to the World Bank's insistence that the country is poised to join the ranks of middle-income countries to the flood of articles about Accra as a cosmopolitan, creative hub, Ghana's star is on the rise.[6] (Apparently, "Accra's Jamestown is electric—it's like Hackney Wick on steroids."[7]) Without undermining Ghana's considerable achievements, this praise—comparative, marked by low expectations, and based on neoliberal rubrics of progress (GDP, consumption, friendliness to global capital)—eludes the experiences of the majority of Ghana's people. A human rights history, on the other hand, excavates the human suffering that has accompanied Ghana's story and uses it to interrogate the national political trajectory.

The NRC was not the first (nor the last) time when citizens used the language of international human rights as a lens through which to parse the substance and content of freedom in Ghana. The first part of this chapter explores the way human rights was utilized by Ghana's government, labor unions, journalists and others during the first ten years of national independence. Human rights was and still is a mutable language deployed for myriad ends by different communities within Ghana and beyond. Its power was and still is in the attempt to mobilize a supra-national moral standard to describe, challenge, and condemn political violence. "Rights talk" in Ghana's early independence period was inherently politically fraught; it was an invitation to consider if, when and how state violence become untenable—and what to do about it. Accordingly, a human rights history of Ghana is not a narrative of moral absolutes and bright lines; we are not entering the "world of uncivilized deviants, baby seals, and knights errant" that David Kennedy criticizes as the consequence of the human rights worldview.[8]

The second part of this chapter uses the NRC's reports of suffering as a guide and touchstone in a brief recounting of Ghana's journey through the late twentieth century. Encountering Ghana's past in this way, through claims of human rights abuse, is controversial. Are these stories proven to be true? Are there other truths that are missing from citizen testimony? Can policies justified in their time now be condemned as intolerable? What separates a human rights violation from other types of violence? A human rights history of Ghana evokes uncertainty and even dispute; it is an accounting that avoids the illusion of consensus and instead magnifies the way Ghanaian political history remains unsettled.

Rights Talk and Ghanaian History

Before the NRC, Ghanaians deployed the language and concepts of international human rights in national politics. As a normative part of global, national, and local politics—indeed, as a "world-wide secular religion"—international human rights is expansive and diverse, including law, rhetoric, policy, and practice.[9] It has the capacity to "construct a wide array of different discourses."[10] This fecundity is evident in decolonizing Ghana, where human rights rhetoric was utilized by diverse communities, for multiple audiences, and to diverse ends. In the era of decolonization, various communities marshaled human rights as the ethical ballast of diverse political agendas. Politicians, newspapers, and public intellectuals marshaled "rights talk" to discuss the global implications of Ghanaian politics, while labor unions, social organizations, and activists employed rights rhetoric to address their national government and the wider world in the same breath.

Contemplating human rights in late-1950s and early-1960s Ghana departs from the scholarship that emphasizes the waning days of the Cold War as the moment when international human rights captured the global imagination.[11] This study presents an earlier trajectory where human rights talk was part of mapping and pursuing freedom in Africa's anticolonial and early independence era. Aligned with Bonny Ibhawoh's exploration of the significance of human rights language in colonial and decolonizing Nigeria, this study traces how Africans in Gold Coast and then Ghana "appropriate[d] and deploy[ed] in diverse ways the same language of rights and liberty that was so central to the British imperial agenda."[12] Kwame Nkrumah, the Ghanaian anticolonialist and nationbuilder, utilized the rhetoric of human rights as a pragmatic political language, alternately marshaled at opportune moments in the halls of the United Nations and then later discarded as an emblem of Western political hypocrisy. Although the historian Jan Eckel describes Nkrumah's ambivalence as evidence that human rights was a "marginal" concept in decolonizing Africa, this study challenges the idea that human rights pragmatism signifies a limited engagement.[13] Rights talk, whenever and wherever it has been deployed—in the post–World War I League of Nations, in Geneva in 2016, or in the colonial Gold Coast—can never be separated from its political utility. Fundamentalist notions of human rights as a language of true believers mask the ways rights talk is always and everywhere a political weapon.

Writing in *Foreign Affairs* as the prime minister of a newly independent country, Kwame Nkrumah explained to "American readers" that in Ghana, self-determination was an "inalienable right." "We are more concerned with fundamental human rights than with any particular skin color," he explained, attempting to both assuage US fears of Pan-Africanism as racial chauvinism and to criticize American Jim Crow.[14] Nkrumah's attempts to win global hearts and minds were troubled by rival Ghanaian politicians who used the language of global human rights as a weapon against him. Foremost among these was Kofi Abrefa Busia, an esteemed Ghanaian politician and social scientist who vocally criticized Kwame Nkrumah's leadership in the global public square.

Less than six months before Ghana's independence in 1957, Busia urged the British government to compel Nkrumah's party to include the European Convention of Human Rights in the new Ghana Constitution.[15] Binding the newly independent Ghana's constitutional order to the European Convention, according to Busia, was a necessary "safeguard." He continued along these lines even after independence. In London in 1961, Busia criticized Europeans for failing to speak out against Nkrumah's government in Ghana. "Is the cause of democracy served," he admonished, "by accepting different standards of tolerance, or freedom, or veracity, or human rights?"[16] Three years later, in another speech, this time to the Ghanaian Students Association, Busia again railed against Nkrumah's leadership, specifically focusing on the cause of political prisoners and using the language of human rights. "We've got so used to it we don't even stop to ask what it means to be inside a prison in detention," Busia exhorted the students. "Do you know how they are being fed? Or when they sleep? Or what happens to them? We don't. I have tried to get reports, I appealed to the Human Rights Society in the U.S., I appealed to the International Commission of Jurists."[17] For Busia, the language of human rights was a way of pursuing an international community response to Nkrumah's excesses.

Over time, Kofi Busia's missives from abroad became more strident. No longer was human rights simply a critique of Nkrumah's flawed rule. Now, the pursuit of human rights justified actively undermining Nkrumah's government. In a pamphlet entitled "Ghana Will Truly Be Free and Happy," Busia laid out the opposition-in-exile's plan to overthrow the Nkrumah state. The fourth point of the platform was to rewrite the constitution in order to "express the people's identity and aspirations, ensure fundamental human rights and personal freedom, and establish a truly free, independent, and respectable judiciary." He ended his missive confidently, inviting Ghanaians to "cast away their fear and defeatism . . . to do their part" and know that Ghana would be free. "Be prepared. More will follow."[18] Scholars who claim that "the UN was the only real place where anti-colonialism and human rights intersected," overlook the machinations of the Ghanaian opposition who deployed human rights, in earshot of the world, to question Kwame Nkrumah's capacity to lead.[19]

Politicians in exile were not the only ones who voiced criticism of Nkrumah's government in the key of human rights."[20] In 1959, when the famous Railway Workers Union derided the new Industrial Relations Act, which required all unions to join the government affiliated Trades Union Congress, they claimed that it "contravene[ed] the United National Declaration on Human Rights. On Ghanaian soil, critics used the idiom of human rights to describe Ghana's increasingly restrictive laws as betrayals of the ideals that Nkrumah championed during the anticolonial struggle. "We fought for independence to be able to live as freemen governed by principles of the UN Declaration of Human Rights as well as Ghana's own coat of arms motto: freedom and justice," Kwow Richards, then secretary of the United Party, admonished.[21]

While opposition groups made their discontent known at home and abroad, Nkrumah's Convention People's Party (CPP) government also found human rights a fertile ground for ideological battle. Human rights universalism was an opportunity to parse the hypocrisy of the global order. C. L. R. James, a vocal ally of the CPP, bristled at the audacity of European countries knee-deep in colonial atrocity presuming to criticize independent Ghana on human rights grounds. "Who are the backward ones in the Belgian Congo today? Who are the advanced and who are the backward ones?" wondered James.[22]

During the 1959 Nyasaland crisis, Nkrumah's CPP again sought to use Britain's commitment to international human rights to win concessions for Africans. In 1959, the British government sent three thousand troops to Nyasaland (now Malawi) to put down a pro-independence movement. In the resulting violence, 51 people were killed, more than 1,300 were detained, and many more were wounded.[23] Ghana's CPP organized protests in solidarity with the Nyasaland freedom fighters and marched to the UK High Commission in Accra. "We are trying to prove to the whole world that Africans are conscious of their human rights," the general secretary of the CPP explained.[24] However, pro-apartheid forces elsewhere in Africa would not cede the moral and political high ground to Kwame Nkrumah's Ghana. The Rhodesian European National Congress fired back that they too would organize a national day or mourning—for opposition activists detained without trial in Ghana.[25] For some critics, the Nkrumah government's authoritarian policies undermined Ghana's ability to act as a credible human rights advocate abroad. "Two wrongs do not make a right," stated one letter writer in the 1959 *Ashanti Pioneer*. Those speaking out about Nyasaland should also "agitate without further delay for the release of Ghana's political detainees."[26] An editorial in the same newspaper was similarly critical. "On what grounds," the writer demanded, "do CPP and their government stand . . . as champions of suffering humanity elsewhere in Africa?"[27] Indeed, when the British prime minister faced questions about Nyasaland during a visit to Accra in 1960, he quickly parried, reminding the questioning journalists of their own government's harsh emergency measures and full jail cells.[28] In the early independence years, the language of human rights was a double-edged sword, used to both defend and criticize the Ghanaian government.

In this milieu, Kwame Nkrumah continued to wield human rights as a tool of African liberation, insisting that European states must live up to their own expressed ideals and clear the way for African liberation. Standing before the United Nations in 1962, Kwame Nkrumah compared South African apartheid to the towering, bright-line example of international human rights abuse: Nazi Germany. "The essential inhumanity [of apartheid] surpasses even the brutality of the Nazis against the Jews," he explained. A state-funded political magazine, the *Ghanaian,* took up the cause, echoing Nkrumah's stance about the moral hypocrisy of the "so-called free West" who "look on unaffected with only occasional protests while the lives and liberties of millions of Africans wither in the iron hands of apartheid South Africa."[29] Eventually, Kwame Nkrumah would provocatively suggest that possession of any colonial holding should disqualify countries from UN membership.[30]

In the first years of national independence in Ghana, Kwame Nkrumah deployed human rights to undermine the moral authority of Western nations. Meanwhile, a collection of critics including Kofi Busia insisted that Nkrumah's government must be cried down as a human rights violator. These debates about whether rights talk would justify Pan-African liberation or apartheid and which leaders and nations might don the mantle of human rights advocate reflect the moral and political complexity of African countries' entry into the global political order.

Following the 1966 National Liberation Council (NLC) coup d'état, with Kwame Nkrumah in exile and the CPP banished from Ghanaian political life, human rights continued to be part of the debates about Ghana's political future. Immediately following the February 24 action, the NLC released a pamphlet entitled *The Rebirth of Ghana: The End of Tyranny*, which established that "Ghanaians in all walks of life have been denied their fundamental human rights."[31] Independent Ghana's first coerced regime change was supposedly an attempt to restore human rights—or so said a number of editorials published in the *Legon Observer,* a University of Ghana–based publication that sprang up in the aftermath of the NLC coup.

In the *Observer,* Franklin Oduro described the Nkrumah years as a time of propaganda and distortion. These were days when the politician responsible for administering the Preventive Detention Act might turn around and give an eloquent public speech about "fundamental freedom, the right of men to be treated as men … the right of men and women to the serenity and sanctity of their homes and hearths, the right of children to play in safety under peaceful havens … the right of old men and women to the tranquility of their sunset."[32] "It is incredible," Oduro quipped, "that a man who had such love for freedom would detain so many people without trial."[33] The *Observer's* editorial pages were marked by such critiques about the gap between human rights rhetoric and reality in Nkrumah's Ghana.

There were also musings about the role that the human rights concept might play in building a better Ghanaian future. Five months after the NLC coup, an *Observer* editorial pondered whether constitutional language about human rights might "nip an incipient dictatorship in the bud" and thus safeguard the future.[34] This particular author concluded that human rights language would not guarantee Ghana's political fortunes, noting that "no sequence of words, no matter how morally stirring or upright, could guarantee that human rights would be respected.[35] Ghanaians utilized the language of human rights to describe both what had befallen Ghana and how the country might be set to rights. During the first decade of Ghana's independence, politicians, journalists, and citizens marshaled rights talk, domesticating it for use in local political conflicts and simultaneously confronting the inequity and imbalance of the global political order. This trend would continue. By the time Ghana embraced a truth and reconciliation commission (TRC) in the early twenty-first century, a malleable human rights rhetoric had long been part of Ghanaian political life.

1957–1966

No single Ghanaian has been subject to as much praise or vilification as Kwame Nkrumah, Ghana's first prime minister and president. Differing versions of Nkrumah's legacy—visionary anticolonial icon, father of Pan-Africanism, paranoid African president, authoritarian leader—form a tangled and volatile bulk in the public sphere. From his own ideological pragmatism to the authoritarian inheritance of the British colonial state and the Cold War pressure chamber, Kwame Nkrumah's transformation from the man deemed *osagyefo,* or "redeemer" in the Akan Twi language, to his pyrotechnic political demise in Ghana's first coup d'état in 1966, is a foundational tragedy story in modern African politics.[36]

Pose the following question to any group of Ghanaians—did Kwame Nkrumah's CPP government abuse peoples' human rights?—and a volatile and protracted debate will ensue. The question is provocative because it calls for a moral assessment of the leadership of one of Africa's most imposing thinkers, theorists, and diplomats.[37] A simple label (abuser or respecter of human rights) is ill-fitting for a leader who both articulated the value of African self-determination and established himself as the head of a one-party state in which "of dissensus there was little evidence."[38] In 2012, a Ghanaian writer called for a "presidential commission involving intellectuals" who would "write the history of Dr. Nkrumah for an objective and non-partisan view."[39] Little did the writer know that such a history has already been produced. This nonpartisan accounting of Nkrumah's legacy was not articulated by a group of esteemed professional historians; it was curated by Ghanaian citizens themselves within the national reconciliation process.

The NRC archive's stories and petitions challenge the narrative of Kwame Nkrumah as either demagogue or savior. Ghanaians told stories establishing Nkrumah as the architect of the 1958 Preventive Detention Act (PDA), a law that empowered Ghana's government to detain citizens preemptively and without trial. Nkrumah's government defended preventive detention as a policy to protect the sovereignty of a lone independent nation surrounded by European colonies and in the midst of global Cold War. Over the course of eight years, hundreds of Ghanaians were swept into jail without recourse. In the NRC, Ghanaians remembered the PDA as an act of political violence; this was a policy that effectively incarcerated large numbers of citizens who, for diverse reasons, had made themselves enemies of local, regional, or national branches of the CPP government.

Indeed, there were persons like Kwablah Darquah, who participated in national reconciliation expressly to describe how people swept into prison as young men emerged years later, scarred, disillusioned, and bitter. "My being here today is to inform . . . about what the PDA did to a lot of able-bodied young Ghanaians and also to educate the public about the hardship we underwent."[40] Emmanuel France, arrested in 1958, explained that the "PDA had no moral roots," that "it was just passed as a tool to turn Ghana into a one-party state."[41] Detaining people extrajudicially and indefinitely, France claimed, licensed further atrocity. There were "prison officers [who] maltreated and tormented the detainees far beyond what they could bear," and proud Ghanaians emerged from cells damaged, plagued by "physical disability [and] emotional and psychological sores."[42] Preventing detention, many NRC participants explained, was a policy easily hijacked by those who would prosecute petty and local conflicts using state power. Petitioner Nicholas Dompreh blamed his detention on a physical altercation between himself and Kwamina Otoo, a local Akim Oda man. When Dompreh was later arrested by police, supposedly for "hurling insults at Kwame Nkrumah," he insisted that Otoo, his rival, used the cover of the PDA to engineer his arrest.[43]

The violence of preventive detention is not the only image of the CPP years lodged in the NRC records. Ghanaians injured by acts of terrorism also came forward to share nostalgia-tinged stories about the days when the government cared enough about Ghanaians to provide health care for those in need. Kwame Nkrumah was "profoundly motivated by an ideological vision of radical socioeconomic development;" he recognized that human development was the necessary precondition for economic growth.[44] This was part of the message of Joseph Allen Blankson, whose father was critically injured during a 1962 bomb blast. At the time, the elder Blankson was a music teacher for the Young Pioneers, a youth organization associated with Nkrumah's CPP government. While leading a public march, a bomb exploded and Blankson was hospitalized. After he lost one of his legs, the CPP government made his health a priority and "catered to" his needs, even sending him abroad to Britain to be fitted for a prosthesis.[45] With the demise of Kwame Nkrumah's government in 1966, the health of the elder Blankson also declined. Petitions like these reveal that there are those who mourned the end of the Nkrumah era as the passing of a vision of government in which human welfare was central to the work of political independence.

Although the petition of Joseph Allen Blankson focuses on the care-taking activities of the CPP government, it also illuminates the context in which Kwame Nkrumah's PDA was launched. This was a time of existential and physical threats to Ghanaian sovereignty. Kwame Nkrumah's effort to remain politically nonaligned amid the Cold War's polarization had created powerful enemies. As public places became sites of bombings and Nkrumah responded with increasingly draconian measures, Ghana's dissidents drew on the Cold War's inflammatory language to discredit Nkrumah's leadership. These appeals were not lost on the US government, which began to fear that Nkrumah had taken an "ugly lurch to the left," and expended resources to ensure that Ghana would not be "lost" to global communism.[46] By February 1966, Nkrumah's fears had become a reality: a coalition of Ghanaian police and army officials calling themselves the National Liberation Council (NLC) and acting with the support of the US Central Intelligence Agency seized power. A month after the takeover, Joseph Ankrah, one of the leaders of the NLC, wrote a letter to President Lyndon Johnson and spoke of Nkrumah as a menace to human rights and Ghana as one the USA's proxy states. "The Army and the Police Services were compelled to intervene to stem the tide of a growing communist menace in Ghana," Ankrah wrote. "We watched with dismay the destruction of our civil liberties. The cherished rights of the individual were contemptuously disregarded. . . . You can depend on me, my Government and the people of Ghana to support your democratic principles and your way of life," Ankrah wrote.[47] On both sides of the Atlantic Ocean, those who justified this interruption of Ghana's politics depended on images of Nkrumah as a violator of human rights, and particularly the history of the PDA, to make their case.

1966–1969

On February 24, 1966, when the NLC seized control of Ghana's government, the leadership was adamant about "liberating" the country from the grip of an authoritarian dictator. By decree, this army and police junta dismissed the president, dissolved the National Assembly (parliament), and shuffled the judiciary.[48] Just like that, Ghana embarked upon a cycle of military inter-ventionism, becoming the prototype for what would come to be called an "endemic problem . . . in African political life.[49] Scholarly assessments of human rights in this era tend to favorably compare the NLC years to the preceding Nkrumah government and praise the NLC for returning Ghana to civilian rule.[50] Not so the NRC archive, which illuminates the violence of the 1966 regime change and the subsequent years. Alongside the petitions of Ghanaians who mourned the end of the Nkrumah state's caretaking practice and those who confirmed the existential threats to Ghana's sovereignty, there was also a raft of petitions showing that Kwame Nkrumah's government was not singular in using extrajudicial detention as a weapon against political dissent. In the citizen accounting, the PDA was not exceptional; rather, it was part of a broader history in which a succession of diverse governments used extrajudicial detention to express authority.

One of the first acts of the NLC was to release hundreds of Ghanaians detained under the PDA. At the same time, the NLC instituted new "protective custody" policies that detained the functionaries and attachés of the former government. Again, Ghanaians were sent to cells without judicial review, clear sentencing periods, or formal processes of recourse. As the targets of Nkrumah's CPP were released from detention, people associated with Nkrumah's CPP were shepherded into the newly emptied jail cells. Philip Dade Armah, an intelligence office employed at Flagstaff House, was one such person. Armah spent almost a year in "protective custody" at Nsawam Prison. Although other former CPP security agents were released earlier, Armah noted that "those of us who did not know anybody" spent longer stretches of time imprisoned and were subjected to daily beatings with soldiers' guns.[51] Emmanuel Amartey Adjaye, another Flagstaff House guard, was assaulted, detained, and paraded before hostile crowds in Accra.[52] At the inaugural Accra public hearings on January 14, 2003, the sixty-seven-year-old Adjaye tearfully told his story of assault and detention. The police and army men "turned our ears into drums [that they] beat at will . . . My testicles turned to a football" and "my lips [into] a punching bag." Adjaye also remembered the crowds who "booed and hurled profane and unprintable words at us."[53]

Samuel Boadi Attafuah, also known as Nana Domena Fampong I, also described the 1966 liberation as an act of profound and indiscriminate violence. On February 24, when the radio announced the NLC takeover, a mob poured onto the campus of the Kwame Nkrumah Institute of Economics and Political Science and targeted "lecturers, students, and workers," whomever they could find. This mob, consisting of "hefty-looking soldiers" and "irate civilian[s] . . . under the influence of alcohol or other strong substances" was bent on destruction. The crowd dragged Attafuah from Africa Hall and beat him within inches of his life. According to Attafuah, the violence was both ideological and opportunistic. He heard his assaulters urging each other to "hurry up to finish [him] quickly and go back to campus to join the people up there to collect some of the booty." He also heard the mob encouraging each other to "take part in the demolition of the 'devil's effigy' (apparently referring to a 30 foot bu[r]st of President Nkrumah, overlooking the Institute.)" "Divine intervention" came at the moment a soldier left Attafuah for dead after smashing his left cheek with the butt of a gun.[54]

In this telling, the excesses of the NLC period are substantial and consequential. "As of now, I still suffer from severe pains in my left eye and ear as well as the joint of my cheekbones and find much difficulty even to yawn or masticate food on that side. I also experience constant headache as a result of the permanent injury on my cheek." Beyond the physical debility, Attafuah carefully listed the possessions (seven gabardine and woolen suits, one hundred classical and local records, three quality kente cloths, and two very expensive long neck chains) he had lost due to the looting of his apartment at Africa Hall. Attafuah mentioned that he was later hired by the Labor Department to research the "large-scale unemployment" that followed the 1966 coup d'état.[55] This first military intervention, like all the others that would follow, had deleterious economic consequences.

Similarly, Emmanuel Adjaye complained of new legislation that held citizens responsible for the economic delinquencies of the Nkrumah state. Adjaye's petition listed in succession the NLC decrees "numbers 3, 7, 10, 23, 40, 92, 111, 131, and 141," which "further restrict[ed] [him] from enjoying [his] fundamental human right [sic]."[56] Based on the premise that Nkrumah and his attachés had looted the public coffers, these laws were ostensibly intended to recover the nation's wealth from private hands.[57] Months after the NLC coup, the legal scholar William Burnett Harvey questioned the indiscriminate application of these restrictive laws, noting that persons ranging from "financial advisor to the Presidency" to common "Lorry Drivers" and "C.P.P. Activists" all suffered economic consequences as a result.[58] This was precisely the argument of Emmanuel Adjaye, who called these decrees "ruthless" and "unmerited." As a guard at Flagstaff House, Adjaye insisted, he was simply doing his job. Why, then, should he be punished for working "in lawful service to the nation"?[59]

The citizen petitions also count collective losses that cannot be valued monetarily. "It is regrettable to mention," remembered Attafuah, "that thousands of valuable books from the Institute's rich library were destroyed and burned by the new principal of the Institute."[60] By including this brief description of book burning among the accounts of past human rights abuse, Attafuah's narrative urges us to consider the consequence of coup d'état on education, archives, and cultural patrimony. "There were many casualties of [the NLC] coup," historian Jean Allman similarly explains, "but one that has not been fully appreciated is postcolonial knowledge production about Africa, or 'African Studies.'"[61] By 1969, the NLC had succeeded in managing a transition back to civilian rule, including commissioning a new constitution and holding parliamentary elections. The Progress Party, led by Kofi Busia, emerged victorious and Ghana returned to civilian rule.

1969–1972

Just as Kwame Nkrumah's government was undone by the Cold War's exigencies, Dr. Kofi Abrefa Busia's government also capsized on the shoals of an unfavorable global political economy. The similarities were not lost on Nkrumah, who penned an open "letter of consolation" to Busia dripping with schadenfreude. "My dear Kofi, I have just heard on the air that your government which came to power barely three years ago has been toppled by the Ghana Army. . . . Most of the evils of which my government and I were accused . . . were apparently the same reasons that motivated the army takeover of your regime."[62] Although Nkrumah and Busia charted entirely different courses, in the NRC archive's narrative, they both made Ghanaian people victims of their broader economic and political agendas.

In contrast to Nkrumah, Busia unreservedly sought to work within the economic constraints set out by the Cold War's politics. His belief that sharing the economic vision of the Western nations would translate into material support for Ghana was sorely tested during his short tenure as prime minister. When Busia attempted to service Ghana's debt according to the stringent austerity measures imposed by the International Monetary Fund (IMF) and the World Bank he "managed to alienate virtually all those groups who had first given [him] enthusiastic support: the intellectuals, the trade unions, students, wage earners, businessman, lawyers and judges, and most critically Ghana's military officers."[63] There is perhaps no clearer evidence of Busia's miscalculation than the words of his own finance minister, J. H. Mensah, who publicly distanced himself from the austerity policies even while signing the loan documents. "It is impossible to convince any Ghanaian that public money should be spent on paying such debt rather than on developing the country," he stated in the closing days of the Progress Party regime.[64] As fuel, food, and transportation prices rose, Busia finally suspended the deep austerity measures championed by the global lending institutions. As the World Bank and the IMF withheld relief and limited lending, Ghana's economic distress only increased, and Prime Minister Busia was left to twist in the wind.[65]

The NRC archive's stories about the Busia era describe the human suffering that accompanied the austerity policies of late 1960s Ghana. Joseph Broni Amponsah, a former policeman, came to the NRC to complain about forcible unemployment during the Progress Party years. Although Amponsah claimed that he was dismissed because of his hard-hitting investigation of election irregularities, legal research done by the NRC staff found that his dismissal was intelligible in much more mundane ways.[66] Amponsah was among the Apollo 568, a contingent of civil servants summarily and abruptly dismissed in 1972.[67] While the Busia government insisted these cuts were a straightforward and necessary means of cutting government expenditure, many of the victims, like Amponsah, claimed they were targeted because they acted with integrity and nonpartisanship in their respective roles.

The distress of the Apollo 568 found a voice in the court case *E. K. Sallah v. Attorney General*. Ghana's highest court agreed with Sallah, a dismissed civil servant who insisted that this mass layoff was illegal. The court ordered the Busia government to rehire Sallah and pay him damages but the prime minister balked, refuting the ruling in a televised national address. "No court, no court," an openly defiant Busia insisted, "could compel the government to employ or redeploy anyone it did not wish to work with."[68] A government that campaigned on upholding the rule of law, accountability, and strong institutions was openly flouting Ghana's judiciary. A public outcry ensued and Busia was criticized for abandoning liberal political principles for the sake of expediency.[69]

Alongside the petitions about the Apollo 568 controversy the NRC records also describe the violence of the Alien Compliance Order. In 1969, the Busia government passed a law requiring all "aliens" living and/or working in Ghana to obtain the proper migration papers or exit the country forthwith. As with Apollo 568, Busia justified this policy as a reaction to Ghana's fraught economic situation. Within a matter of months, thousands of West African migrants, many of whom had been living in Ghana for decades, if not generations, were compelled to leave Ghana posthaste. The suffering that ensued is described clearly in the executive summary of the NRC report, but only faintly appears within the citizen petitions and testimonies. "Faced with financial and economic ruin," the national reconciliation commissioners wrote, "some aliens committed suicide; others sold their houses and businesses for a song. Some greedy Ghanaians seized the properties of aliens or entered unconscionable agreements with them as to their disposal. Much suffering was caused by this attempt to enforce laws which had been left dormant for years in recognition of the mobility of the population in West Africa. It left considerable bitterness and destroyed many homes."[70] The report mourns the impact of the compliance order on Ghana's immigrant communities but says little of the Alien Compliance Order's economic justifications or its relationship to the Busia government's externally directed austerity agenda.

The citizen petitions bear only the faintest trace of this xenophobic policy. Dora Puplampu brought a petition asking for help locating relatives who emigrated, lived in exile, and died under the shadow of the compliance order. "At the time of the Aliens Compliance Order my sister . . . left Ghana with [Mr. Danyaro] and seven children. We learnt later that both Mr. Danyaro and my sister died and up till today, we do not know the whereabouts of the children. I am appealing to the Commission to help . . . as all previous efforts to trace the children have proved futile."[71] In this study's sample of the NRC files, Puplampu's request for help is the lone citizen petition about "the first time in the history of Africa [when] a neighboring government [drove] out of its country fellow Africans like cattle and oxen in open trucks."[72] Nevertheless, even the absence of citizen complaints about this devastating policy is illuminating. Perhaps there were few citizens in twenty-first-century Ghana who were willing to reveal their ties to communities previously marked as strangers. Perhaps the justifications offered by the Busia government—that border control is the right of any sovereign nation, migration is a drain on the economy, life will be better for citizens if strangers are expelled—had taken seed and grown. There are many possible reasons why the history of the Alien Compliance Order may be hushed in the NRC citizen records and remembered in the official NRC report. Considering each of them, minding the gaps and silences is part of the revelation of the NRC archive's human rights history.

Nevertheless, the Alien Compliance Order, like the mass dismissal of government workers and other austerity measures did not generate sufficient goodwill among the Ghanaian population.[73] Busia's government was short-lived and the measures described above provided a justification when Ignatius Kutu Acheampong and his soldiers abruptly closed the curtain on Ghana's Second Republic.

1972–1979

The National Redemption Council coup d'état of 1972, like the 1966 NLC takeover, was based on the idea that only military intervention could set Ghana back on course. In contrast to Kofi Busia's government, which was hamstrung by "excessive international influence," Acheampong espoused a staunch economic nationalism, immediately revalued the Ghanaian cedi, and publicly decried looming foreign debt as ethically indefensible.[74] To great public excitement, Colonel Acheampong launched the Yentua, or We Won't Pay, policy, repudiating foreign debt and calling for the review of existing loans.[75] He initiated Operation Feed Yourself, which was designed to develop food crops and increase meal and poultry production.[76] He insisted that self-reliance was a collective enterprise involving all Ghanaians and launched campaigns calling on Ghanaians to Eat Local Foods, Patronize Locally Manufactured Goods, and Rely on Our Own Human and Natural Resources.[77] These policies were ideologically different from those of the preceding Busia government, but they similarly expected Ghanaian people to bear the brunt of their government's economic agenda.

In the NRC archive, Acheampong's stirring vision of self-determination is remembered as a weapon wielded against vulnerable individuals. The story that Emmanuel Badasu and John Owusu brought to the NRC begins in 1973, when the two men were accused of stealing underground telephone cables. A new subversion law made "any act with intent to sabotage the Ghanaian economy" a capital crime judged by military tribunal and as a result, Badasu and Owusu were sentenced to death. Appearing at an NRC zonal office decades later, Badasu insisted—as he had in 1973—that he and Owusu were innocent "escaped goats [sic]" of the bosses at the Tema Cable Construction Company who blamed their workers in order to cover up their own corruption, theft and mismanagement.[78] There was little recourse for these workers under the strident Acheampong regime. "Once [this] matter was dealt with by the Military Tribunal" the NRC legal officer explained, "its decision was final." An "ordinary citizen . . . wrongfully convicted by the Military Tribunal had no other forum where he/she could exonerate himself/herself and would have to suffer any punishment meted out to him/her."[79] Badasu was able to secure a stay of execution but languished in jail until 1982.

Stories like Badasu's expose the underbelly of a brand of economic nationalism that blamed individuals for Ghana's economic missteps. "If anybody wants to be an enemy in this economic war we are waging, he will be an economic prisoner of war," warned Acheampong. "He is only thinking about himself, he is not thinking about the country and if we have such people in the country we will never succeed. . . . Anybody who wants to challenge me, who wants to be saboteur in this exercise will find me very difficult."[80] Acheampong's program blamed recalcitrant citizens, not failed policies or even a hostile international economic climate for Ghana's economic stagnation. Only by moving citizens through pressure or coercion—or by removing them through imprisonment—would Ghana's growth be propelled.

This government directive trickled down into society and Ghanaians were recruited to inform on their fellow citizens. For example, according to Samuel Adovor, the Acheampong government "made a declaration that anyone who gives an [sic] information leading to the arrest and recovery of contraband good would be rewarded with 50% of the proceeds from the goods' sales," and so he embraced this culture of surveillance.[81] His NRC complaint was that in 1975 he had led soldiers to recover quantities of petrol and kerosene at Abrepo, Kumasi, and only received 10 cedis. Decades later, still looking for the promised payout, he came to the NRC asking the commission's aid in "recover[ing] what is due."[82]

The Acheampong years show that robust and visionary rhetoric do not automatically translate into effective policies. Neither Acheampong's nationalist rhetoric nor his policies generated the promised wealth, stability, and growth. These were years "characterized by falling agricultural and industry productivity, a runaway inflation, shortage of essential inputs and spare parts, a breakdown of the infrastructure, and incredible rise in the cost of living and general moral degeneration." [83] Ghanaians were subject to an increasingly draconian government determined to control the groundswell of criticism and popular protest. Finally, Acheampong concocted a controversial proposal to abolish political parties and install the military permanently in national leadership through a concept he called Union Government. At this point, Acheampong's deputy, Lieutenant Fred Akuffo, seized the chairmanship of the Supreme Military Council in a 1978 "palace coup," pushing Acheampong out of office and into prison. However, this shift did not sufficiently address the regime's corruption, stem the economic crisis, or resolve popular dissatisfaction. By June 1979, a new faction of soldiers, from the lower ranks of the armed forces, staged a coup d'état.

1979–1981

On June 4, 1979, a new faction of soldiers, led by Flight Lieutenant Jerry John Rawlings, seized control of Ghana's government. In a drama "rivaling . . . the extravaganza of the James Bond films," Rawlings morphed from a junior army officer held in a condemned cell to the most powerful position in the country at the helm of the Armed Forces Revolutionary Council (AFRC) within the course of two weeks.[84] Despite the brevity of the AFRC rule—a scant eighteen months—its impact on Ghanaian political consciousness cannot be underestimated. Riding a wave of populist rhetoric, Rawlings presided over a purge that impacted all sectors of Ghanaian society, from the army to the marketplace.

The AFRC's "house cleaning" exercise resulted in unprecedented public violence. All living former heads of state, including Akwasi Afrifa, Fred Akuffo, and Ignatius Kutu Acheampong were executed on June 26, 1979. Soldiers also burned down public markets throughout the country, blaming traders and market women as central culprits in the economic woes of the Ghanaian working man. The AFRC leadership and supporters justified all of this as cleansing violence that would deliver Ghana back into the hands of its people.[85] However, the NRC's accounting challenges this revolutionary populist narrative by displaying how ordinary working Ghanaians suffered in this era of soldier violence. The NRC report criticizes the AFRC that presided over a "total breakdown of law and order making it possible for arbitrary arrests, beatings, abductions, killings, detentions and seizure of money and personal property" to take place.[86] Moreover, hundreds of Ghanaians lodged harrowing complaints about the violence that was unleashed during this period. In the NRC records, assaults against market women and traders peaked during the AFRC years.[87]

However, this cacophonous archive also includes justifications of the AFRC violence. In his NRC petitions and testimonies, Osahene Boakye Gyan, former spokesperson of the AFRC, describes the violence that engulfed Ghana during this period as inevitable and politically necessary.[88] According to Boakye Gyan the AFRC regime was distinct from previous coup makers because it unseated a military regime which itself held power by force. "The

[AFRC] did not overthrow a constitution and a civilian government under it. It did not dismiss a parliament of the peoples' representatives and their mandate. It targeted mainly the members of the Armed Forces in search of justice, peace, and stability."[89] Boakye Gyan's petition continued: "Any act of human rights abuse . . . occurred while pursuing acceptable ends of justice in Ghana. . . . Any acts or omissions may be accepted as miscarriage of justice committed in good faith."[90] Boakye Gyan's parsing of the means and ends of different types of coups stands in stark contrast to the citizen reports of market women flogged in public, families separated by imprisonment and exile, and men made to stare at the sun or frog-jump in the noonday heat. This disparity is itself a revelation; it provokes a discussion about the complexity of assessing political violence in African history. How do we weigh the suffering of vulnerable populations against the lofty goals of nation builders? Can a utilitarian philosophy of means and ends comprehend the intimacy and irrevocability of individual suffering and loss? Conversely, can the fundamentalist language of human rights make space for the hard choices of politics?

True to its word, the AFRC returned Ghana to civilian rule and held national elections on September 24, 1979. Hilla Limann of the People's National Party was the victor and presided over the country for a brief period. On December 31, 1981, Rawlings intruded into Ghanaian politics once again and seized control of the state. In his "second coming," Rawlings established a military order that would direct Ghana's fortunes for the next decade and beyond.

1982–1992

The 31st December Revolution reestablished Rawlings as Ghana's highest political authority. The intrusion of the Provisional National Defense Council (PNDC) as a military government was justified much like the AFRC regime had been: as a "holy war" against corruption and an effort to restore power to the Ghanaian people.[91] Accordingly, the PNDC suspended the national constitution, banned political parties, detained party leaders, created public tribunals, and set up a "peoples' government" that empowered local PNDC affiliates.[92] Under this structure, civil-society, labor, and community-based organizations were banned or dissolved and reconstituted as extensions of the PNDC; the military became central to Ghanaian public life. The final report lists, over the course of many pages, Ghanaians who were disappeared, tortured, and killed in the decade between 1982 and 1992. Trivial events, including driving a fancy car or arguing with soldiers about the right of way, could lead to assault, detention, or even death.[93]

During these years, the leader of the people's revolution also embraced structural adjustment programs that caused considerable hardship for many in Ghana. Rawlings explained this about-face as a matter of pragmatism and sound economic policy. "The time had come," he explained, for "populist nonsense to give way to popular sense."[94] Austerity, in this period, was ushered in on the coattails of PNDC authoritarianism.[95] In the words of the Ghanaian historian Albert Adu Boahen, "We have not protested or staged riots not because we trust the PNDC but because we fear the PNDC! We are afraid of being detained, liquidated or dragged before the Citizens' Vetting Committee."[96] The NRC was an opportunity for Ghanaians to finally open their mouths about the violence of the years between 1982 and 1992. In the NRC report, the Rawlings years consisting of the PNDC and the AFRC governments "stood out in the excessive use of repressive measures in dealing with citizens."[97] Ghanaians poured into the NRC offices to lodge complaints about the years between 1982 and 1992. The heavy representation of the PNDC and AFRC years in the NRC files is at least partially related to temporal proximity. At the 2001 inauguration of the NRC, for most Ghanaians alive the Rawlings period was the stuff of recent memory.

During the later PNDC period Rawlings became the rare dictator who remakes himself as a democrat. In the early 1990s, he oversaw Ghana's transition to civilian constitutional rule, complete with political parties, a moderately free press, and democratic elections. The PNDC transformed itself from military authority into a political party, renaming itself the National Democratic Congress (NDC), with Rawlings at the head.

1992–2000

Eight more years of Rawlings' rule, within the context of a constitutional and democratically elected government, saw the progressive liberalization of Ghanaian politics. New human rights organizations were created, including the Commission on Human Rights and Administrative Justice and the National Commission on Civic Education. As usual, the NRC archive complicates this record of the NDC years as a time of flourishing human rights. Citizen stories challenge the totality of the transition; there was not always a clear boundary between the years of military government and the coming of democracy. This was the NRC testimony of James Agyapong Addai, who made the mistake of believing that democracy had truly returned and penned an article critical of Rawlings in the *Pioneer* in September 1992. "Critical analysis . . . reveals that the man J.J. Rawlings is not a law-abiding citizen of this great nation Ghana," Agyapong wrote.[98] He was promptly detained, questioned, and tortured by the Bureau of National Investigation. Although the PNDC had become the NDC and Rawlings would soon be a United Nations goodwill ambassador, Ghana's democratic opening was predicated on a constitutional indemnity clause ensuring that Rawlings, the PNDC, and all of its agents would not be held accountable for the violence of the earlier period.

After prevailing in the 1992 and 1996 national elections, NDC chairman Rawlings was no longer eligible to stand for the presidency. More than two decades of Rawlings' rule came to a close when Ghanaians elected John Agyekum Kufuor of the rival New Patriotic Party as president in 2000. On the campaign trail, Kufuor promised that if elected, he would confront the unresolved violence of the previous era. In his first message to the Ghanaian Parliament, President Kufuor presented his plan for a national truth and reconciliation commission.

Conclusion

Approaching Ghanaian history through the lens of human rights abuse involves confronting the legacies of Ghana's leaders and the considerable hope attached to the country's independence. Amid this minefield, the NRC testimonies and petitions are a touchstone pointing inexorably to the question of how people were living and who was suffering within the turbulence of Ghana's political and economic history. Although individual citizen stories may appear to condemn one leader or another, together they create a collective narrative that exposes the cycles of human rights abuse and the similarities in state repression over time.

This chapter sketches a human rights history which refuses the pretense of a singular or settled narrative about Ghanaian political morality. The NRC petitions and testimonies guide us into the dissensus that follows from diverse citizen experiences of state power. This review unearths similarities in how a diverse procession of postindependence Ghanaian governments justified human rights abuse. From this vantage point, Kwame Nkrumah's defense of a fragile national sovereignty amid the Cold War's peril and Kofi

Busia's capitulation to externally developed economic development programs are related. In both cases, the unfavorable terms of Ghana's integration into the global political and economic system created a sense of emergency and enabled leaders to act ruthlessly. These stories show the language of existential threat to be particularly efficient in masking the presence of human suffering. Similarly, Colonel Acheampong's proud economic nationalism and J. J. Rawlings's unabashed populism are united in articulating bold visions of Ghanaian freedom. Both leaders dared to dream of a nation unfettered from the political and economic status quo bequeathed them by colonial history. And both faltered by blaming individual Ghanaians for the national economic plight. Ideologically dissimilar regimes were united in treating different populations within Ghana in much the same way: as problems to be controlled, contained, and transformed.

CHAPTER 3

Kalabule Women

[Victim's voices] are like lightning flashes that illuminate
parts of the landscape: they confirm intuitions; they
warn us against the ease of vague generalizations.
Sometimes they just repeat the known with an unmatched
forcefulness.

—Saul Friedlander
*The Years of Extermination: Nazi Germany
and the Jews, 1939–1945*, xxv

Thursday, January 16, 2003. The setting is Accra's Old Parliament House. Jacqueline Acquaye appears before the National Reconciliation Commission (NRC) to tell her "gruesome story." The following day, the *Ghana Review* reports that not even a "glass of water and tissue paper" could stop her tears.[1] In 1979, about a month after an ambitious flight lieutenant named Jerry John Rawlings vowed to deliver Ghana from corruption, more than ten soldiers came to Acquaye's house in Akwapim-Akropong and accused her of hoarding scarce commodities. Acquaye tried to explain, to no avail, that the 260 bags of flour in her possession were neither smuggled nor hoarded. Flanked by soldiers, she was taken from her home to the local police station. "You bring some meat?" an officer called out when she arrived. Shaken, Acquaye spent the night in Akwapim Cells, a place she described as filthy with human excrement. At dawn the beatings began. First hands were used, then guns. She was transferred to a place called Acheampong House, where the violence continued. An army officer ground hot pepper together with gunpowder and forced the mixture into her vagina. Bleeding, weeping, Acquaye was made to "walk on her knees" on a mixture of broken glass and gravel. She lost consciousness. She awoke at the 37 Military Hospital. Weak and disoriented, she was informed that she would have to undergo emergency surgery and was rushed to Korle Bu Teaching Hospital. "They removed the uterus to save my life."[2] At this point, with tears flowing down her face, the sixty-five-year-old woman bared her stomach to reveal a five-inch scar, a reminder of the surgery to remove her uterus. The crowd gasped as the three female commissioners present, Florence Dolphyne, Henrietta Mensa-Bonsu, and Sylvia Boye, abandoned their seats at the high table. Rushing down to the floor, the three begged Acquaye not to publicly bare her body and physically tried to shield her from the cameras. Acquaye did not budge, presenting her body, scars and all, as evidence of her experience.

Most of the women who came before the NRC were traders like Jacqueline Acquaye; their suffering was connected to the work of buying and selling commodities. Historically, market trading has been more than a profession among Ghanaian women; it is a social and political identity of significant consequence. The West African market woman: fiercely independent, cooperatively organized, with no small measure of economic and social agency, is an icon of the prominence and power of women in West African societies.[3] This indigenous feminine power has been a source of anxiety for those who would govern West Africa—European colonialists and postindependence regimes alike. Although trading women's resistance to colonial intrusion is the stuff of history and legend, in the postcolonial era these same qualities of independence and collective organizing have often antagonized national governments.[4] In Ghana, there is a tradition of public backlash against market women that stretches from the colonial era to the present day.[5] When the Ghanaian economy dips downward, the iconic market woman who was once praised as a shrewd entrepreneur may very quickly become a scapegoat. The word *kalabule*,[6] a Ghanaian colloquialism that connotes unseemly, exploitative, and thieving business practices, has been used at least since the late twentieth century to describe market women as agents of corruption and economic stagnation.[7]

In coming to the NRC, Jacqueline Acquaye and many others like her marshaled body and voice to testify to the presence of economic, physical, and sexual violence in Ghanaian history. Their stories and their telling of them display the power of public victim testimony; in these narratives we witness the value of truth and reconciliation commissions (TRCs) as vehicles for citizen voice.[8] As the embodiment of a great reversal in which the last are made first, or as performative ritual, or even as a step toward national therapeutic catharsis, the very fact of TRC testimony is stunning. Nevertheless, this chapter pushes beyond the valorization of victim testimony to explore its substance. What do the so-called victims create with this "officially-sanctioned testimonial space"?[9] To what ends and purposes did market woman thrust their broken bodies and voices before the nation, exposing the violence that occurred at the intersection of gender and politics in Ghanaian history? At the national level, their suffering-soaked stories challenge the stigma of market women as *kalabule* women: purveyors of greed, venality, and exploitation in Ghanaian history. At the same time, once spoken, these testimonies are amalgamated into a global discursive field where images of African women's victimization abound, freely circulate, and function as both dogma and propaganda. The abused and debased African woman is a stock image of colonial vintage that is used to justify externally directed military intervention, promote an attenuated version of global feminism, and other questionable goods.[10] What happens when market women's stories are taken from the NRC archive and added to the chorus of suffering African women? In this chapter, the NRC is a site where Ghanaian market women stepped into the public identity of the human rights victim, to ambivalent ends.

Saul Friedlander, the historian and Holocaust survivor, establishes victim testimony as the key to unraveling the conundrum of historical violence. Victim voices, he claims, penetrate the opacity of stunning violence by gesturing toward, hinting at, and circling around that which cannot be explained by standard historical methodologies.[11] In "outburst[s] of pain and despair that . . . reject the possibility of order and coherence," Friedlander finds meaning and insight. We are living in an "era of witness," a moment when we privilege the individual voice as a way of knowing the past. The TRC emphasis on individual testimony is part of this broader shift.[12] Supposedly victim voices do not only explain the intricacies of violence, they also urge us to intervene. Human rights organizations confirm the idea that victim testimony is endowed with the power to call into being a concerned global community, to draw together those who live comfortably in wealthy nations with their brethren living in poorer nations riddled with conflict or constrained by scarcity.[13] The hope of human rights testimony is that it will mobilize new publics who by bearing witness to violence are compelled to act.[14]

Although victim voices may light afire global conscience, they do not always reflect historical or ethical complexity. There is a risk to these "circuits of suffering."[15] Brigittine French's warning that "survivor narratives are all too often presumed to be transparent" strikes a cautionary note—not only about the verifiability of victim testimony, but also about its opaque collusion with unspoken cultural and political agendas.[16] Amos Goldberg sketches a trajectory in which victim voices—the writings of Anne Frank, the memoirs of Elie Wiesel, movies like *Schindler's List*—once shattered the scholarly conceits of Holocaust historiography but now have become their own limiting analytical orthodoxy. As these first-person, intimate narratives became ubiquitous, the "excessive voices of victims . . . exchanged their epistemological, ontological and ethical revolutionary function for an aesthetic one."[17] Familiarity has not quite bred contempt, but it has produced contemporary audiences who pursue the sentimental catharsis—what Goldberg calls the "melodrama" of victim testimony. Victims' voices are now required; mundane; objects to be consumed by audiences seduced by the "melancholic pleasure" of emotional intimacy with those who suffer.[18] This emotional identification often generates sympathy, shock, and pity but does not move toward critical analysis or enduring solidarity.[19] Can a robust transnational solidarity be built upon this shaky ground of reductive, partial, or sentimental representations of political violence? This dilemma of human rights testimony as a spur for inadequate representation and nescient reaction is even more pronounced when the victims of violence hail from the continent of Africa and are marked as women.

More than four decades ago, the Guadeloupian author Maryse Conde lamented the "heap of myths . . . rapid generalizations and patent untruths" associated with the African woman.[20] Since then, scholars and activists in gender studies, human rights law, and African studies have impugned this narrative of African women as victims of violence and parsed the damage that it does. The imperative of "white men saving brown women from brown men"—and the concomitant circulation of images of African women's suffering—were neither incidental nor marginal to the European colonial enterprise.[21] This notion of "third world women as a homogenous, 'powerless' group . . . located as implicit victims," continues to be resilient in the postcolonial era because it continues to be useful for contemporary cultural and political agendas.[22] Clearly, no universal African woman exists, but the shadow of the suffering African woman continues to stretch far and wide over the global landscape, invoked in development reports and literary analysis alike.[23] This narrative of implicit and relentless victimhood undermines feminist solidarity by erecting roadblocks to partnership between women in the global North and South and circumvents a rigorous understanding of culture, gender, and global politics. Most importantly for this study, this distorting narrative makes it difficult for African women to speak and for the international community to hear.[24]

Part of the "tragedy of victimization rhetoric" is that if and when an individual African speaks about her suffering, she is heard within this already existing drumbeat.[25] Thus, "women cannot speak out against injustices or rights violations in their countries without risking the label[s]" and terms of this objectification.[26] Although victim voices are supposed to initiate specificity and thus greater understanding, I, like the literary scholar Salome Nnoromele, am "troubled" by the heft of the hegemonic representations of African women as victim. "*Even as* African women are beginning to speak for themselves," their words are co-opted into so much fodder to feed the "popular misconception of African women as slaves, brutalized, and abused by a patriarchal society" (emphasis added).[27] In this context, a testimony is not always revelation or clarification. For African women, daring to speak or write about one's suffering runs the risk of participating in the continuing objectification of self or community. Stories like Jacqueline Acquaye's, in all their intimate candor, cannot escape this entanglement of history, testimony, and melodrama. Immediately upon utterance, Acquaye's testimony of sexual violence becomes part of this global media context in which African women's suffering bodies are hypervisible. The following vignette illustrates the ethical and political complexity created by the "single story" of African women's victimhood.[28]

In 1997, Regina Danson arrived in the United States from Ghana without proper immigration papers and applied for asylum on the grounds that she faced sexual violence in her country of origin. Her name, she said, was Adelaide Abankwah; she was the daughter of a royal family in Biriwa, a town near Saltpond in Ghana's Central Region. After the death of her mother, Abankwah inherited the position of queenmother, a role that required her to be a virgin. However, Abankwah had already fallen in love, become a Christian, and engaged in sexual intercourse with a man. If her community elders discovered this, they would subject her to female genital cutting as a punishment; and so Adelaide Abankwah escaped.

Although Abankwah's initial request for asylum was denied, a team of human rights advocates took on her case and pressed high-profile American women, including then first lady Hillary Clinton, the thinker and activist Gloria Steinem, and actors Julia Roberts and Vanessa Redgrave, to stand with Abankwah and keep her safe in the United States.[29] A flood of publicity followed. Within the course of a few months, *Marie Claire* magazine published two articles on Abankwah; she was also interviewed by NY1 news channel. The Women's Commission for Refugee Women and Children joined in, urging the US Immigration and Naturalization Service to release Abankwah from detention on humanitarian grounds and grant her asylum. There was one problem: Danson's story—the pretensions of royalty, the vengeful "tribal" elders, the threat of female genital cutting—was false. The words of Nana Kwa Bonko V, the chief of Biriwa, who traveled to New York expressly to testify against Danson during a perjury trial are instructive. "We are not savages!" he thundered. "We Fantes do not practice female genital mutilation either as a custom or as a way of punishing anybody. We are a peace-loving people who believe in the sanctity of human beings." Nana Kwa Bonko V "[took] exception to a lie of this magnitude where a whole community and country are portrayed as cannibals."[30]

Regina Danson was eventually convicted of perjury and deported. However, her lie, and the sociopolitical dynamics in which it flourished, remain. Danson did not create this narrative in which African women, as a whole and without exception, must be victims of sexual violation. She was simply willing to accept the terms of this debate and to wield these as part of her individual pursuit of economic and social gain. Tongue-in-cheek, one Ghanaian-American professor in the United States explained this tension well. "This young woman has told a good lie and fooled the American system. I 'congratulate' her and 'wish her well' as an Akan; remember, I should not be envious of her 'shrewdness.' Neither should I be angry with the juridical system and the often ignorant 'support groups' who will believe and fight on behalf of any oppressed individual (especially if they are women . . .) escaping from and/or fighting outmoded non-existent customs in 'uncivilized countries.'"[31] The overdetermined narrative of African women's victimization is part of a global human rights apparatus that metes out violence to states marked as perpetrators of human rights abuse and distributes scarce political goods like citizenship, steady income, and travel opportunity to authentic victims. The premise of refugee status is that suffering people must reveal, narrate, and/or create "trauma stories [which] then become the currency, the symbolic capital with which they enter exchanges for physical resources."[32] And so these "representations take on a life of their own;" they are often not subject to corrective feedback because of their ambiguous political, social, and economic function.[33] The story of Adelaide Abankwah found support because it sounded *true* (as Danson knew it would) to the American audiences she encountered; this "shrewd" story was necessary for Danson to gain passage in a world of economic stratification and surveilled borders.

Is there any difference between the "false" story of Regina Danson and the "true" story of Jacqueline Acquaye? Both are graphic testimonies of the sexual violation of African women. Is the NRC archive just another site featuring stories of Africa's human rights failings and atrocity? By shifting the lens away from the global discourse of African women's sexual victimization to the domestic Ghanaian framework, the stories of Jacqueline Acquaye and other Ghanaian market women can be read dramatically differently. Both Kimberly Theidon and Silvia Rodriguez Maeso urge us to pay attention to the way TRC testimonies immediately cross swords with already circulating domestic, regional, and international explanations and justifications of violence.[34] Within Ghana, market women's stories of violence challenge the *kalabule* narrative that scapegoats trading women as the cause of Ghana's economic stagnation. These testimonies are precise and robust interventions into this ongoing domestic debate about economic power and social responsibility in Ghana. In the NRC, trading women's suffering was not consumed only by an international community who might hear these stories as part of a generalized African violence. Market women exposed their scars and thrust their damaged flesh and broken spirits before a national community that was familiar with the damaging *kalabule* woman rhetoric. In seizing the language of international human rights in this way, Ghanaian market women illuminate the shifting potential of TRC testimony in national and international spheres.

Histories of *Kalabule*

Anti–market women rhetoric is of long vintage in Ghana. Even before national independence, when colonial authorities sought to introduce a price control system during World Wars I and II, the Gold Coast administration blamed high food prices on market women, whom they described as parasites "burden[ing] the consumer with useless layers of profit and hoarding scarce goods."[35] In response, early Gold Coast nationalists such as the legendary J. B. Danquah were compelled to defend market women, "our hardworking mothers," against a colonial state that described them as obstacles to a successful and modern economy.[36] However, even after independence in 1957, the detracting rhetoric of exploitative market women proved remarkably durable. This, despite the visibility of market women in the Gold Coast's anticolonial movement. Market women popularized boycotts, marches, and other public events, winning the praise of theorist and historian

C. L. R. James, who reported that "in the struggle for independence . . . one market woman was worth any dozen Achimota graduates."[37] However, the newly elected Nkrumah administration, when faced with the challenge of transforming a colonial economy into a platform for growth in the midst of the Cold War, singled out "market women's monopoly on food distribution" as one of the local problems requiring remedy.[38] By the last months of the Nkrumah years, market women accused of violating price controls were dealt with as criminals.[39]

A rumor circulating in urban Accra at the end of the Nkrumah years highlights the anxiety surrounding market women's place in the nation. Allegedly, a night watchman at a bank was attacked by three Makola market women, who transformed themselves into python snakes and regularly visited the bank in the dead of night, gaining access to the strong room and making away with large sums of money.[40] To Ghanaian writer M. N. Tetteh, the rumor of the Makola snake women was "a mischievous piece of fun," a laughable attempt to "destroy the reputation of the hard-working Makola women who were strongly behind Dr. Kwame Nkrumah."[41] However, following Luise White's study of rumor as a means of communicating the anxiety produced by colonial violence in Uganda,[42] the Makola snake women stories may also be understood as public manifestations of an anxiety that market women's wealth was illicit, with origins in nefarious activities.

After the 1966 National Liberation Council military coup d'état, scrutiny of Ghanaian market women continued as a matter of policy. One of the new government's first decrees after the regime change was to dissolve and seize the assets of the Market Women's Union.[43] Just three months after the 1966 coup, the *New African* printed an article trying to make sense of Ghana's spiraling economic decline during the Nkrumah years. In its very first sentence, the article bemoans the "well-organized and powerful market women [who] profited from and profiteered on short crops" during the era of Kwame Nkrumah. "Any type of socialism or social democracy [was] anathema to the few thousand market women with £500–£5000 net incomes" who "regrettably" dominated the Convention People's Party national women's organization.[44] With such people in the nation, the article insinuated, Nkrumah's attempt to transform Ghana's economy was doomed. Accordingly, monitoring and controlling market women's activities continued to be at the center of government price-control initiatives even decades later.[45]

In the late 1970s and early 1980s, with Ghana's deepening economic distress, Rawlings's revolutionary government enacted price controls as a way to address income inequality and inflation. Fixing the Ghanaian economy, according to the Armed Forces Revolutionary Council's (AFRC) 1979 "house cleaning" exercise, required removing corrupt individuals from the system.[46] Officially the victims of this purge were supposed to be government workers, members of the armed forces, and private businesspersons, but traders were also routinely scrutinized, fined, and assaulted.[47] During the early Rawlings years, *kalabule,* as a synonym for individual corruption with national consequences, was a national crime, and market women were the most obvious (and vulnerable) offenders. Ghanaian newspapers followed the regime's lead, condemning market women as "exploitative parasites hoarding their wealth and essential goods while people starve"[48] and as "human vampire bats" draining Ghana of its life force.[49] Women were flogged, their goods were seized, and they faced fines and imprisonment for *kalabule*. When Rawlings returned to power in 1981, market women's organizations proactively trumpeted their support for the Provisional National Defense Council (PNDC) government, perhaps hoping to avoid a repetition of the violence they experienced in 1979. When groups of market women charted ten buses to publicly offer Rawlings their support at his headquarters, they were turned away at the gate. The Rawlings regime was established on an uncompromising stance toward corruption and would not recognize market women as appropriate partners in Ghana's development.[50]

Throughout this period, market women's bodies stood in for economic realities that were often invisible—inflation, decline in trade, corruption, and incompetence.[51] In the NRC public hearings, it became apparent that market women as a class were tarred with the *kalabule* brush, regardless of their individual business practices. When former military corporal Kennedy MacCoy Segbawu appeared at the Accra public hearings to answer for his role in the aftermath of the December 31st revolution, national reconciliation commissioners Professor Florence Abena Dolphyne posed a number of questions about why Segbawu had arrested Madam Yaa Anima. Was there a ban on the sale of wax prints at that time? If not, what gave Segbawu the authority to arrest people who were going about their legitimate duties? As Segbawu sat silently, the interpreter intoned, "My Lord, no answer." Commissioner Uborr Dalafu Label II continued with the questions. What criteria had Segbawu used to determine whether Madam Anima sold the wax prints above the approved price? Segbawu could only say, "the People's Defence Committee people told me she was selling at an exorbitant price so I arrested her." When the commissioner then asked whether Segbawu himself knew what the control prices were in those days, Segbawu answered in the negative.[52] These exchanges at the NRC public hearings made it plain that soldiers treated market women as "de facto deviants" whose work was assumed to be criminal.[53] Weeks after the 1979 AFRC revolution, the rhetoric of the *kalabule* woman culminated in the burning of Ghana's major markets. Soldiers attacked Accra's famous Makola Market first, then, from Kumasi to Sekondi to Tamale to Koforidua, major Ghanaian markets were razed to the ground by soldiers. This act of massive public violence was celebrated in the *Ghanaian Times* of 1979 as a "happy tragedy"; now, the article wrote, the Ghanaian working man would be free from the tyranny of *kalabule* women.

Even while Ghanaian soldiers were pouring kerosene on kiosks and stalls, the stereotype of the wealthy market woman was largely rooted in myth. The "vast majority of women in urban marketing barely earn[ed] enough to meet their daily subsistence needs."[54] According to Claire Robertson, the rhetoric of the *kalabule* woman and the violence it birthed was fueled by the intersection of gender and class anxiety. Ghana's moribund political economy created a tinderbox in which market women were pushed beyond the circle of national sympathy. Although years have passed since the days of this public violence, the debate about market women's work and place within Ghana still continues. In October 2011, former president Rawlings revisited and justified the razing of Makola Market in a speech at the University of Ghana. Rawlings insisted that in the face of the revolutionary anger of the Ghanaian soldiers, the public flogging of market women was the best possible outcome.[55] In Ghana's NRC, the much-maligned market women spoke for themselves. The public platform offered to former president Rawlings and to scholars who have written about this era is rarely offered to the women who were themselves stripped naked, detained, flogged, and assaulted. Market women's self-presentation at the NRC cannot be reduced to a narrative of victimization.

First, Ghanaian market women established the public intention of their stories by addressing themselves to the nation. Kate Abban, who introduces herself as the head of the International Association for the Advancement of Women in Africa and mentions residences in both Cape Coast and Accra, described her 1979 incarceration and assault at Burma Camp as an event of national importance. "I want this to be put on the record for future generations. . . . I want what happened to be known." She also requested that the "nation" apologize for what she suffered." At Burma Camp, "someone slapped me from behind. I remember that as a result of the slap, my pearl earring got shattered. I was also hospitalized at Korle Bu Teaching Hospital for three months as a result of the slap."[56] How much force shatters pearl? What type of "slap" hospitalizes an adult woman for three months? In this petition, Abban's suffering stands alongside her economic privilege. Multiple residences, pearl earrings, and brutal physical assault are all part of the same story. Abban was among the rare petitioners who did not ask for any compensation; the NRC was an opportunity to finally address the nation. Other market women's stories reveal just how rare such a platform was.

For Abena Kitiwaa, "the whole trouble started" in 1983, when she and a group of other Cape Coast bakers pooled their money and bought a large quantity of flour.[57] Soldiers accused Kitiwaa of hoarding flour; she was detained and beaten but released without charge. While recovering at home, Kitiwaa was surprised to see her name splashed across the *Daily Graphic* under the title "Baker Suspended for Indiscipline." Insisting that she had neither committed nor been charged for any crime, Kitiwaa confronted the *Graphic* publisher and asked for a retraction or a rejoinder "to cleanse the mind of those who had read the stories."[58] The publisher refused, saying, "Hey, Madam, don't you know the *Graphic* is a governmental property?" In those times, it was exceedingly unlikely that Kitiwaa's version of events would ever find a public voice. After living under the stain of this accusation for years, Abena Kitiwaa came forward to publicly tell her story at the NRC and clear her name.

Second, in many of these stories, market women challenge the stereotype of *kalabule* woman's wealth, dominance, and greed by graphically revealing the full extent of their suffering. As described above, Jacqueline Acquaye literally forced Ghana to see her scars, to view her most intimate losses. Yaa Anima presented herself at the Accra hearings dressed all in black, wearing mourning attire from head to toe. Her dress was a visual statement; this mourning attire was not a reference to a recent bereavement, but an homage to the many losses she had suffered as a victim of state torture.[59] In 1981, Yaa Anima was a textile trader in the Nima neighborhood of Accra when Corporal Segbawu (mentioned above) seized 140 half-pieces (six yards each) of wax print, arrested her, and brought her to Gondar Barracks. Over the course of two weeks, Anima and other detained women were beaten regularly and made to sweep Accra's streets. In one sadistic game, they were sent to Labadi Beach and made to collect and haul bags of sand. On another day, one "tall soldier" pulled the hair off her head and caned her until she bled from her vagina. This abuse left Anima with chronic headaches and partial deafness and traumatized her to the point where she abandoned large-scale trading altogether. With four children to support and few options for gainful employment, Anima fell into despair and contemplated suicide. Tears punctuated her story as she chronicled her path from textile trader to market porter, one of those called *kayayo*, a person who does the most unskilled labor in the markets, "moving from village to village, carrying wood and all kinds of things just to make ends meet." Today, she noted, her children had not received adequate education because she was unable to provide for them and so they were also marginally employed as "truck pushers and hawkers."[60] By mentioning her children, Anima joined the many traders whose NRC presentations included careful descriptions of the many people depending on them to provide.

Third, in the NRC, market women revealed themselves as caretakers who embraced the responsibility of providing for their families and were thwarted by the state's repression. "I was baking to look after the children's schooling, but due to [detention and seizure of goods] these children have to stop schooling," said Acquaye. "I am now jobless. . . . I found it very difficult to feed them and one [has] even died at 37 Military Hospital as I couldn't afford to buy drugs prescribed for her."[61] Far from the image of a wealthy woman profiteering, Acquaye framed her business as a poor widow's attempt to provide for her children. In the NRC, market women spoke the names of dependent husbands, needy children, and extended relatives who all suffered because market women were treated as public enemies. By revealing their social networks, market women urged Ghanaians to view their labor in the context of community. Market women's insistence that the nation recognize them as mothers, caretakers, and providers stands in contrast to the *kalabule* rhetoric which explicitly sought to cancel out or ignore these identities.

Victoria Ainadjei, an Accra market woman, testified that when she was detained, she was three months pregnant and one of the soldiers pressed down on her swelling midsection. "Upon seeing my belly, one of [the soldiers] said that I had hidden so much money there that my tummy was big," she recounted. "He used both hands to roughly touch and squeeze my tummy from my abdomen up and was saying if this was not money what was it?" The soldier's message was clear: as a *kalabule* woman, Ainaidjei would not be treated as an expectant mother. Soldiers would use her body as more evidence of criminality. Ainadjei's nightmare seemed to end when her husband, who was also a soldier, secured her release. However, there were consequences. "My daughter, who I was carrying when the soldier squeezed and punched my stomach ha[s] been suffering from convulsions since she was born. I was informed by the doctors that it was caused by what the soldiers did when I was pregnant."[62] Her daughter's illness would serve as a constant reminder of the events of this day when she went out to sell her wares and became the victim of assault.

Similarly, Gifty Adom recounted the long-term consequences of a soldier assault. This is how her petition begins: "I have to inform you that I, the mother of the above-named blind boy in 1979, was pregnant and expecting a baby."[63] While selling fish in Mampong, Ashanti, an unknown soldier removed his belt and began beating her body with it. At the time, she was more than nine months pregnant. When her son was born one week later, he was blind. A specialist at the time asked her "whether something had knocked her stomach during the pregnancy." The remainder of her petition focuses on her son, Ibrahim Afrifa, who struggled to complete the Akropong School for the Blind because "the beating had affected both his eyes and his brain." Although he was taught the vocational skill of weaving doormats, he subsequently was unable to find employment. At the public hearings, Adom called Ibrahim Afrifa to sit beside her. In the video recording, the camera focuses on the downcast face of a young man who walks slowly up to the front of the room. Ibrahim is helped to find the seat beside his mother and sits in silence for the remainder of this testimony.[64] In her petition, Adom's only request was on behalf of her son. "I do not need money but employment for my boy as a craft instructor at the Ghana education service."[65] Similarly, at the hearings, her last words focused on Ibrahim. "Whatever [the commission] can do to assist this boy because I don't know when, probably I may die and leave this boy, and if I leave him who is going to take care of him? So I am humbly appealing to the Commission to come to my aid as to how I can look after this boy."[66]

At the time that Gifty Adom suffered her ordeal at the Mampong market, Catherine Cojoe was both a dealer in textiles and the owner of a provisions store and drinking bar in the Accra area. When Cojoe was confronted by five soldiers who seized and auctioned her textiles, she immediately ordered her husband to go to the store and sell everything in the place "at giveaway price." He was too late. By the time he arrived at the provisions store to sell off the inventory cheaply, soldiers were at the door. When Cojoe heard this news, she rushed to the store to see whether anything might be salvaged. "I had a four month old baby girl at my back. They asked me to remove her so that they could shoot me because I was a '*kalabule*' woman." Cojoe refused: "I challenged them to shoot the two of us. I spoke Ewe in prayer to God." This harrowing exchange ended when one of the soldiers, also from the Ewe community, interceded on her behalf. Cojoe kept her life, but her family went into a tailspin. Her traumatized husband could no longer work and her business was devastated. "I sold all my properties to look after my children. Now I have no money and my husband is a sick man," she said. "I need help."[67]

The stories of Ainadjei, Cojoe, Adom, Abban and Anima describe a dystopian world in which pregnant women are brutally assaulted and mothers are asked to take their babies off their back so that they might be shot. These women, whether they were petty traders of saltfish or formerly prosperous owners of textile shops and bars, presented themselves as providers, mothers, breadwinners, and caretakers. Although the anti–market woman violence of the AFRC and PNDC era, with its damaging *kalabule* rhetoric, negated the complexity of these women's identities, at the NRC, these women revealed the depth their suffering, their place in the community, and the enduring social consequences of soldier violence. National reconciliation was an opportunity for market women to insert their voices and perspectives into a national historical record that has, in turn, theorized, praised, and blamed them. They utilized their bodies, attire, tears, and voices to assert a social rationale for their economic activity, to reveal their suffering, and thus, counter the dehumanizing narrative of the *kalabule* woman. When they insisted that they be seen as mothers, sisters, wives, caregivers, entrepreneurs, and citizens, the appointed commissioners heard them. The NRC report mourns the fact that in the past, "women, the mothers of the nation, have been humiliated in public and suffered acts of indignity that disgraced womanhood."[68] Classifying the victims of violence as mothers (and not as market women) seems to render the violence against them more heinous and unjust. Even at the time of the AFRC and PNDC revolutions, the few voices publicly defending market women spoke in this same vein and used the language of motherhood to inspire shame in the Ghanaian public. "The only public defenses of market women portrayed them as impoverished, helpless mothers, rather than respected social actors," Gracia Clark recalls.[69] Both Clark and Robertson view this invocation of the maternal as a reactionary strategy in difficult times. Supposedly, only by hiding their business acumen, denying their agency, and highlighting their domestic and reproductive roles could market women escape the stigma of *kalabule*.

In contrast, in the NRC archive's citizen records, market women did not separate their public or private identities. If the NRC commissioners insisted that these women were "mothers," the market women themselves claim the complexity of their various social roles. The NRC promise of redress, perhaps spurred the market women's desire to articulate *all* their relevant losses, both personal and professional. Ofosuah Komeng began her petition in this way: "I am a very responsible single mother with seven children and a trader." For Komeng, the destruction of Makola Market was devastating. "Being the sole caretaker of my family . . . [this loss] demoralized my whole life to the extent that life lost its meaning to me." Her efforts to educate her children "all went to waste [and] many of them became drop-outs." The demise of her family and profession were intertwined. "The thought of my past as compared to these times make me shed tears," she claimed. "For now, I am just a petty trader that sells the wares in front of my house."[70] Far from being the successful business woman at Makola, Komeng was now working as a petty trader; her losses also include her professional identity. Similarly, Araba Quansah was a young woman selling small items in Takoradi during the PNDC era. While selling the ground cassava meal called *gari*, soldiers with guns appeared and auctioned off her goods. Quansah did not receive any of the money and that day's experiences halted her education. "I wanted to be a medical nurse, but because of what happened to me, I could not further my education," she noted. "This has prevented me from becoming a nurse." By way of reparations, Quansah requested that the government help her pursue a nursing program, she hoped that continued education would allow her to "help the nation."[71] Both Komeng and Quansah (and many other petitioners) did not avoid describing the professional costs of the violence meted out against them.

In the NRC records, Ghanaian market women strategically present their histories and their social identities anew. Their stories counter monolithic formulation of market women's wealth and practice. Alongside the shattered pearl earrings, there is also the saltfish seller who lacks economic support, has "no one to help her," and is working just days before giving birth. The connection between these women of different economic and social status is that they were all made into victims when Ghana's soldiers and military government demonized their productive labor. Moreover, in contrast to the *kalabule* rhetoric denigrating market women's social identity as an abomination and a site of disorder, in the NRC archive, these women describe themselves both as responsible mothers taking care of their families and successful entrepreneurs. Caretaking labor is not separated from professional labor; in fact, market women's ability to maintain effective social bonds is closely related to their success as traders. These stories within the NRC archive focus on the diverse ways that women contribute to the reproduction of Ghanaian society.

At first glance, Ghanaian market women's testimonies in the NRC may appear to evoke the overdetermined narrative of the brutalized African woman victim; however, this study considers the different discursive contexts in which these testimonies move. Stories that seem to simply confirm generalities about sexual violence and African women sound fundamentally different within their domestic Ghanaian context. By considering the audience to which market women directed their stories, and the strategy of their curated submissions, this study traces how Ghana's marginalized communities utilized the national reconciliation experiment to expand the historical record. In the national context, human rights testimony is more than a vehicle for the consumption of victim voices and emotional identification à la carte. These stories, in all their visceral revelation, combat the long-lived rhetoric of the *kalabule* woman as predator, deviant, and national scourge by revealing Ghanaian market women as physically and emotional vulnerable, economically generous, and socially connected. But these testimonies also enter an international discursive space where the suffering bodies of African women are overexposed. Part of the riskiness of victim testimony is in the way assertions of suffering and violence resonate differently within local, national, and global spheres. The individuals and communities that participated in the Ghana's national reconciliation embraced a risky victimhood with disparate national and international consequences.

CHAPTER 4

Family Histories of Political Violence

My imprisonment has caused the death of my mother.
She fell into a coma after my arrest and died a few days
later. My father went on a hunger strike and died later.
My family is accusing me that I caused the death of
my parents. I am a Christian; I've forgiven those who
wronged me. I've nothing to do with them. The problem
is now between myself and my family; how they will
accept me back into the family.

—Emmanuel Kwaku Badasu
"Reconciliation Witness Stuns House
with Emotional Delivery"
Ghana Review, January 21, 2003

At Ghana's National Reconciliation Commission (NRC) market women displayed the rippling violence that accompanied the *kalabule* woman narrative. Soldier violence affected not only the individual market women but also the family members and community who depended on and cared for her. This was another pattern within the NRC archive: Ghanaians defining and describing human rights violations in terms of withered families. Emmanuel Kwaku Badasu's story of imprisonment leading to a mother's death, and then a father's hunger strike, and then a bitter family feud, describes mounting and compounded losses. Ghanaians made the family central to their accounting of the consequences of state violence. Stories about imprisonment, torture, exile, poverty, and other types of political violence are simultaneously accounts of family estrangement, divorce, unhappy homes, and distorted filial expectations. In these documents, seemingly discrete acts of assault or incarceration do not harm only the person whose body is bruised or locked up, they ripple out across society, impacting those whose lives are entwined by bonds of blood and affection. Human rights abuse was manifest in the loss of intimate relationships and the destruction of key social bonds. Political violence, then, is domestic violence—the home should be central in how we assess the policies and practices that change the ways people dream, live, and love.

The language we use to describe suffering *matters*. Telling stories of violence communicates our values; in representing loss we remake the self and reappoint our communities. The obituary, in Judith Butler's estimation, is also an act of nation building. Not everyone who dies is rendered visible, let alone publicly grieved. There is, after all, "no obituary for the war casualties that the US inflicts," Judith Butler writes about the American public sphere, nor can there be.[1] Death notices make particular human endings visible, mark them as losses and worthy of grief, and in so doing affirm the community's values. Similarly, Melissa W. Wright's study of contemporary Mexican state violence insists that activists' choices in articulating suffering are often sophisticated critiques of state violence. "Return them alive!" exclaim today's Mexican activists, calling out for those who have been lost to the machine guns, unmarked graves and machetes. By insisting that their dead are "disappeared" and demanding their return, these Mexican activists connect their national condition to the devastating wave of state violence in late twentieth century Argentina, Chile, Guatemala, Peru, and other Latin and South American countries. Referencing these "decades of struggle" is itself an assertion: the violence afflicting Mexico today is akin to the state terror that was created by erstwhile neoliberal governments operating in the context of US-funded repression and exploiting social hatred in Latin and South America.[2] Rendering Mexico's dead as "disappeared" illuminates the continuation of neoliberal state violence in the twenty-first century.

What do the Ghanaian NRC archive's family histories of political violence build and illuminate? To what ends did Ghanaians map the concentric circles of suffering that surround a single act of assault, exile, or forced unemployment? This chapter explores the historical and political consequences of Ghanaian citizen narratives that used the language of human rights violation to render visible the layers of intimate harm associated with the Ghanaian state's violence.

By applying the language of human rights to social suffering, the ruptures that "seep into . . . ongoing relationships and become a kind of atmosphere that cannot be expelled to an 'outside,'" Ghanaians diverged from the individualism that is conventionally part of the international human rights concept.[3] Among the many critiques of international human rights discourse's reliance on the liberal conception of human beings as autonomous, distinct, and separate individuals, Judith Butler's meditation on loss as inherently social, resulting from "our socially constituted bodies" which are "attached to others, at risk of losing those attachments, exposed to others, [and] at risk of violence by virtue of that exposure," is particularly illuminating.[4] Where grief is concerned, Butler explains, the idea of individual loss is inadequate. Human grief is composed of intimate absences which exceed the loss of the single person who has been disappeared, exiled, imprisoned, or even killed. These acts of violence take from us the "relationality that is neither merely myself nor you, but the tie by which [we] are differentiated and related." Human rights discourse has been loath to account for these losses— the absence of a person that is also the loss of a relationship, and the dissolution of the self and community made by that relationship. For this, Butler notes, "there is no ready vocabulary."[5]

And yet, the NRC archive's family histories of political violence highlight suffering that is relational and social. These stories leave behind the framework of individual loss to map the ways a mother's untimely death is also the loss of all that the mother would have done in the future: the school fees she would have paid, the support she would have provided, the doors she would have opened for her children. As grown men and women sobbed openly about absent parents at the NRC hearings, the multiple and exponential losses of their condition become apparent. Losing a person is also the destruction of social and personal identities. To all who have suffered and grieved, the NRC archive's revelation that we experience violence through our attachments and relationships is perhaps unsurprising. However, these citizen stories are arresting as part of a national truth and reconciliation commission (TRC) rooted in the framework of international human rights.

A diverse body of law, practice, ideology and theory together constitute a global human rights regime that is "characterized by deformalization, indeterminacy, and a lack of hierarchy" and constituted from a "contradictory welter of instruments, documents, statements, cases, and treaties."[6] Amid this complexity there are historical patterns: individualistic understandings of harm dominate and different categories of rights (civil and political vs. economic, social, and cultural) have different legal and political standing.[7] Despite these trends, the power of the human rights concept has always been its mutability and accessibility. Different communities can seize and marshal "rights talk" for diverse ends. The "internationalization and universalization of human rights" according to Paul Tiyambe Zeleza, "is an ongoing process to which all world regions and cultures will continue to make contributions."[8] Historically, scholars have praised regional human rights instruments as the way to pursue this work of redefining, expanding, and shifting the human rights concept. The African Charter on Human and Peoples' Rights (1981) was such an attempt to domesticate international human rights by creating a framework inspired by the "historical tradition and values of African Civilization," and able to "aid the total liberation of Africa."[9] However, even this attempt to move away from the individualistic notion of human rights and toward the codification of collective and community rights enshrines the power and sovereignty of the African state. In both the African Charter and the African Court on Human and People's Rights expanding human rights away from liberal notions of individualism and challenging the focus on civil and political rights also includes shoring up human rights as a pillar of state power. [10] In both these ways—by preserving particular biases and hierarchies and justifying the power of state governments—international human rights as "creed, doctrine and ideology," has too often reproduced the inequalities and injustices within and between states.[11]

Considering that human rights has often been "deployed in the service of domination,"[12] Upendra Baxi issues this call: international human rights must be recalibrated if it is to be redeemed. In the past human rights has been bound to the history, ideological heritage, actions, and interests of powerful states both in the Global North and the Global South. Now, Baxi insists, human rights must be "humanized," it should be tied to the voices, bodies, and liberation of persons who suffer.[13] By going beyond the cultural and geographic critiques, Baxi suggests that the experiences of persons who suffer, and *not the states, governments, or theorists who presume to speak for them*, must be made central in the effort to create the theory, law, and practice that constitute the international human rights framework.

The NRC archive's family histories of political violence that present the substance and texture of human rights as defined by Ghanaian citizens at the turn of the twenty-first century, illuminate this recalibration of an increasingly unmoored internationalist discourse. Within the NRC, Ghanaians unselfconsciously used the language of human rights to describe social suffering. These stories define human rights abuse in terms of an individual's relationship to her communities, and trace how political violence seeps into the economic, social, and cultural lives of citizens. A broad NRC mandate that called forth people "who have suffered any injury, hurt, damage, griev-ance or who have in any other manner been adversely affected by violations and abuses of their human rights" created space for citizens to decide which events should be included in the national human rights review.[14] Then the NRC bill listed "killings, abductions, disappearances, torture, sexual abuse, detentions, ill-treatment, seizure of properties, hostage-taking, interference with the right to work, and abuse of judicial process" as the substance of its review.[15] This category of ill-treatment provided ample space for personal interpretation of the NRC mandate, allowing Ghanaians to insert diverse experiences of suffering into human rights review.

Of course, as already discussed in Chapter 1, citizen stories were medi-ated by interlocking levels of bureaucracy. NRC statement takers, investiga-tors, and commissions decided which stories saw the light of day in the public hearings, which were ultimately deemed nonjurisdictional to the NRC's work, and which met the bar for true victimhood. In spite of this bureaucratic imprint, the NRC allowed Ghanaians from a variety of social, geographical, and ethnic backgrounds to publicly interpret human rights abuse according to their own experiences and sensibilities. This—the ability to represent the definitions, perspectives, and preoccupations of citizens, to preserve "folk constructions of crises"—sets the NRC archive apart.[16]

The 4,240 petitions gathered by the National Reconciliation Commission, in their cacophony, elude the directives of state power and the conventions of human rights discourse. A sampling of approximately a thousand peti-tions includes more than fifty different ethnic identities and fifteen different languages and dialects. Former government ministers, farmers, unemployed hawkers, *kayayee* (market porters), civil servants, and soldiers all presented themselves as victims of violence. Amid this diversity, NRC participants focused on the domestic sphere—on family—when displaying their suf-fering. Their stories trace the course of Ghana's turbulent politics directly through the intimate lives of the country's people and identify human rights abuse as the diverse events and policies that together undermined the stabil-ity, prosperity, and happiness of Ghanaian families. In the NRC narrative, the consequences of state policies are profoundly gendered, affecting the family unit and creating bad parents, broken homes, and bitter children.

Anthropologists of political violence have carefully parsed the language that people use when speaking about suffering. In women's oblique stories about the Partition of India and Pakistan, Veena Das discovers a shrouded but devastating violence. Details of food consumption, household chores, and banal social interactions riddle and mask stories about rape, kidnapping, and murder. In contrast to scholars who dismiss these mundane details as a product of trauma, a psychological recoil from the red-hot pain of violence, Das describe the inclusion of these mundane domestic details as an eloquent testimony of violence experienced as a totalizing force that seeps into the very crevices of an individual's daily life.[17] There is a particular horror when the banality of everyday life—the cooking, the washing up, the food shopping—is punctuated with the brutality of state violence. In this vein, Nthabiseng Motsemme analyzes the quotidian details that riddle South African women's truth and reconciliation commission (TRC) testimonies not as a distortion of trauma, but as a precise reflection of life under apartheid. These domestic details within women's "selected speech" reveal the breadth and scope of apartheid's violence.[18] Similarly, Fiona C. Ross describes the utility of circumlocution within the testimonies of South African women who participated in the TRC.[19] In women's reluctance to engage in "straight-talk," Ross detects an instinct toward self-preservation rooted in cultural and linguistic norms that value metaphor and elliptical speech in regard to matters of sex and violence. For Antjie Krog, the public complaints that some African women's TRC testimonies were "unintelligible" expose the cultural chasms that persist within South Africa. These failures of translation, both linguistic and cultural, Krog suggests, exist both in the TRC and in national political and public life.[20]

Much of this rich literature interrogates how women narrate past political violence. However, in Ghana's NRC, this type of selected speech describing family life as the site for state violence is not restricted to women's testimonies and petitions. Both men and women poured into the NRC offices clutching funeral notices, aged family photographs, and even undernourished children to show the scope of their suffering. Husbands, sons, brothers, and grandfathers linked their domestic hardships to the national political turbulence of the past five decades. Men and women insisted that the state, in its various postindependence incarnations, is the perpetrator of intimate suffering. By identifying the home as a site where the turbulence of Ghanaian political history was manifest, these citizen records urge us toward an expanded notion of domestic violence that transcends the distinction between the public and private spheres. In contrast to standard definitions of domestic violence that focus exclusively on the harms that women and children face in their homes, Ghanaians reveal that imprisonment, forced unemployment, exile, land alienation, and all manner of injustice shape the health and strength of Ghanaian families. The NRC archive is the site of a gendered history of political violence where women and children are affected by national political turbulence and men's suffering is also rooted within the walls of the family compound.

Men's Petitions, Women's Lives

Far fewer women than men participated in Ghana's national reconciliation exercise.[21] This is a collective history in which men's voices are overrepresented, but the archive is nonetheless attuned to the relationship between gender and suffering. Ghanaian men detailed their struggle to fulfill gendered expectations of domesticity and responsibility amid the maelstrom of Ghanaian politics. While men described state policies and practices that prevented them from being "good" fathers, husbands, and sons, their stories often include oblique images of the experiences of their wives or mothers or female relatives. In these stories, women's suffering is the shadow, an apparition conjured repeatedly within Ghanaian men's stories of human rights abuse.

James Owu, a former Ghanaian soldier, described the hardships he faced for refusing to accept the authority of the unelected Provisional National Defense Council (PNDC) government and the rule of J. J. Rawlings. His petition detailed lost property, an escape from Ghana, exile in Sierra Leone, and eventually his capture by Ghanaian troops based in Sierra Leone as part of ECOMOG's (Economic Community of West Africa's Monitoring Group) peacekeeping operations in the 1990s. Detained and deported back to Ghana, Owu was sent to prison from the Accra airport. Later, he learned that from the time he was captured in Sierra Leone, his wife was detained and held at Cantonments Police Station in Accra. She remained there for seven weeks and then was sent to the 37 Military Hospital. This experience of detainment, Owu wrote in his NRC petition, was not something that his wife had yet found the words to describe. "Apart from the detention, my wife was not willing to tell me what treatment was given her at the station."[22] Despite the passage of years, his wife's experience of violence remained unspoken and unresolved within their home. Although James Owu's story—his life as a soldier, his exile in Sierra Leone, and his capture and repatriation— was described in Ghanaian newspapers, there is no such public account of his wife's experience. Both in the public sphere and in their own home, the details of Mrs. Owu's experience of detention remains hidden. Her husband's NRC petition is the only public record of her suffering and even he can only gesture at a violence that is incompletely known. Men's narratives will always be unworthy substitutes for women's voices; however, in the NRC archive where family is paramount, men's stories offer oblique and imperfect glimpses into the trials facing Ghanaian women.

At the NRC, George Addai described his father's arrest for economic crimes during the 1979 AFRC "house cleaning" exercise. Persons holding more than 50,000 cedis in a bank account had to account for the source of their wealth and despite his protestations, the elder Mr. Addai was imprisoned under "deplorable conditions" and suffered assault at the hands of soldiers. George mentioned that his sister "had to get involved in a relationship with one of the guards" at the Accra prison so that she could visit their father and look after his safety and needs.[23] Addai's petition provides no further information about his sister's experience and she herself did not appear to submit her story to the NRC. There is only this single line suggesting that a young woman was compelled to barter either her affections or her body in order to protect her father. The consequences of detention and imprisonment in the NRC family histories extend beyond the individual placed behind bars.

There were also some women who did not submit petitions claiming their own victimhood but who appear in the archive as supporting witnesses. Jacqueline Nasser appears in the NRC records as a witness for her husband, Sammy Nasser. In 1982, soon after the PNDC takeover, while Sammy was visiting his ancestral country of Lebanon, the family learned that he had been stripped of his businesses and property and warned never to return to Ghana. Allegedly, Sammy's brother used connections to the newly installed PNDC government to prosecute a feud between the two brothers and acquire full control of Sammy's properties and businesses. However, Sammy could not stay away from Ghana. In 1988 he returned and was detained at the Kotoka International Airport. There, security agents told him that he could be released if he immediately renounced his Ghanaian citizenship and consented to his deportation. Nasser refused and spent the next four years in prison. The Nasser NRC file includes the letters that Jacqueline Nasser wrote to the PNDC government during these years, begging for her husband's release. Sammy Nasser's return to Ghana was not an act of treason, she insisted, but an expression of his love for his home country. "My husband is and has always considered himself to be a Ghanaian," she wrote. "He has lived his whole life, is established in Ghana, and has such sentimental attachment in this country that he cannot live anywhere else."[24] Asking him to renounce his citizenship was an impossibility. In his wife's words, "He has no other nationality except Ghanaian."

Although the Nasser NRC file focuses on the injustice of imprisonment and lost property, these acts of violence are compounded by the Ghanaian government's attempt to strip Sammy Nasser of his national identity. The file even includes a faded photocopy of an expired Gold Coast passport. Sammy Nasser, as a young boy, stares solemnly out at the world. The message is clear: before Ghana was even Ghana, when it was still the British Gold Coast, Sammy Nasser was already there. In 1937, when Sammy Nasser came into the world, he was the second generation of his family to be born in Koforidua, in Ghana's Eastern Region. His grandfather had moved to the British Gold Coast in the early twentieth century and had become part of the cocoa industry. Sammy's father, Nasri, was born in Koforidua in 1914 and worked in both cocoa and textiles. By describing his family's history in this way Sammy Nasser claimed a Ghanaian nationality, with all the associated rights. In 1982, when he was first accused of financial crimes, because he was "first and foremost a Ghanaian, proud of [his] nationality, and having no intentions whatsoever to destabilize the nation;" he sought to return to Ghana and clear his name.[25] When he arrived at the airport and was told to turn in his passport and leave Ghana forever, this was an "infringement on [his] fundamental human rights and freedoms," and he could only decline.[26] In this, Sammy Nasser's NRC file is part of a long-standing debate about where persons of Lebanese descent fit into Ghanaian history.[27] There are many scholars who describe the nonintegration of Lebanese within Ghana. In contrast, Sammy Nasser publicly displayed his family's deep roots in Ghana, revealing bonds of birth and affection that would not be shaken.[28]

For our purposes, however, this particular NRC file is also a record of the life and times of Jacqueline Nasser. As with the women in the NRC files of James Owu and George Addai, Jacqueline's experience appears dimly, as a silhouette. When her husband was imprisoned, Jacqueline was required to raise her own voice to defend her family. Her stories are glimpses of the suffering at the crossroad of PNDC repression and the Lebanese diaspora's gendered caretaking practices. Lebanese-born, Jacqueline came to Ghana as the bride of Sammy Nasser. In the early 1980s, when her Koforidua-born father-in-law, Nasri, fell ill, he moved to Lebanon and Jacqueline also returned in order to care for him. Jacqueline's role as wife and daughter in this transnational Ghanaian-Lebanese family was burdensome. "Looking after my ailing father-in-law and my four children in the very difficult situation of the seemingly unending strife in Lebanon made my health deteriorate seriously."[29] Even her husband's presence in Lebanon following the PNDC's rise to power did not ease her burdens. Sammy was "never happy" in Lebanon, and although returning to Ghana in these time was folly, he could not resist. When he was arrested at the airport, the hardships facing the family multiplied. Charged now with supporting her family and engineering her husband's safe release, Jacqueline wrote long letters to the authorities: "The continued detention of my husband is causing the family serious hardships and emotional distress." Even in this file, there is no picture of Jacqueline, no passport; she is not officially a petitioner. Nevertheless, her experience at the junction of the Lebanese civil war, Ghana's military rule, and her filial expectations is preserved in witness statements and past letters. Her words illuminate how gender mediates both the experience of diaspora and the experience of violence.[30]

Such experiences are found throughout the NRC archive. Courageous wives, mothers, and sisters appear in Ghanaian men's narratives; they trace disappeared relatives, step in as sole breadwinners, smuggle out goods and people, and visit those languishing in prison. Women maintain a critical presence within an NRC narrative overwhelmingly created by men. The political implications of women's caretaking activities bear further scrutiny. In Pamela Reynolds's study of the South Africa antiapartheid movement, the "behind the scenes" activities of African women are politically significant. In "tracking down their children, going from prison to prison, from officer to officer, withstanding rudeness and physical abuse, in smuggling messages, in taking advantage of opportunities to write, to send food or clothing," women strengthened their communities and must be remembered as key players in the antiapartheid struggle.[31] In the same way, the NRC archive leads us to reconsider the role of women within Ghanaian political history.

On Absent Fathers and Broken Families

When the NRC opened a petition-taking office in the town of Hohoe, it collected a number of stories about absentee Ghanaian fathers exiled during the first ten years of independence. That these petitions came out of the NRC's Volta Regional Office is not a coincidence. The conflict about integrating the territory formerly known as the Trans-Volta Togoland into independent Ghana was, according to the NRC report, part of the volatile inheritance of colonial rule in independent Ghana. Once part of German West Africa, then split between French and British administrations as a League of Nations trust territory, this region's future was uncertain in the period surrounding the

Gold Coast's 1957 independence. At a time when many in Ghana were jubilant over their country's political independence, "there was a large group of
persons" within the new country, "who did not wish to be a part of Ghana and
would not abandon their agitation . . ." toward a sovereign and independent
Togoland.[32] The dream of an independent and unified Togoland—a polity
that required the secession of the Volta Region from Ghana—had its supporters within Ghana. In the Nkrumah years, these Togoland patriots were
accused of fomenting treason and often crossed Ghana's eastern border both
to escape state repression and to plot against the Convention People's Party
(CPP) government.[33] Although the economic and political consequences of
British Togoland's uneasy integration into independent Ghana have been
documented,[34] the NRC archive urges us to consider the intimate and domestic impact of this would-be nationalist movement.

One of the NRC participants was Robert Kwame Antor, the son of
S. G. Antor, the founder of the Togoland Congress Party. The elder Antor's
detention in 1961 "hampered the progress of his children."[35] When he later
died in exile, the school bursaries of the Antor children were revoked. At the
public hearings, Robert Kwame Antor, with tears in his eyes, described his
efforts to seek work that would enable him to look after his younger siblings.
In response, Commissioner Emmanuel Erskine expressed regret that children of politicians were made into victims because of their parent's political
activities and ideologies. The NRC archive, however, makes it is clear that it
was not only the children of politicians who suffered in this way. A number of
young men from the Volta Region submitted testimonies seeking reparations
because their fathers crossed over into exile and left them without support.

Daniel Agusa, Japhet Akpakpla, Edmund Nukro, and Hayford Akumiah
ranged in age from twelve to twenty-two when they lost their fathers, but
their stories are similar. Each claimed his father was part of the United Party
(UP), an opposition political party banned by Nkrumah's CPP government in
1964. However, even before the UP was made illegal, its members faced political surveillance and repression. All the petitioners described their fathers'
desertion as politically motivated. The patriarch left "when it became unbearable for him,"[36] "when he saw that his life was in danger," [37] or because the
"Convention People's Party wanted to arrest him."[38] They placed the blame
for their absent fathers squarely at the feet of Kwame Nkrumah's government
and described their current economic hardships as a consequence of these
early losses. "Because of my father's self-exile in Togo our education suffered,
Daniel Agusa noted.[39] Said Akpakpla: "Because he was away, most of his

properties got lost and farms were destroyed. He was not able to look after me in school. Hence, I ended up my education in primary class six."[40] Nukro and Akumiah remembered their fathers' absence in the same way—as a hardship that marred not only their childhoods, but the rest of their lives:

> He left me and my other brothers and sisters at a very young age in the care of my poor mother who was also unemployed. She was not able to do much with regards to our educations. This affected us to this day. Hence we have no employment. We only do subsistence farming.[41]

> When he was leaving to Kpalime Togo, he left behind a wife named Elizabeth Kro and eight children including myself. My mother was unemployed so she could not look after us in terms of our education. . . . This has affected us till today because we do not have any good job.[42]

The petitions are remarkably similar in drawing the connection between absent fathers, limited educational opportunity, and persistent poverty. In fact, Edmund Nukro and Hayford Akumiah claimed that their fathers, Wahrenfried and Isiah Kofi ran away to Kpalime, Togo, together. Despite the passage of time (here, nearly half a century), adult men publicly mourned the loss of their fathers. The image of the absent father is an explanation for the grinding poverty that these men endured through their lives and in these stories, exile is a harm that continues even after the family is reunited. When Wahrenfried Nukro returned to Ghana in 1966 after the overthrow of Kwame Nkrumah's government, he was in ill health and his many assets were lost. Similarly, when Isiah Kofi Akumiah came back in 1967, his son remembered that "he had to start from scratch" but was unable to do hard work because of his ill health. He died in 1971. In these narratives, fathers return home changed, diminished, and without resources. Others perish in exile or come back only to lay down their bodies to rest. Their children, whose school fees have not been paid and who have had to go to work rather than to gain an education, have already missed their opportunity. These stories communicate that state violence echoes across generations when poverty is a vise that can rarely be broken. The suffering of a father's exile is compounded when a child's trajectory is determined by a single factor: school fees. In detailing the domestic consequences of political exile, these petitioners simultaneously indict the web of poverty that grips and orders the live of Ghanaian children.

Political exile was not the only factor that separated Ghanaian families. In the NRC archive, imprisonment and unemployment were twin acts of domestic violence that broke family bonds. Christian Blukoo was a rapidly-advancing security officer during the Nkrumah years.[43] Before the 1966 regime change, Blukoo was working at Peduase Lodge, the president's retreat house in the Akuapem Hills. The entire Blukoo family was settling into mountain life; they had secured land and were farming and raising poultry. Then, during the 1966 regime change, Christian Blukoo was arrested and hauled to Nsawam Prison. The day he was taken from his home in Akuapem was the last time he saw his wife alive. "I came out of prison to be told of my wife Amma Dupre['s] death. My daughter Vivian Blukoo also died later in 1971. Everything I had at Peduase Lodge . . . all perished." The eighteen-month detention utterly changed his life. Blukoo's narrative does not talk much about what happened behind bars at Nsawam; his story is preoccupied with the loss of his wife and daughter. "As far back as 1966 I have gone through sorrowful events," he wrote. "Because how my wife died, I did not know. Where my wife was buried, I was not shown." When he was released, Blukoo, like many associates of the former CPP regime, struggled to find work. This hindered his ability to act as a father should; he "could not see [his] only son, Francis Blukoo through any proper education."[44] Christian Blukoo spent the next decades struggling to secure the pension he was owed for his life in the service.

John Bomo Ackah, also stationed at Peduase, was detained for two years and released in February 1968. Detention was physical and emotional torture, but it was caused a rupture in Ackah's private life. "What was most painful was that I was about to engage my fiancée," he recalled. "By the time I was released from prison, my fiancée had married another man." Intimate relationships were irrevocably altered when civil servants and soldiers found themselves suddenly behind bars following the coup d'état. The remainder of Ackah's petition details the difficulty facing an ex-prisoner seeking employment and social connection after two years of detention. "I believe there is not much I can do regarding the unlawful detention and the maltreatment I received. . . . However, I feel I ought to be compensated for the loss of my personal effects/belongings."[45] Among these personal belongings were the items he had hoped to use for his engagement.

Mary Anthonia Kumeni's story reveals that women were also subject to detention, and also described the consequences in their homes and relationships. In 1972, Kumeni was an organizer for the Progress Party when Acheampong seized control of the government. When soldiers arrived at her door in Hohoe, Kumeni was pregnant. By the time she returned home from Ho prisons, she had lost her baby. "When I was brought to the Ho prisons, we were made to sleep on bare iron bedsteads. I started bleeding and had treatment at Ho district hospital. The bleeding ceased after a week's treatment at Ho district office. . . . Later on I had a still-born baby." Soon afterward Mercy Kumeni lost her husband as well: "My husband also divorced me on the grounds that I was involved in party politics." He feared that he and his family would have to bear the brunt of his wife's political activities. In Kumeni's story, gender was not incidental to her experience of prison life. State violence affected her in the most intimate of ways: by harming her reproductive capacity and taking her partner from her. These overwhelming losses left her "weak, old, and dejected."[46]

Other petitioners also blamed the state for the dissolution of their marriages. Like Kumeni, Samuel Dwira was arrested and detained during the Acheampong coup d'état. While being hauled away to cells, Dwira "inquired why [he] was incarcerated" and was told that he was being kept because "[his] government has collapsed." With the overthrow of Busia, those citizens who had most vocally supported the Progress Party were now under scrutiny and sometimes became targets. After one year's detention, Dwira returned home to an empty house. "On my release I met my room empty as my wife had [parked] everything from the room thinking I was dead and left for her hometown Enchi in the Western Region. I made all efforts to bring her back but the relatives said they do not know when I will be arrested and detained again, so they will not allow her to marry me again."[47]

In these petitions, detention is a stigmatized status with consequence for a person's social status and prospects. Moreover, the stain of political activity may extend to family and friends; Dwira's in-laws and Kumeni's husband sought to distance themselves from persons who, overnight, were marked as enemies of a newly established government. In this context there are high costs to participating in Ghanaian politics: identifying with a party may jeopardize one's freedom, family or friendships.

The intimate consequences of political participation were clear in Kwadwo Owusu-Sekyere's petition. A lawyer, former ambassador to Egypt, and long-time politician, Owusu-Sekyere's NRC petition details the horrors of detention in the Sunyani barracks during the AFRC period. He describes urinating on himself, begging for mercy, and the experience of watching his son shaved by a broken bottle. Owusu-Sekyere's teenage son had also been arrested alongside him, and at the barracks, soldiers ordered the two men, father and son, to beat each other. "I was surely shaken. I was at that time 49 years old and feared [for my safety]. . . . I reluctantly summoned all my strength and really gave my son a slap on the right cheek. . . . I immediately broke down and sobbed uncontrollably, but I was shouted down to stop." This trauma drove a wedge between father and son. Immediately after this incident, Owusu-Sekyere's son Patrick found a way to leave Ghana and moved to Britain, where he has remained up until the present day. "[Patrick] came to Ghana in July and sitting down at the living room with him, he told me and I quote 'Daddy, do you know that I cannot look straight into your eyes?' I asked him to forget and leave the past to history."[48] For Owusu-Sekyere, the loss of his relationship with his son was devastating. "At the autumn of my life, my son . . . would have been by best, reliable, and constant companion and adviser but for that brutish and inhuman act perpetrated on us, he has no desire of living in Ghana again."[49] The emotional and geographic distance between father and son continue to testify to the brutality that transpired within the Sunyani barracks.

In the NRC archive Ghanaians described seemingly mundane problems such as joblessness, missing pensions, public dismissal, and nonpayment of wages as human rights abuses because of their impact on Ghanaian families. The language of human rights violation is not limited to a categorical list of particularly heinous crimes, but instead includes any number of events and policies that wreaked havoc on Ghanaian families. As new regimes detained soldiers and citizens associated with the previous government, they also cast off civil servants. Within the Ghana Education Service, the Ghana Publishing Corporation, the Cocoa Marketing Board, and numerous other state-run businesses, workers were summarily dismissed and replaced, because of Ghana's cyclical coups d'états. Although forced unemployment may appear insignificant compared to exile or imprisonment, in the NRC archive, it, too, has devastating consequences.

A former police officer named Francis Anane testified that in 1981, his wife was listening to the radio when she heard his name announced in a list of persons dismissed from service by the new PNDC military administration. In shock, she suffered a miscarriage and a distraught Francis Anane "almost committed suicide."[50] In this NRC petition, the announcement of forced unemployment inaugurated a period of family crisis that included not only the miscarriage, but also social notoriety and economic hardship.

Similarly, Anthony Bartz-Minlah connected his abruptly-ended career at the Ghana Education Service to four deaths—those of his wife, twin daughters, and mother-in-law. In 1979, Bartz-Minlah was abruptly retired in the course of the AFRC revolution. Soon after, when his wife fell sick, the family could not afford proper medical care and she passed away on Christmas Day. By March, his twin infant daughters had also fallen ill and died. "Where was the money" to pay for their medical care? he asked. The petition ends with his mother-in-law dying, overwhelmed by heartbreak. The anger and sorrow in Anthony Bartz-Minlah's petition is palpable. When he lodged his petition at an NRC statement-taking office, he brought copies of his wife's and daughters' funeral programs and included a portrait photograph of his mother-in-law. Their lives, he insisted, all had to be counted among the casualties of state violence.[51]

There is a story preserved within the NRC archive about a Ghanaian soldier who allegedly confronted J. J. Rawlings about the injustice of summarily stripping citizens of their jobs as part of regime change. Why, Frederick Affoh wanted to know, were army officers being forced out of the service as part of the 1979 revolution? How did this align with the Rawlings regime's populist rhetoric? Supposedly, Rawlings explained that those being dismissed were senior officers who were "corrupt" and had to be "dealt with."[52] And yet, in his NRC petition, Frederick Affoh insists that he was not corrupt and still his life was disrupted when he was dismissed without any recourse. "I had nothing to live on and became almost destitute." At the time, he "had a family to look after, [and] children still in school." Moreover, in 1988, Affoh's father passed away. "I could not . . . ensure a fitting and decent burial for the old man, an event that any dutiful child would want for his father," he wrote.[53] In Affoh's eyes, he had never received an explanation for why he had been prevented from fulfilling his filial duty to be a good provider for his children and a dutiful son at the time of his father's demise.

Forced unemployment also wreaked havoc in the life of Grace Tetteh, the wife of a Ghanaian diplomat. During the 1979 AFRC revolution, the Tetteh family was stationed in the United States but were living on furlough in Ghana. They were targeted by Ghanaian soldiers who arrived at their rented bungalow in search-and-raid mode and accused the family of participating in the previous regime's corruption. "I was told that some soldiers in a big truck had come to seize . . . all our belongings we had brought from Washington, USA. Our furniture, cooking utensils, important family documents . . . personal belongings, our children's clothes and just about everything we ever owned. It was devastating. . . . My husband, children and I were extremely devastated. . . . We accepted that we had to start life all over again."[54]

Eventually, when Tetteh's husband received a new assignment for Angola, Grace stayed behind in order to settle the children in Ghanaian boarding schools and then joined her husband. Just then, the news broke that Rawlings and his soldiers had again seized control of the Ghanaian government again. This unexpected upheaval was overwhelming: "The events in Ghana at the time coupled with the problems we had led me to suffer a breakdown. . . . It felt like the carpet was being pulled from under my feet." The family returned to Ghana under a cloud of professional uncertainty; eventually Mr. Tetteh was officially dismissed. In her NRC petition, Grace Tetteh quoted the dismissal letter, now decades old. "Due to the ongoing revolutionary process, it has been decided to relieve you." Her husband's "frustration, disappointment and ill-health" led to his untimely death at sixty-three years old. In telling her husband's story to the NRC, Grace Tetteh also spoke on behalf of "wives like [her] who sacrifice their professions in support of our husband's career."[55] In this petition the suffering associated with forced unemployment is multiple, compounded, and devastating.

Conclusion

In telling their stories of state violence, Ghanaians focused on their families. They located human rights abuse in a mother's inability to safely carry her child to term, a son's thwarted wish to properly bury his father, and the love lost between spouses following a lengthy detention. The NRC archive details the ways that government violence—in acts of commission and omission alike—intruded into their intimate lives, producing inadequate mothers and fathers; frustrated, wayward children; and broken relationships. Ghanaians did not always define human rights abuse as a matter of heinous physical atrocity; instead, they mourned the unspooling of violence in their homes and relationships.

If narrating the experience of suffering also instructs the listening audience on how to view and relate to violence,[56] there are consequence to this NRC archive that places social suffering at the center of Ghana's human rights history. First, using the language of human rights abuse marks particular state policies and practices as ethically untenable. What is a human rights violation after all, but something that never should have happened? By describing forced unemployment, political detention, intergenerational poverty, and economically-restricted education as injustice and abuse,

Ghanaians delineated the breadth of political violence in the national history. Second, these stories reveal that all types of violence have social consequences, even acts that appear to be directed toward a particular individual. Harming human beings creates barriers between people and distorts the functioning of community. The NRC petition of fifty-two-year-old Margaret Nimo made this point eminently clear. In 1979, during the June 4th Revolution, soldiers came to Nimo's home in Abossey Okai Zongo, Accra, looking for her husband. "My husband had gone to work but did not come home for reasons I don't know," she recounted. "I told the soldiers he was not around, they told me I would replace him." Three soldiers then beat her unconscious. Around 11 p.m., the last remaining soldier in the house forced himself sexually on her. "My two children who were five years and 2 years at the time watched on helplessly and cried."[57] On the next day, the nightmare continued when the soldiers took Nimo and the two children first to Gondar Barracks, then to the Nima Police Station, and finally to the police hospital. During the three days she spent in the hospital, her only visitor was her brother who came from Kumasi to see her. When she was discharged, she immediately moved to Kumasi with her children in order to recover and seek additional treatment.

In her petition, Margaret Nimo mentions psychological trauma, physical pain, and economic loss among the results of this incident. In addition, the petitioner wrote, this incident "destroyed" her marriage. "As of now I do not know the whereabouts of Mr. Frank Mensah. He is no more my husband following the incident and he refused to care for the two children I had with him. My father insisted that I should [no longer] marry him since he did not find out my whereabouts [up to] one year after the incidents. I agreed with my father's decision." Margaret Nimo's losses, the suffering located in her intimate life, had only continued and deepened with the passage of time. In her file, there is no accompanying letter from Frank Mensah; there is no record of why he stayed late at work on that day of horror or why he came neither to the police hospital in Accra nor to Kumasi to find his family. In these records, this silence is palpable and sorrow-stained. Margaret Nimo's NRC file does include an accompanying statement from her daughter who tells the nightmare story from 1979 from her own child's eye view. Margaret Nimo requested that the government provide her with capital to start a new business; she also asked whether the government "could compensate [her] children" who had suffered much.[58] Stories like Nimo's highlight how violence ripples out through society and shapes the most intimate spheres of family and self.

In ways both known and unknown, a single assault may pull the surrounding community into the orbit of suffering.

By inserting these family histories into a national reconciliation experiment charged with recommending appropriate redress for victims, Ghanaians posed a particular challenge for historical justice initiatives. How does a state confront and repair the damage that traverses public and private spheres and which has settled into individual consciousness, family functioning, and social life? This is the challenge posed by this collection of NRC records: reparations and reform policies that focus solely on individuals as the victims of violence, while neglecting to consider the complexities of intimate and social relations, will inevitably be inadequate. Clearly, this challenge to count the real, social and relational costs of imprisonment, unemployment, and poverty extends far beyond Ghana. These family histories of political violence are an invitation to consider where intimate loss and social suffering fit within the work of political reparation. These family histories of political violence illustrate why survivor voices must be made central when counting the costs of and contemplating solutions to political violence. A crucial political history lies hidden in the mouths of everyday people; only they can map the violence that settles into the bones of those living in the eye of the storm.

CHAPTER 5

The Suffering of Being Developed

Nonjurisdictional Petitions

Not all stories submitted to the National Reconciliation Commission (NRC) offices were treated equally. Among the more than four thousand petitions, staff classified approximately three hundred statements as outside the scope of the NRC's human rights review. Zonal-office statement takers, investigation officers, and/or the executive secretary determined that these stories did not fit within the commission's temporal or substantive mandate. Mainly excluded from the public hearings and overlooked by the media, these stories still remain part of the expansive NRC archive, dutifully listed in the final report and physically preserved among the other file folders stored at the University of Ghana's Balme Library.

The nonjurisdictional petitions at the heart of this chapter are evidence of the NRC's sorting process, making plain the places where citizen and government visions of historical violence diverge. The notations of statement takers and legal advisors are glimpses of both the workings of the NRC bureaucracy and the contrasting definitions of human rights animating Ghana's truth commission.

In two collections of nonjurisdictional petitions, Ghanaians described the violence of two Volta Region development initiatives that alienated marginalized communities from land. For these petitioners, the NRC provided an opportunity to speak out about a history of economic and geographic displacement and to show that initiatives that forcibly separated people from their land, whether championed by the government or multinational corporations, constituted a human rights abuse.

The first selection of petitions came from communities resettled as part of electricity generation projects in Ghana. By 1965, when the famed Akosombo

Dam was built as part of the Volta Hydroelectric Project, eighty thousand people had been displaced by planned flooding that destroyed homes, farms, and shrines. The second collection of stories came from the communities abutting the Songor Lagoon, the site of West Africa's largest salt flats. There, artisanal salt harvesting (or "salt winning") was central to the economy, culture, and identity of the local Ada communities for generations;[1] it currently supports the livelihood of approximately sixty thousand people living in the region.[2] From the mid-1970s onward, two companies, Vacuum Salt Products, Ltd. (VSPL) and Star Chemicals, sought to privatize salt winning on the Songor Salt Flats. Local community members who continued to harvest salt faced assault, harassment, economic marginalization, and displacement while private companies claimed exclusive control of this natural resource. The competition between business and the local indigenous community erupted into violent conflict as VSPL conscripted Ghanaian soldiers and police officers to protect private interests. Assault, imprisonment, intimidation, and torture were among the techniques used to build Ghana's salt industry.

Decades later, in the national reconciliation experiment, individuals and organizations revisited the suffering accompanying the construction of the Akosombo Dam and the privatization of salt winning on the Songor. The NRC bureaucracy, however, was ambivalent about whether these stories were relevant to the national human rights review. The stories shared by the Akosombo resettlers and the Ada salt winners were marginalized within the NRC Archive and deemed nonjurisdictional. In Chapter 4, I described the expansiveness of the NRC's mandate: the human rights review covered the vast majority of national history (1957–1992) and included the category "ill-treatment" which allowed ample space for citizen definitions of suffering and harm. However, from the moment of submission, a petition was subject to the NRC bureaucracy consisting of statement takers, legal officers, investigators, and commissioners who each had the discretion to classify a citizen complaint as misaligned with the NRC's work.[3] In the cases below, these NRC officials concluded that human rights abuses had not been sufficiently proven and refused to accept the Akosombo resettlers' and Songor salt winners' claims.

In the past, the Ghanaian government championed both the Akosombo Dam and the privatization of the salt industry in Ada as opportunities to propel national economic development. By claiming that development in Ghana spawned violence instead of creating growth, these citizens joined a sustained and robust debate about the ambivalence of the global development imperative. In the 1990s, Claude Ake described the Janus-faced "ideology of development" in postcolonial Africa: it is both a stirring call to substantiate political freedom through economic transformation and a foil with which beleaguered state leaders justify their rapacity.[4] Around the same time, global anthropologists coined the term "development refugee" as a way to communicate the suffering of persons displaced in order to make way for development projects.[5] The rural Ghanaians who participated in the national reconciliation exercise were not alone in mourning a mode of development that stripped already-marginalized communities of land and autonomy. From India's big dams to Ethiopia's land grabs for commercial agriculture to the Standing Rock Sioux's resistance to oil pipelines in the United States, "evictees have one thing in common," wrote the legal scholar Paul Ocheje. "They are the poor and marginalized in society. . . . Their views on the development of the lands which they occupy and on environmental stewardship are dismissed without careful consideration."[6] In the NRC archive, the Akosombo resettlers and the Ada salt winners join this chorus by detailing how economically disenfranchised and politically marginalized communities become victims of national development initiatives that are ostensibly meant to uplift. In their stories, development initiatives reflect, reproduce, and reinforce the very inequality and exclusion that they claim to combat.

Resettlement Dreams and Disasters

When he arrived at the petition-taking office in Accra, George Nartey described the displacement and resettlement of communities affected by the Akosombo Dam as an abject failure.[7] Nartey spoke from his own experience as part of the Dede/Sewirako resettlement in the Fanteakwa District of the Eastern Region. A community that began in 1964 as six thousand people had dwindled to approximately one thousand; all who were able to leave had sought greener pastures elsewhere. This second scattering of the community was a consequence of the original sin of shoddy resettlement; Nartey's petition detailed the myriad problems facing the community. The land in the Fanteakwa District was fertile, but due to the "vagaries of the weather," the resettlers had never been able to establish themselves as farmers. As acquiring food in sufficient amounts became more difficult, Nartey could only reminisce about the early days in the resettlement, when the community received food rations from Kwame Nkrumah's government. After the 1966 coup that drove Nkrumah into exile, rations were "arbitrarily withdrawn" and hunger became a constant companion. The settlement was dotted with "dilapidated" houses, and the community was compelled to fetch "raw untreated water" at some distance. Infrastructure—particularly health care—was sorely lacking. "Apart from some Catholic medical NGOs who visit at random," he noted, "there is no hospital or clinic worth its name" in the area. Those who had the misfortune of falling ill traveled miles of "rugged road" to Begoro town for medical attention. Ironically, this community, whose lives were altered by the Volta Hydroelectric Project, still lacked electric power. "For almost forty years now, these folks ha[ve] been denied supply of electricity—the main reason why they gave up their lands," Nartey wrote.[8]

If Kwame Nkrumah had been present to hear Nartey's story of unclean water, persistent hunger, and intermittent charity-based health care, he would surely have been disappointed. In the early years of independence, Ghana's Volta River Project (VRP) was a symbol of the joint political and economic hopes of the Black Star Nation's new identity. Electrification would spur industrialization, and a new Ghanaian economy would propel the country forward from colonial dependency toward self-determination. More than a source of electricity, the VRP was a "symbol of confident nationhood," representing the creativity, purpose, and ambition of a new African nation.[9] Although the Volta Basin had been identified by the British colonial government as a possibly lucrative economic investment, Nkrumah transformed the hydroelectric dam from a scheme to mill colonial bauxite into aluminum on behalf of Mother England to a cornerstone of Ghana's pursuit of modernity.[10] Under Nkrumah's visionary eye, the VRP included "the hydroelectric dam, an aluminum smelter to process Ghanaian-mined bauxite, new cities, a deep sea harbor and other infrastructural investments."[11] In these years, a massive public-information campaign trumpeted the value of the VRP as a national triumph and a collective necessity. In 1961, Kwame Nkrumah insisted that Ghana could not develop without controlling its own power supply. "Newer nations, such as ours, which are determined by every possible means to catch up in industrial strength, must have electricity in abundance before they can expect any large-scale industrial advance."[12] In 1965, Nkrumah eloquently explained that the project "transcend[s] any political consideration and is . . . in the truest sense, an expression of our national unity and of our national purpose and aspirations."[13] For Nkrumah, the economic potential and national pride generated by the VRP were foundational to Ghanaian independence and, thus, unimpeachable.[14] It is no wonder that esteemed visitors to Ghana, including Che Guevara and Queen Elizabeth II, were ushered to see the Akosombo Dam at various stages of completion.[15]

Amid this proud vision, Nkrumah's government articulated a plan to provide for the communities that would be displaced from their home lands by dam-related flooding. The successful resettlement of displaced communities was part and parcel of this vision of independence and modernity. The parliamentary act creating the Volta River Authority (VRA) explicitly stated that no persons should "suffer undue hardship" or be "deprived of necessary public amenities" as a result of Ghana's rush toward electrification.[16] A few years later, Nkrumah reiterated this message: "No one should be [made] worse off" by a project conceived as a national good.[17] This history of Ghanaian officials publicly seeking to mitigate the negative impacts of development makes the petitions of George Nartey and others particularly jarring. Today, as Ghana is plagued by national leaders with visions significantly more parochial and venial, the VRP is a residue of better times, a memory of a bygone era of big dreams and national optimism.

In the twenty-first century, the pride associated with the Akosombo Dam is much worse for wear. The dam is still responsible for a majority of Ghana's power supply, but environmental and economic pressures have made it clear that Akosombo is insufficient for Ghana's contemporary needs. Power outages have plagued the country in recent years; reliable electricity is a scarce resource available only to those whose wealth affords them relief from the national plight.[18] Today, it is tempting to recoil from stories like those offered by George Nartey, which seem to tarnish the legacy of a bold African leader who dared to dream of actualizing economic independence through a self-sustaining national economy. Indeed, the NRC expressed doubts about including these critical stories about the Akosombo resettlement and the VRA in the human rights review, claiming that "it would not be in the public interest to permit persons to come forward forty years after the event to make fresh claims" about submerged properties, land, and homes.[19] The NRC bureaucracy reduced Nartey's critique to a tardy compensation claim. However, the stories of Ghanaian people defy this characterization; by marshaling the language of human rights abuse, the Akosombo resettlers were insisting that Ghana recognize failures of national development as acts of violence with moral and political consequences.

By the early twenty-first century, big dams had become flashpoints of protest about the right to land and self-determination for rural and indigenous communities around the world. From southern Brazil to India's Andhra Pradesh

state to Costa Rica, big dams are no longer unimpeachable modernist jugger-
nauts. Instead, they are catalysts for organized resistance around indigenous
rights and environmental justice. In 2003, as Ghana's NRC held its public hearings, the Icelandic writer Elísabet Jökulsdóttir grabbed a microphone during a
domestic Icelandair flight to speak out against the construction of the Karahnjukar Dam.[20] That same year, Burmese communities declared their intent to
stop construction of the Tipaimukh Hydro-Electric Multipurpose Dam with
their "last drop of blood."[21] And contemporaneously in Sudan, students affected
by the Merowe Dam began a protracted struggle to obtain compensation for
loss of land and livelihood. These stories about Ghana's famed Akosombo Dam
join this global chorus about large dams that "epitomize social exclusion" rather
than propelling equitable development.[22] Inevitably, the global critics of big
dams explain, it is the already-marginalized communities whose homes, lands,
and bodies marked as obstacles in the path of progress.

These citizen narratives illuminate the particular pathways by which
development initiatives become sites of violence. These stories are not whole-
sale rejections of the premise of national development; the NRC participants
do not exhibit general skepticism about statist economic intervention or the
cynicism that describes development as a technology of state control and surveillance.[23] In their petitions, Ghanaians do not describe or long for a pristine
past before the intrusion of the Akosombo Dam. Instead, resettlers offered
nuanced critiques of an authoritarian approach to national development that
substituted the will of technocratic experts for the voices and agency of the
subject communities. By relying on models of progress and growth that sup-
plant the authority and insight of the local community, Ghanaians explained,
development leads to suffering.

The economist William Easterly has described contemporary global economic development practice as a "tyranny of experts" in which the land and
civil rights of indigenous, often marginalized populations are trampled in the
name of poverty eradication.[24] Key global institutions like the World Bank, the
International Monetary Fund, and the United States Agency for International
Development, embrace antipoverty initiatives that are undemocratic and
authoritarian; too often, the will of expert technocrats—many with decidedly
shallow local knowledge—is made law for poor people around the world. The
accompanying violence is not only at the level of representation and voice;
governments and companies around the world have not shied away from
using deadly force to clear the ground for development.[25] In the NRC archive,
authoritative development practices shaped the Volta River resettlement.

For Kwame Nkrumah's government, successfully resettling flooded communities was part of realizing the dream of national electrification. The newly-established VRA was expected to ensure that resettlement would not harm or diminish local residents, and instead would improve their lives. However, determining the substance of and pathway to a better life was a technocratic challenge for the VRA. As professionals from diverse fields, including social work, rural planning, and agricultural technology, were brought on board, the Volta resettlement agenda fell headlong into the "expert-solutions-mindset."[26] Mitigating the possible harms to displaced communities fell to the wayside and the Volta River resettlement became a chance to enact a progressive rural transformation showcasing Ghana's move toward modernity. "I am confident," Nkrumah boldly stated in a 1965 speech four years after the planning for resettlement began, "that the . . . people will not only command a higher standard of living than before, but they have the tools and opportunity to develop scientific mixed agriculture and healthy community living."[27] Similarly, the VRA's chief resettlement officer, E. A. K. Kalitsi, described resettlement not just as a geographic move, but also as a way to give people the "opportunity to participate much more than they have . . . in the development of the country for their own benefit and for the progress of the country."[28]

The practice of technocrat-led resettlement, however, foundered. As conceived by the VRA, professionals from Ghana's urban capitals like Kumasi and Accra would be the vehicles and architects of modernization.[29] These experts were charged with planning "an improved life" for resettled communities. They decided where people would live and what type of agriculture they should practice; they audaciously ordered space and people with the goal of propelling Ghana forward into the future. However, the pitfalls of development reliant on "conscious direction from the center" despite the "lack of sufficient knowledge at the center" became apparent.[30] In this case, the government experts who sought to remake the lives of affected Volta River communities often ignored the contours of those same communities.[31] Only a few years before the completion of the Akosombo Dam, the VRA remained "uncertain how many people were living in the lake area."[32] Dam construction was quickly outpacing the research studies that would ensure resettlement success. The rushed time line and the lack of information were compounded by the perception that rural subjects could easily be molded into modern citizens. However, Ghanaians in the flood areas would soon make it clear that for better or worse, human beings were not clay to be molded according to seven-year development plans.

Government experts decided that resettlement was an opportunity to introduce "scientific farming" methods that would increase yield. They chose sites for resettlement that were suitable for mechanized farming, and the VRA promised that seed for cash crops, tractors, and other necessary instruments would be forthcoming. "A resettling population," it was believed, "could be persuaded to make a radical change from traditional to modern farming methods more easily than one already entrenched on the land."[33] The attempt to engineer the livelihoods of these communities ultimately proved one of the clearest failings of the resettlement agenda. Constrained by time and resources, the VRA could not provide the promised resources. When displaced people arrived at their new home sites, many had neither the means, the implements, nor the training to embark on mechanized farming. As early as 1965, initial reports suggested something was amiss in the agricultural plans for the resettlement towns. Chief Resettlement Officer Kalitsi noted that as a result of the delays in acquiring agricultural tools, "the people are getting idle and some have started drinking and reports of acts of hooliganism are drifting in from some places."[34] Kalitsi cautioned that people would eventually leave the resettlements unless they could find a way to earn a livelihood. "The spectre of a ghost town hangs over the settlements we have built," he ominously warned.[35] Decades later, George Nartey's NRC petition lamenting the dwindling numbers at the Dede/Sewirako resettlement confirms the prescience of Kalitsi's warning. There were obstacles facing individuals who wanted to revert to commercial agriculture by traditional farming methods—the land allotments were too small, and attempts to farm outside the prescribed land brought resettlers into direct conflict with host communities—and many chose to leave. At the NRC's public hearings in Ho, the petitioner Albert Sunkwa described the lack of appropriate farmland in the resettlements. His community had to migrate again, this time to Kwahu, in order to build viable lives.[36]

Housing was another arena where resettlement experts fell short and where citizens turned to the NRC in order to settle the score. Neat, orderly, and modern housing was part of the Ghanaian government's vision of resettlement as modernization and development. However, both George Nartey's submission and a collective petition submitted by the Anyaboni Resettlement Centre described the resettlement housing as "dilapidated."[37] Apparently, the years had not been kind to what had originally been described by VRA experts as "modern model villages of which the nation could be proud."[38] As early as 1970, just a few years after the creation of the resettlements, displaced residents were complaining that these new, modern houses did not account for the rural climate or the social needs of the resettled families. Proudly built according to the notions of progress championed by architects and town planners, these new modern homes were hot during the day and cold at night, unlike the mud and thatch homes the residents once inhabited. The houses' fancy honeycomb design, theoretically supposed to allow for the free circulation of air, instead let in water during rainstorms and dust on windy, dry days. Beyond the physical design and in line with assumptions about the nature of modern households, these homes were built for nuclear families, usually with a single sleeping room. For polygamous and extended households, this type of housing was uncomfortable at best, untenable and volatile at worst. Finally, these homes constructed on the rushed timeline of the hydroelectric project were of dubious quality. In 1965 fierce storms ripped the roofs cleanly off these new houses and resettlers began to question the value of the homes they had been given.[39]

Housing problems were of particular concern because the VRA's new houses were supposed to stand in as equitable compensation for the land lost on the Akosombo's flood plains. Confronted with the displacement of thousands of citizens, the VRA experts created a plan to avoid the logistical nightmare and expense of parceling out cash compensation to everyone who lost land and homes. Instead, allocating new and improved housing would serve as compensation in kind. From the VRA's perspective, "it seemed that the innumerable variations and details of compensation could in most cases be smothered and eliminated in the one standardized act of presenting each family with a core house."[40] These new houses were not only symbols and vehicles of Ghanaian postindependence modernity, they were also a way for the Ghanaian government to avoid paying out compensation to the affected communities.

As described above, in both size and design, the "improved" housing did not meet the needs of the displaced communities. This problem became even more evident when resettlers sought to "improve" the housing to meet their own needs by building attachments and sheds to the structures they were provided. VRA officials worried that such "unauthorized structures" would change the "modern, beautifully planned and designed model townships" they had built. Fears that the resettlements would "degenerate[e] into disorganized old fashioned settlements or slums" began to crop up in the VRA records.[41] From house design to agricultural modes to the upkeep of the towns, the VRA expected displaced residents to buy into and comply with plans developed by state experts. The result was "houses that were not homes"; dwellings that could not satisfy people's needs.[42]

Both the ill-fated push toward scientific farming and the problems with housing reveal the folly of assuming that development agendas representing the will of technocratic experts can simply be imposed on citizens. The Ghanaian state is not unique in overlooking the voices of affected citizens. "Development in Africa," warns Paul Ocheje, "remains by and large, what the government does to people, not a process in which the people participate to shape the decisions that affect their lives."[43] The prevailing assumption was that communities targeted for development, because of their poverty and need, were ill-equipped to be agents, much less true partners in the process. Some VRA studies from the 1960s describe the communities marked for resettlement as "simple" people in need of transformation. These were "primitive farmer[s] . . . eke[ing] out a precarious existence" or "villagers and rural people . . . unused to long hours of pressured work." The challenge of modernization, according to the VRA Resettlement Office, was to overcome the "natural conservatism of rural people" and move them toward an improved life.[44]

To be sure, many staff members involved with VRA resettlement were aware that local buy-in was necessary for its success. Kalitsi approached his task as a "matter of creating conditions satisfactory to [the displaced communities]."[45] Indeed, the example of the Tema Port resettlement (1953–1959), where local communities had not been consulted and reacted by holding "wild demonstrations . . . where people swore public oaths . . . that the move would take place only over their dead bodies," had made the Ghana government aware that displacement and resettlement were fraught and potentially explosive.[46] In light of this history, the VRA dutifully created a social welfare office staffed with sociologists and social workers, many of whom had been involved in the earlier Tema resettlement and presumably had learned from their mistakes. This time, the VRA was committed to seeking input from the communities that would be displaced. The VRA recruited community development assistants who "were sent forth into the field both as missionaries and relatives" to "persuade [people] to accept evacuation happily."[47] Two social surveys would collect the people's perspective on matters both small and large. The research agenda was quite rigorous. "At the family level, we hoped to assess the needs of each household and to be able to allocate new houses so that people would be near those they preferred as neighbors."[48] At the community level, these surveys sought input about resettlement preferences regarding geography, neighboring communities, culture, and other matters.[49] However, this extensive consultation and outreach did not necessarily translate into the resettlement policy.

Although the VRA sought out local voices, there was no concomitant emphasis on actually listening to and translating these voices into action. With neither money nor time allocated to ensuring that these local studies affected the VRA's practice, this research program created an illusion of partnership on the part of the VRA and an illusion of choice for the displaced communities. In May 1962, nine months after construction on the Akosombo Dam had begun, no resettlement program had been created, nor had staff been assigned to develop it.[50] Even if the chief resettlement officer himself was committed to seeking community input, his office exerted limited leadership power within the resettlement at large.[51] In fact, some VRA sociologists and social workers had criticized the resettlement housing, raising the same concerns that NRC petitioners would raise decades later. Following resettlement, VRA personnel expressed "disappointment" at the lack of impact their research had on the final outcome.[52]

At the time, however, the social welfare team, perhaps prematurely, praised their success in giving "people a feeling that VRA was really interested in their future."[53] The outreach, which gave these communities an opportunity to state their choice of neighbors, adjacent villages, and other preferences, was designed to assuage the sentiment and pride of displaced communities; it was not perceived as a necessary foundation for making decisions about resettlement. This dynamic was evident when disagreements arose between the community and the VRA on fundamental matters, such as where a resettlement should be located. The social welfare staff "had to go back to the people again" and "employing all sorts of techniques and pressures," convince them to accept the VRA's decision.[54] Needless to say, no such pressures were levied on the VRA to see the community's point of view. Moreover, the VRA outreach officers could not answer the most common question posed by the people targeted for resettlement: how much compensation would they receive and when?[55] Reflecting on the immediate aftermath of resettlement, a VRA sociologist explained that the "lesson learn[ed]" was to conduct social surveys earlier.[56] The other, perhaps more expansive, lesson is about the folly of development initiatives that seek out the voices of target populations yet make no provisions for hearing—much less relinquishing decision-making power to—those populations.

Although the VRA approached the displaced communities as objects to be acted upon, resettled communities came before the NRC decades later to highlight their legal and social rights, assert themselves as citizens, and criticize both the process and the outcome of the state's modernization agenda.

Their formally worded petitions challenge both the premise and the practice of the VRA's authoritarian resettlement. For example, complaints about democracy (or the lack thereof) reoccur in these nonjurisdictional petitions. The Anyaboni community was frustrated at being subjected to the edicts of the VRA representatives—these "self-imposed managers and trustees" who "would not heed a word from the community regarding housing renovation.[57] The Anyaboni described the VRA "trustees and so-called managers" as "dictators with suppressive iron hands" who prevented residents from bettering their lives on their own terms. Residents proposed a remedy: the government should allow resettlers a chance to "exercise their freedom of choice . . . share their likes and dislikes . . . and enjoy the benefits due to them as Volta Flood Victims."[58]

The resettlers appearing before the NRC asserted their own authority and expertise. Before George Nartey described the woeful conditions in his resettlement community, he announced himself as a "citizen" of Dede/Sewirako. From this place of authority, he reviewed the history of the resettlements, asserted the failures of the program, and articulated particular solutions. First, Nartey called for the Ghanaian government and VRA to provide greater resources to the resettlements to ease tensions between the displaced residents and the host communities. Greater resources, he argued, were required to help "forestall [the] clashes" between the communities.[59] Nartey also addressed health care access. After unequivocally calling for pipe-borne water, Nartey criticized the existing social service delivery system, which relied on nongovernmental organizations (NGOs) to provide essential services to poor people. The "Catholic medical NGOs that visit at random" were insufficient to meet community needs. In this vein, Nartey also criticized public-education failures. In decades, his resettlement had yet to produce a single university graduate. Government-sponsored educational scholarships, he said, could address this woeful state of affairs. Finally, taking direct aim at the hydroelectric project, Nartey demanded free electricity for the Dede/Sewirako resettlement. It was unacceptable, he said, that resettlement communities were still in darkness after decades.

The NRC narratives illuminate the folly of authoritarian development models in Ghana. By retelling the story of the communities displaced by the VRP and focusing on the missteps of technocratic experts who shunned local wisdom and hoarded decision-making power, these citizens inserted their voices, authority, and expertise into the ongoing debates about national development and economic growth in Africa. They also addressed the use of force in such projects. Alexander Sunkwa's NRC petition claimed that some residents of the resettled communities were not fully apprised or consulted about how, and when, they would leave their ancestral lands. In Krachi, people were "bundled one day by a group of soldiers into trucks amidst protests" and expected to make a new life in an "inhospitable environment."[60] Surely, the VRA would question the veracity of this image and point to their months of outreach preparing communities to evacuate.[61] Nevertheless, Sunkwa anchors the resettlement of the Krachi people in this beginning nightmare of soldiers forcing people into trucks against their will. This image of coercion and suffering, applied to the Volta resettlement history, illuminates the thin margin between these visions of beneficent development and authoritarian violence.

The Struggle for Salt

The NRC records chart the unintended consequences of the Akosombo Dam, Ghana's most famous national public works project. The second collection of citizen stories details the suffering associated with another twentieth-century development initiative: growing Ghana's salt industry. Unlike the Volta River resettlement stories, here, the agents of development were private business companies. The most notorious among them was company called Vacuum Salt Products Ltd., which pursued a lucrative salt mining industry at the expense of artisanal salt winning on the Songor salt flats.

The Songor Lagoon's salt industry predates Ghanaian independence in 1957 and the creation of the Gold Coast Colony in 1867 by generations. Salt winning has "from time immemorial" been part of life along the Songor.[62] Traded as far as the Sahel and beyond, the salt harvested here has long been part of the regional economy. The local community has traditionally managed this resource according to a principle of open accessibility in which none of the surrounding clans, or the religious leaders, can claim ownership of the salt flats.[63] When salt is present, *all* people (even beyond the local community) are welcome to the harvest. This traditional resource management system became an obstacle for twentieth-century development schemes (both government and private) that depended on limiting public access to the salt.

In the early 1970s, private companies convinced the leaders of the Ada Traditional Council of the benefits of developing the salt flats.[64] In 1970, the "dynamic Ghanaian entrepreneur" Samuel Christian Appenteng created VSPL after acquiring the Greek-owned Panbros Salt Company.[65] Buoyed by the pro-privatization atmosphere of Busia's Second Republic, VSPL overcame local skepticism to secure a ninety-nine-year lease for a portion of the salt flats. When the relationship between VSPL and the local community crumbled years later, this lease would be heavily scrutinized. Did the Appenteng family use false promises of social and economic revitalization, or even bribes to gain this foothold in Ada?[66] Over the next three decades, the history of salt winning and the potential of the salt industry would be fiercely debated, erupting into violence and leading to court cases and, eventually, to the NRC.

However, in the 1970s, the collective economic possibilities made possible by salt were at the forefront of everyone's minds. There were other private companies, like Star Chemicals, Ltd., which boasted some local Ada representation among its management and sought to compete with VSPL. After the Acheampong government overthrew the pro-business Busia government, in March 1974, a new Executive Instrument 30/74 established that the entire lagoon was a collective natural resource that must be administered by the government for the national good. Nationalization, in this case, consisted of simply leasing the land back to the private companies that did not adhere to the tradition of open and communal salt winning. Here, counterintuitively, government intervention further restricted access to a resource that previously was available to all Ghanaians.[67] VSPL posted signs in the region warning "all persons fishing or in any other way using the Songaw[sic] Lagoon" that "it is from now on FORBIDDEN TO FISHING or in engage in any other occupation inside that portion of the Lagoon which has been enclosed."[68] The company informed the local inhabitants that "the land has been leased to our company by the Ghana Government" and "all trespassers will be dealt with according to the law."[69] For VSPL, developing the salt industry on the Songor required exclusive control over the land. For many among the indigenous inhabitants, the idea that the development imperative required them to relinquish their right to fish, gather salt, or even move freely through the land was impossible to accept. Emboldened by their government lease, VSPL now marked local salt winners as trespassers and thieves and hired soldiers and police to guard their concession from the community that had used the land for generations.[70] Clashes between the company and local salt winners ensued and the salt flats were transformed into a battlefield.

The community's persistent poverty posed perhaps the greatest challenge to VSPL's vision of trickle-down development. Throughout the 1970s and 1980s, much of Ada was mired in "abject poverty" at a time when these companies sought to drain the wealth out of the area.[71] Although VSPL promised that its activities would benefit the Ada people, the company employed local people only as low-wage workers without standing or protection. Unsurprisingly, some in the local community refused to be reduced to trespassers or exploited labor on their ancestral lands. Being incorporated into the development agenda at such a rudimentary level was insufficient for a community who saw the salt flats as their collective patrimony.

Imagine the hopes of the traditional salt winners when Rawlings's Armed Forces Revolutionary Council burst onto the political scene in 1979. Rawlings's populism and rhetoric about purging corruption resonated with a community disenfranchised by this partnership between private enterprise and government power. However, the military government's actual intervention into the conflagration on the Songor was decidedly ambivalent. In 1985, the Provisional National Defense Council (PNDC) banned VSPL and ownership of the salt flats passed into the hands of the central government.[72] However, the same questions of decades past persisted: What did it mean to declare the Songor a national natural resource? Would local communities be able to use it freely? Whose vision of development (chiefs, salt-winner cooperatives, or technocratic experts) should prevail? The PNDC did not offer new approaches to unraveling these dilemmas.

The petitions and statements about the painful history of the Songor salt flats in the NRC archive reveals a suffering that is neither past nor sufficiently repaired. In these citizen stories, the violence surrounding the development of a salt industry has formed into a hard pit at the center of modern Ada identity. This conflict spans decades and different governmental regimes; in their petitions, citizens describe the salt flats as an indigenous natural resource that is central to Ada identity. This struggle over salt has created a powerful social movement that, to this day, challenges the ideals of neoliberal globalization in this particular context.[73] Many of the NRC petitions were lodged by persons linked to this social movement; national reconciliation allowed local activists to thrust themselves onto the national stage.

When Benjamin Apronti-Ofotsu appeared before the NRC in 2003 he carried a collective petition and came forward to represent the "interests of all those . . . who in diverse way suffered atrocities meted out . . . at the hands of soldiers hired . . . by Stephen Appenteng of the Management of VSPL." Apronti-Ofotsu's file included a petition he submitted to the Commission on Human Rights and Administrative Justice five years earlier; this was not his first time approaching the government seeking "Payment of Compensation for Various Forms of Atrocities against the Indigenes around the Songor

Lagoon." He reported that three soldiers, accompanied by Samuel Appenteng, arrested him, tortured him, and sent him to Accra's Burma Camp, where he was detained for three weeks. When he returned to Ada, sick and broken, the salt he had gathered was burned, presumably by the same soldiers.[74]

Apronti-Ofotsu and other petitioners described the role of the Ghanaian soldiers and police officers who acted as the hands and feet of corporate violence. Bringing these stories before the NRC was itself an assertion that the government must be held accountable for the harm created at the nexus of corporate and state violence. Mentioning Burma Camp, the central headquarters of the Ghana armed forces, highlights the collusion between VSPL and the Ghanaian government. Salif Fierdzinu's story was similar to that of Benjamin Apronti-Ofotsu: two soldiers (again accompanied by Appenteng) confronted Fierdzinu while he was on the way to gather salt and physically assaulted him. He was sent away, first to the VSPL office, and then eventually to Burma Camp.

And of course the bullet that killed Maggie was fired from a police officer's gun. The death of Margaret Kuwornu in May 1985 was a watershed moment in the Songor salt struggle. During a police raid on local salt harvesters, a young pregnant woman known locally as Maggie was struck by a stray bullet and killed. The uproar surrounding her death catalyzed the PNDC government to take a public stand; Chairman Rawlings ordered Maggie's remains to be flown to Accra and publicly mourned.[75] The Ada Songor Salt Cooperative, formed in the 1980s, created a collectively written pamphlet explaining the history of the salt struggle; it was entitled *Who Killed Maggie?*[76] "For all the years since 1971 until Maggie's death, the wailings, the cries, the clamor, the sufferings and the written pleas of our people apparently never penetrated the ears of our government" is how one chapter of this pamphlet begins.[77]

Maggie's death is also a reference point in the NRC stories; through it, individual petitioners connect their personal complaint to the larger, collective story of the salt struggle. When Amakwor Anim brought a petition to the NRC, she described herself as a companion of Maggie's on the day of the shooting. She, too, was on her way to Christiana Abbio's house when they encountered a police raid. Her story is an eerie echo of Maggie's. Both women were pregnant; both were shot by police bullets—but Amakwor Anim survived. The bullet grazed her stomach, and she suffered a miscarriage, but her friend, Maggie, was killed.[78] Another petition tells of events that occurred in the week before Maggie was killed. Awoyo Puplampu was arrested with twenty bags of salt and brought to a VSPL office. When Puplampu told her torturers that "salt mining was a job for the Ada people," Stephen Appenteng told the men surrounding Puplampu to pick up a nail-studded piece of wood and slap her.[79] With deep cuts in her head and blood dripping down, Puplampu was made to chew salt and to hold a block and jump. She was also beaten. She sought compensation both for her lost salt and for the suffering she endured.

The prevalence of women's voices in these petitions reflects a history in which salt winning was traditionally women's labor. Consequently, VSPL's violence disproportionately affected the women of Ada. Mamle Mansa Sebi claimed that she and her husband were transporting 225 bags of salt from Ada to Kwahu Tafo, when soldiers arrested them. Sebi and her husband "were subjected to severe beatings." Sebi recounted, "My husband bled all over . . . his whole face was swollen"; he never recovered and died four months later. Her story recorded the injustice of her husband's assault and also revealed the economic consequences of this loss. Sebi's life was preserved but she was now a sole parent of nine children. She asked the NRC for assistance to meet her financial duties.[80] In the same vein, Korleki Obuor testified that when soldiers seized her truckload of salt, she was so despairing about her family's financial future that she contemplated suicide.[81]

In contrast to the imagined male subject of political violence, petitioners established that women's bodies were particularly vulnerable in the salt struggle. When Moses Ayornu was accosted by soldiers while ferrying thirty bags of salt from the lagoon to Lufenya, he was beaten and forced to chew salt. Along with describing his continuing gastrointestinal pain, Ayornu spoke of the suffering of his two female assistants. After the brutality and a three-week detention, the women lost their reproductive capacity. According to Ayornu, they "have been barren up to today, possibly due to the large intake of salt."[82] During the Accra public hearings, Madam Aku Sebi told a harrowing story about VSPL's brutality toward women. Sebi was five months pregnant when she was found winning salt at Awudikope. She was slapped, beaten with a belt, and asked to gaze at the sun burning over the salt flats. Stephen Appenteng himself, she claimed, forced her to chew salt and drink a cup of odorous, bitter liquid. While locked in the guardroom, Sebi began to miscarry. "I used my cloth to wrap the fetus and deposited it in a rubbish can," she wrote. She remained in custody for six long days, unable to inform the soldiers of her condition, using her cloth to stanch the blood flowing down her legs. Two decades after her trauma, she is still frightened whenever she hears of salt winning.

The statue of Margaret Kuwornu erected at Bonikorpe shows that her baby has been born and is nestled on her shoulder, wrapped in her cloth. It depicts her in a time that never came to pass. The particular and gendered suffering of women is central both to the local community's experience of the violence and the archive's record of the salt struggle.

Soti Abdulai's petition demonstrates the lack of recourse available to Ghanaians harmed by VSPL on the Songor. Abdulai was at home when a group of policemen and VSPL came to arrest him because residents of Toflokpo town had been gathering salt in VSPL's concession. Beaten and jailed in Tema, Abdulai returned home a week later determined to seek justice. When he approached the district secretary of Adangme East, urging him to "look into the atrocities . . . meted out to people in [this] area," the government representative advised him to go to the police. However, when Abdulai arrived at the Dawa police station to report a crime against his person, he was arrested again and detained for another week. "After my second release, I decided not to do anything about the case, for fear of another arrest," he wrote.[83] VSPL's ability to hire state agents, both police and soldiers, to prosecute their agenda on the Songor, damaged the relationship between the Ada people and the public officials who should have been in their service. Abdulai's story of suffering, protest, and silence in the 1980s reveals precisely the importance of Ghana's early twenty-first century NRC. For many, the opening provided by the NRC's human rights review was long awaited.

Along with exposing the brutality against women, the deleterious economic consequences of VSPL's activities, and the complicity of local government officials, the petitions in the NRC archive energetically describe the salt struggle as a matter of indigenous land rights and autonomy. Benjamin Apronti-Ofotsu drew contrasts between the value of traditional salt-harvesting techniques and the extractive approach imposed by VSPL. Established "over the centuries" and central to the spiritual and political life of the community, Apronti-Ofotsu's description was echoed by Awoyo Puplampu's assertion that salt mining was part of the Ada people's identity. These references to tradition, culture, and spirituality establish the value of the salt flats apart from capitalist economic growth. Local history and spirituality have proven to be critical in the indigenous social movement around salt; this "rootedness" has been a "strong source of resistance and alterity."[84] Apronti-Ofotsu's claim that VSPL "resorted to dehumanizing methods" to "keep its head above the waters in the salt trade" criticizes not only the physical violence of soldiers and police but also the epistemic violence of corporate definitions of development.[85]

The stories Ghanaians committed to the archive invite a long-overdue conversation about what constitutes development, who it is for, and who gets to decide. Despite its contemporary relevance, the NRC bureaucracy briskly sidestepped the substance of this citizen critique of national development. The legal notes attached to the citizen petitions reveal how and why this critical history of the salt struggle was deemed nonjurisdictional within the official NRC review. By approaching the petitions as isolated, individual complaints disconnected from an ongoing collective struggle between VSPL and the Ada people, NRC officials—statement takers, legal investigators—undermined and downplayed the stories that Ghanaians shared. For example, the brutal physical assault of Awoyo Puplampu, described above as a symbol of VSPL's gendered violence and assault on indigenous Ada identity, was reduced by one legal investigator to a "misunderstanding" between VSPL and "the inhabitants who claimed the land belongs to their ancestors."[86] Another petitioner, Jonathan Teye Duonsi, a farmer from Agbedrafor-Ada, described a 1974 purge of his community following the killing of a VSPL watchman. After the death of the company's watchman, 150 people were arrested and detained for years. They were subjected to abject prison conditions, including "severe malnutrition, overcrowding, insect bites which later developed to skin diseases, malaria, TB, pneumonia, etc."[87] The suffering spooled out across generations: "This incident has made many children fatherless, poor, deprive[d] of formal education," Duonsi explained.[88] An NRC investigator dismissed Jonathan Teye Duonsi's petition on the grounds that the Ghanaian courts had already dealt with this matter. Duonsi and the other detainees were accused of killing the VSPL watchman, the investigator explained, and all had been detained, stood trial, and were eventually acquitted. From the official NRC perspective, justice had already been done, so his petition was dismissed.

The skepticism of the NRC bureaucracy is also evident in the note attached to the complaint of Tetteh Puplampu, a farmer living at Hwakpo-Ada. "In the course of investigation the petitioner was invited to contact the investigatory to clear certain aspects of his claim," the investigation team noted. "He failed to respond." The NRC then asked the local police, stationed at Kasseh-Ada, to track down Puplampu and obtain a statement from the witness. Puplampu's original story included details of arrest and torture at the hands of Ghanaian soldiers. Other petitioners, like Soti Abdulai, described how local police forces were often complicit or active participants in the violence meted out to the Ada community. Given this context, dispatching local police to take a statement may have eroded Puplampu's trust and contributed to his silence. Moreover, the NRC bureaucracy took the discrepancies between the police's story and Tetteh Puplampu's original petition as evidence of Puplampu's mendacity. The grand size of his claim of loss was the last straw for the NRC bureaucracy. "It appears that there is no truth in the petitioner's claim that he lost 160,000 bags of salt. This is so because he has no salt mine of his own from which he could mine such huge quantity."[89] Frankly, this single line strikes at the crux of more than three decades of conflict on the Songor Lagoon: can anybody claim to own of the quantities of salt produced on the salt flats? There is a tradition in which these "huge quantities" have been made available to all, in Ada and beyond. Approaching these citizen stories through the lens of individual ownership and without the context of decades of struggle skewed the NRC investigations.

One NRC investigator was openly suspicious of the veracity of Teye Bosumprah's story, particularly about the claim that in 1982 VSPL workers set fire to 170 bags of salt. The investigator disbelieved Bosumprah's description of the facts in the strongest of terms. "It is ridiculous to believe that anybody could set salt on fire," the note scoffs. "Opinions sought from some of the people who mine salt indicated that it is impossible to destroy salt with fire as [is] being alleged."[90] However, Bosumprah was not the only one who described this practice; a number of petitioners within the NRC describe the way VSPL workers would burn the thatch surrounding heaped salt in order to destroy the load. By undermining the veracity of these individual stories, the NRC avoided contemplating or adjudicating this challenging, ongoing debate about the violence of development on the Songor and beyond.

This marginalization was most evident on a warm day in June when the notorious Appenteng brothers, Samuel and Stephen, finally appeared before the NRC in Accra. Their team of young lawyers cross-examined and attempted to discredit the testimonies of the witnesses from Ada. As mentioned in Chapter 1, the lawyers suggested that Aku Sabi, despite being beaten and drilled, had miscarried because she did not take good care of her health. Similarly, in these public hearings, Sammy Appenteng implied that traditional salt winners were engaging in illegal activity and thus deserved the consequences. They had been arrested "either by military personnel or custom security men engaged . . . to check illegal mining in the VSPL concession," he insisted. Why should he be held responsible? When salt was confiscated by these soldiers, he noted, they deposited the proceeds into the government's chest. He insisted that as legitimate businessman who leased the land on the salt flats, neither he nor his brother could be blamed for any suffering that had occurred.[91] The Appenteng brothers would offer no apologies nor any admission of guilt. Both perpetrator denial and bureaucratic skepticism froze the potential for a much-needed conversation about authoritarian development and land rights in Ghana.

Conclusion

In the NRC, Ghana's rural communities presented the consequences of land alienation cloaked in the trappings of economic development. Their stories reflect the pitfalls of a development model in which growth is predicated on transforming target communities along lines they do not choose and from which they will not benefit. The stories from the Volta River Project resettlements reveal the shortcomings of an authoritarian development mode that persists even as technocratic experts undertake copious research and seek out local voices. In today's context, "local partnership" is a foundational principle in development practice even as economic exigencies, pressures of time and funding, attenuated local networks, and biases (conscious and subconscious) may ensure the leanness of this "partnership." The lesson of the NRC archive is that authoritarian development does not require authoritarian speech and that discourses of democracy may coexist with practices of autocracy in national and international realms.[92]

Both collections of citizen petitions floundered within the NRC bureaucracy. These stories were marked as nonjurisdictional by investigators, legal advisers, and statement takers who decided, for various reasons, that these stories should *not* be considered within the country's human rights review. Confronted with citizen complaints about the Volta resettlements, the commission turned to the VRA—described in many citizen petitions as the perpetrator of violence—and received noncommittal and evasive responses. "We are unable to investigate particular cases of petitioners who have not indicated the names of the original owners. . . . We request that the petitioners produce their [identification] cards for further investigations."[93] By focusing on the procedural complexity of these petitions, the VRA neatly sidestepped the substantive critiques raised by residents of the resettlement towns. The official commission response followed this same line, claiming that "more than adequate notice was given to local inhabitants" about their displacement and that "it would not be in the public interest" to discuss compensation.[94] Patronizing at best, this official NRC response closed the door on yet another opportunity to consider the political and social fallout of the Volta River hydroelectric project and other national development initiatives. Despite these obstacles, the NRC archive immortalizes the citizen-expert version of this history. Nonjurisdictional or otherwise, the voices of Nartey, Dunkwa, the Anyaboni Collective, and others are preserved in the public record and continue to speak.

Although the petitions and testimonies about the Songor salt struggle exposed the violence unleashed by private businesses claiming to deliver economic progress, the Ada salt winners were dispatched in the same manner as their counterparts from the Akosombo Dam flood areas. Citizens influenced by the movement that has developed around the decades-long struggle for salt in Ada came to the NRC and sought to thrust their stories of a violent and unjust neoliberal development onto the national stage. However, the NRC bureaucracy did not engage with the fundamental questions of who owned the salt and the violence of particular visions of growth. Instead, investigators, statement takers, and attorneys challenged the veracity and accuracy of individual stories.

For example, in these petitions, many self-described victims named members of the Appenteng family, the owners of VSPL, as active participants in the violence. When Benjamin Apronti-Ofotsu stated that three soldiers detained him, forced him to chew salt, roll on the ground, and suffer other painful drills, he claimed that the soldiers were accompanied by VPSL head Samuel Appenteng.[95] Similarly, when Salif Fierdzinu told his story about being assaulted and tortured by soldiers in 1982, he, too, placed the Appentengs at the crime scene. Awoyo Puplampu insisted that Stephen Appenteng himself had ordered soldiers to slap her when she articulated her right to win salt. As a point of historical fact, citizens' claims that the owners of a large private company personally participated in rough intimidation, violence, and assault that was part of the day-to-day maintenance of the VSPL enterprise may appear far-fetched. However, the truth of the citizens' argument may be found in this dogged refusal to separate the violence unleashed by police, soldiers, and mercenary citizens from the corporation at the center of the Songor salt struggle. The perpetrator of violence, each of these petitioners insisted, was VSPL, the company and its economic agenda, not only the individual policeman or soldier who did its bidding. How better to make this point than to place the Appenteng brothers at the scenes of torture? As a result of these citizen stories, the Appentengs were compelled to present themselves at the NRC in order to clear their name. Through a team of lawyers, they summarily denied any responsibility for the atrocities the petitioners described. They were legitimate business owners who surely could not be blamed for any violence resulting from their desire to protect their leased land or grow their company.[96] The Appentengs' denial of responsibility, coupled with bureaucratic skepticism, resulted in the neutralization and dismissal of many of these petitions about the salt struggle.

In the stories from the Volta River resettlement and the indigenous salt winners in Ada, Ghanaians displayed the suffering that accompanied the displacement of rural and poor communities in the name of national development. These stories of suffering are part of a vital, long-overdue conversation about the tragedy of exclusive visions of national growth that require the poorest Ghanaians to sacrifice traditional land and property rights. Ghana's NRC inspired this rare record of citizens condemning exclusive and authoritarian models of economic development. Unfortunately, the NRC swiftly marked these stories as marginal to their pursuit of historical justice in twenty-first-century Ghana.

CHAPTER 6

Soldier, Victim, Hero, Survivor

At the center of the global truth-and-reconciliation-commission (TRC) phenomenon is the human rights victim, the person who has suffered much and is deserving of succor. In their ideal form, TRCs foreground victims' voices and usher a previously marginalized person back into a restored political community.[1] If TRCs are not always able to deliver the full measure of reconciliation and progress that postconflict societies require, at least they listen empathetically to those voices and thus provide "a sense of satisfaction, acknowledgement, reduction of uncertainty, empowerment, and healing" to those who have suffered.[2] Ghana's National Reconciliation Commission (NRC) was one such "victim-centered process" in which commissioners listened to, sympathized with, and "encourage[d] witnesses to put behind them the bitterness and pain so as to get on with their lives."[3] The NRC's focus on victims' voices was not always well received. Critics accused commissioners of bias and criticized the version of historical truth that might emerge from these voices.[4] Foregrounding victims requires also identifying and chastising perpetrators and Ghanaians cast in the latter role chafed at this characterization.

The TRC's romance with the language of victims and perpetrators comes at a cost. Reading (and writing) history through this dichotomy obscures the complexity of political violence, the "gray zone in which categories of perpetrator and victim blur."[5] This framework of innocent victim/guilty perpetrator is not only historically obfuscating, it also limits postconflict political futures. If perpetrators are "deemed, by virtue of their crimes, to have forfeited their voice and contribution to the formation of their society's future," how then should a nation proceed?[6] Mahmood Mamdani warns of the risks of governing according to a vision of victims' justice. In places where people must find a way to live together, the moralistic language of victimization and guilt may be impracticable.[7] For Mamdani, the campaign to characterize the violence in Darfur as genocide was an example of the naïveté of victims' justice. Unleashing this label—the black mark of *genocidaire*—further entrenches the divisions within the Sudan. Resisting the label of genocide, Mamdani explains, protects the possibility of a political solution that requires both sides of the conflict to meet and compromise. Resisting this act of naming is not an attempt to ignore the breadth and depth of violence; such resistance is, instead, knowing enough about the violence to understand that essentializing victims and perpetrators erects obstacles to the peace that must come.

The cacophony of the NRC's collective history writing does not allow the Ghanaian past to be sifted out into innocent victims and guilty perpetrators. In these records, the passion play of innocence and evil quickly gives way to a jarringly complex political history. In 2003, President Kufuor himself, who sponsored the NRC, described Ghana's human rights victims as complex political actors. He framed the NRC as a "release valve" to mitigate the possibility that suffering people would "take up cudgels and cutlasses and go after those people they think hurt them."[8] Today's victim might become tomorrow's perpetrator; the thin line between these two identities, and the speed with which they might be reversed, was part of Kufuor's justification of a Ghanaian truth commission. Godfred Kissi, one of the earliest citizens who lodged a petition at the Accra office, identified himself as one of these volatile victims-turned-perpetrators. When Kissi's father's died (through the violence of Provisional National Defense Council [PNDC] policies), his son was unable to secure a good education and struggled for years. Along with his petition, Godfred Kissi's NRC file includes a letter from March 28, 2003. "Please I am remembering you to look at my file number 16. . . . You have not call me yet for the hearing and if I am cheated by the government then I will also be an enemy of the state." Quite quickly, Kissi warned, he could change from state supplicant to state enemy. In contrast to the victims' justice framework based on the presumed innocence of those who suffer, in the NRC archive there are whispers of the potential volatility of Ghanaian victims.

This is a national political history that includes victims who are not innocent and perpetrators who, in their suffering, cannot simply be dismissed as guilty. The first part of this chapter addresses stories from and about Ghanaian soldiers. Part of the complexity of the archive is that these soldiers (many of whom were accused of violence) claimed that they, too, must be counted among the victims of national history. In these records, the dichotomy in which victim and perpetrator are distinct, discrete identities, blurs. What are the consequences when the African soldier, whose notoriety has been established through the colonial and postindependence period, claims that he, too, has suffered? Is he to be believed? Can victimhood be claimed by those who have held the guns and brandished them against others? These soldier stories reveal where the language of victim/perpetrator falls short when responding to political violence. This chapter explores how the language of *survivors* captures the complexities of the NRC archive's soldier stories and may be a path beyond the limitations of victims' justice.

The second part of this chapter explores the images of resistance that appear in the NRC archive. Like the soldier stories, these images of Ghanaian resistance defy easy categorization. In these stories the power of the state is paramount, and yet, the resilience of individuals who sought to mitigate, counteract, and resist state violence is also accounted for. The images of ambivalent heroism that emerge in the NRC archive, like the soldier stories, are unsettling because they defy easy characterization. Those Ghanaians who resisted state violence were marked as criminals and often suffered the consequences; these heroes are afforded acclaim neither in the present nor the past. Nevertheless, the presence of these resistance stories, however ambivalent, within the NRC's public history-writing project must not be overlooked. The records preserve accounts of Ghanaians who sought to draw boundaries around state violence in their own communities and lives. Together, these records of soldier victims and ambivalent heroes illuminate the moral complexities of life within the crucible of political violence.

Soldier Stories

When they want to call, eh
When they want to call, eh
When they want to call Nigerian government
Them give am name "Federal Military Government"
For Libya dem give am name "Liberation Council"
For Liberia dem give am name "Redemption Council"
For Zaire dem give am name "Revolutionary Council"
Them get different different names
For different different governments
But the correct name for them
Na "soldier go, soldier come"
Soldier go, soldier come!
—Overtake Don Overtake Overtake, Fela Kuti

When you are bearing arms that can spit fire and death, and when you receive orders standing to attention in front of a flag without knowing who will benefit from this order . . . you become a potential criminal who's just waiting to spread terror around you. How many soldiers are going around such and such a country bringing grief and desolation without understanding that they are fighting men and women who argue for the same ideals as their own?

> —*Thomas Sankara: The Upright Man*
> Directed by Robin Shuffield, Marc Ridley, Samuel
> Gantier, Serge Dietrich, and Cyril Orcel, 2006

Soldiers have played a prominent and volatile role in the African continent's political history. The ongoing militarization of Africa, which is evident in ongoing conflicts, a penchant for coups d'état, and high flows of arms, continues to place the spotlight on African soldiers as central figures shaping the continent's fortunes. Images of African soldiers as perpetrators of violence, as "beasts of no nation," abound. This was not always so. In the mid-twentieth century, African soldiers played a role in bringing forth the world beyond European colonialism.

In the colonial Gold Coast, World War II veterans who had traveled the world, fought for the empire, and experienced colonial racism in "Mother England" were conduits of anticolonial consciousness.[9] The February 1948 march of the Ex-Servicemen's Union to the Gold Coast governor at Christianborg Castle is a seminal point in the history of Ghanaian independence.[10]

Similarly, in 1975, the Tanzanian president, Julius Nyerere, described the "soldiers of Mozambique freedom" as a distillation of the country's best tendencies. "Neither age nor sex or color determined who were the soldiers of Mozambique. Children, youths, and old people, all worked for freedom; men and women carried arms, transported supplies, cultivate the land. . . . Blacks, white and people of mixed ancestry, all risked their lives as they worked for freedom."[11] Even in the early postindependence period, the military's intrusion into the workings of the new African governments held the promise of progressive change. The political scientist Ali Mazrui hailed soldiers as representatives of the people; they were a "semi-organized, rugged and semi-literate" class who had "begun to claim a share of power and influence in what would otherwise have become a heavily privileged meritocracy of the educated."[12] By the end of the Cold War, this hopeful narrative of the African soldier would dramatically shift with the procession of proxy conflicts and forced regime changes prosecuted by ambitious military men willing to receive global monies. Since then, representing African soldiers "as the barbaric (African) masculine other," who is a threat to democracy and a purveyor of atrocity, has become the norm.[13]

In the NRC archive, Ghanaian soldiers are not solely conduits of violence. Soldiers identified themselves as citizens, civil servants, and fellow victims of state power. At the public hearings, accused perpetrators were often unwilling to adhere to the script of guilt and remorse. Instead, these soldiers utilized the platform of the NRC to present their own interpretations of Ghana's history of political violence and their place within it. Alongside the complicating voices of Ghanaian soldiers, the NRC includes citizens who eloquently describe the violence of militarism in Ghanaian history.

In 1975, David Okyere was apprentice to a mechanic who had amassed some financial debt. When soldiers arrived to confront Okyere's employer, they found only David there and beat him severely. He lost a tooth, was hauled to jail, and endured hard labor until his parents bailed him out. Two years later, Okyere, who had been living in exile Nigeria, returned to Ghana after learning that Colonel Acheampong had been deposed. His return was fueled by hopes of a new life in Ghana, and he brought with him the machinery and goods he had acquired during his years abroad. Okyere was traveling from Accra and Kumasi with his machinery and goods when soldiers stopped him. They seized the goods he had brought from Nigeria and instructed Okyere to come to the barracks with documentation as proof of ownership. However, Okyere could complete this simple documentation task "because of [his] earlier encounter with the soldiers. . . . I could not make any follow-up due to fear."[14] Just like that, David Okyere, bound by his fear of Ghanaian soldiers, lost all he had worked to acquire during his years in Nigeria.

James Owusu-Ansah told a similar story. During a 1979 fuel shortage, while queuing for petrol, a soldier "assaulted [him] mercilessly" for disturbing the order of the petrol line. This incident had a lasting impact: "I always miss a heartbeat when I come into contact with any soldiers," he later recounted.[15] This fear continued to create limits throughout his life; Owusu-Ansah could not bring himself to cross paths with soldiers, no matter the cost.

Persons who did not experience but witnessed these soldier brutalities were also affected. Manasseh Addo, whose witness statement is stored within another citizen's file, described the 1966 coup d'état as unforgettable. "I saw how Ghanaian soldiers treated the students. Students were dragged from their bedrooms as far as to the down steps. They were tortured by the soldiers."[16] The emotional and psychological distress that followed those who witnessed soldier violence was evident in the petition of Alhaji Mohammed Kwame Osei. In 1979, as a successful merchant, Osei was accused of committing economic crimes, arrested, and drilled. He later learned that his wife, Hajia Nyarkoa, was also arrested. Under the care of soldiers, Nyarkoa had become almost unrecognizable: her back was striped with whip marks and her head had been shaved. Her confinement took place during the month of Ramadan; instead of being allowed to fast, Hajia had been forced to consume milk and also *akpeteshie*, a local liquor. Although Alhaji Osei and Hajia Nyarkoa had since divorced, his petition to the NRC painstakingly detailed the psychological and physical cruelties of Ghanaian soldiers toward his former wife. Moreover, Osei brought a collection of witnesses, fellow residents of Nkawkaw, who had seen and could confirm his story.[17] In response to this history of devastating soldier violence, Martin Budu-Kwatia suggested, in his NRC petition that a regiment of British soldiers should be permanently stationed in Ghana to keep the country's army in line. Neocolonial occupation, for Budu-Kwatiah, was a reasonable response to the potential threat of a possible Ghanaian soldier uprising.[18]

In contrast to the stories detailing the pain and terror unleashed by the state security agents, when Ghanaian soldiers and police appeared before the commissioners, they often described themselves as victims of state violence. While the Ghana NRC, unlike the South African commission, did not include any provision extending amnesty to perpetrators in exchange for their participation, the NRC could compel participation by subpoena. In their "confessional performances," Ghanaian soldiers and police adhered to the conventions of perpetrator testimonies around the world; these stories "rarely involved remorse."[19] These soldiers accused of torture, assault, rape, and terror were often unable to remember or unwilling to explain what had befallen them or their victims.

During the PNDC years, Jack Bebli was known as the Terror. He headed a militarized police commando unit that used AK-47s, rocket launchers, machine guns, and hand grenades to pursue pickpockets, robbers, and enemies of the so-called revolution." Bebli's violence was of mythical proportions. Even his death in 2009 could not erase his legacy; "those who suffered at his hands would not forgive his ghost."[20] There were a number of NRC petitioners who described Jack Bebli as a cornerstone of the PNDC's violence.[21] Alex Kwabena Nsiah remembered Bebli as the leader of a squad that forced him off his bicycle and shot him in the leg in 1983. Bleeding, Nsiah was pushed into a Land Rover full of injured and dead people and dropped at the hospital. Alex Nsiah survived, but his leg had to be amputated. Christian Goka tearfully described Jack Bebli as the man who tortured his brother Mawuli and snuffed out his life.[22] Some even claimed that Bebli was "more fearsome than Chairman Rawlings himself."[23]

Truth and reconciliation commissions supposedly privilege victim narratives, not least through structures in which accused perpetrators are invited only to *respond,* to speak to the timeline, narratives, and accounts already presented by victims.[24] At the NRC, Bebli refused to submit to the narrative of his victims. At his first appearance before the NRC in February 2003, he immediately requested that he should no longer be called Jack. Now a hunched, elderly man, Bebli explained that he was a born-again Christian and had renounced the name Jack, with its "devilish" connotation. His chosen name was Paul. By publicly rejecting even the name that was central to his notoriety, Bebli entirely rejected the perpetrator identity foisted upon him. Instead he spun a new narrative of conversion, self-making, and redemption. Choosing to unveil himself as Paul, Bebli referenced one of Christian Scripture's central redemption stories—Saul of Tarsus's conversion from a persecutor of early Christians to an evangelist for Christ. Referencing the story of Saul becoming Paul, this testament to the possibility and grace of radical individual transformation, was not a coincidence. In Bebli's narrative of divine conversion, there was little use for human accountability mechanisms such as the NRC. "We should let bygones be bygones," Bebli insisted, rejecting the very premise of the NRC. After all, his personal transformation was complete; the new Paul Bebli could boldly state that he had "never shot a bird, let alone a human being." The row of victims standing before him was unrecognizable, all had been washed away by the blood of Jesus. As such, only God could be his judge. "The Bible will tell on the last day if my story is not true, but I will take it easy."[25] By claiming an alternative temporality (heaven), a different name (Paul), and another moral narrative (divine and radical transformation), Bebli found an escape from the accusing eyes of amputees, tearful family members, and the nation.

Leigh Payne describes unsettling perpetrator testimony as ultimately useful for democracy because it elicits "contentious" conversations that draw people into the public sphere.[26] At Jack Bebli's NRC appearance, the crowd erupted into boos and jeers at his evasions and alternative narrative of divine redemption. At this point, one of the commissioners, the Catholic priest Charles Palmer-Buckle, interrupted the uproar. He asked Ghanaians to view Bebli as someone who had also suffered and who, even now, was in need of prayer and "serious compassionate vibes."[27] Palmer-Buckle's response to an audience unwilling to allow Jack Bebli to "forget" the suffering he caused was to exhort them to perceive the elderly man sitting before them as something other than an evil soldier. Might Jack Bebli be a soul in need of prayer, a man suffering illness, a fellow citizen in need of compassion? For Father Palmer-Buckle, there was a value—perhaps emotional, spiritual or politic—in naming and perceiving the agents of political violence differently.

In the NRC archive, Ghanaian soldiers claimed that they, too, must be counted among the victims; the archetypical African soldier—male, adult, with the imprint of a gun in his hand—may be a victim as well as a perpetrator of violence. Ghanaian soldiers described the ways proximity to state power—living in army barracks and housing, hierarchical relationships with top brass—restricted their autonomy and limited their agency and their power to choose particular pathways in life. If citizens blamed soldiers for meting out atrocity, Ghanaian soldiers blamed the government; they were people whose employment brought them dangerously close to a volatile postindependence state

Mike Boafo-Ntifo had served in the Ghana Armed Forces (GAF) for almost twenty years when the PNDC government came into power. In the atmosphere of purge and cull, Boafo-Ntifo was arrested "without any provocation or an offence committed." Living in army housing with his family, his personal effects were ransacked and seized, and he was carried away to Accra, "leaving [his] dear wife and little children behind at the mercy of the Almighty God." The only information he received was that his arrest had been ordered by Chairman Rawlings. He was released back to active service and worked uneasily until his employment was abruptly terminated a few months later. Subsequently, Boafo-Ntifo and his family fled into exile because he received word that soldiers "were looking for him." After years in Cote d'Ivoire, Boafo-Ntifo returned to Ghana in 2001 seeking any record or explanation for what had befallen him. He came to the NRC requesting a proper discharge, his pension, veteran's services, and the goods he had lost twenty years earlier. The violence of the past, he claimed, was being unjustly compounded in the present. "Could it be possible" Boafo-Ntifo wrote, "that one animal is killed and its body is shared twice or thrice?"[28]

Paul Asimeng was also a long-tenured soldier with the GAF. Colonel Acheampong specifically requested his services in the fight against *kalabule* in the mid-1970s. During the Armed Forces Revolutionary Council (AFRC) revolution in 1979, Asimeng was arrested and threatened with death unless he found a way to make himself useful to the new regime. One can only imagine the zeal with which Asimeng may have participated in the AFRC-era destruction. Nevertheless, he was discharged and other soldiers harassed him in his attempts to build a life apart from the GAF; he eventually escaped to Nigeria and then Togo. When Asimeng returned for his father's funeral in 1982, he was picked up by soldiers, then beaten and tortured. As a soldier who had fallen out of favor with the new regime, he was automatically classified as a dangerous dissident, someone whose background and training made him a risk to the regime. "I collapsed. . . . I was brutally handled, even my manhood." When Asimeng left Ghana again, he went even further away—this time to East Germany. If it was dangerous to encounter soldiers, it was also dangerous to *be* a soldier who had fallen out of favor.[29]

And there were many who would fall out of favor. Ghana's cyclical coups d'état meant that individual soldiers were often at risk. At age 68, Kofi Akwandoh Arkoful came to the NRC with a story of decades of service. He joined the army in 1952 in the days when it was the West African Command and proudly served during the transition to national independence. Akorful was specially recognized by Kwame Nkrumah himself for his work decolonizing the army in the aftermath of independence. When the 1966 coup occurred, Akorful's earlier recognition became a mark against him in the new dispensation. He was demoted from lieutenant to staff sergeant and posted far away, in northern Ghana. Akorful described this twist of fate as economically and psychologically devastating. "I was left to start my military career all over again," he recounted. "The mental agony I suffered and continue to suffer is beyond description. My military career was woefully destroyed resulting in my inability to care for my wife and children adequately." The demotion yielded a cascade of unfulfilled dreams: "I have not been able to put up a house or at least buy a plot of land for my family." Akorful's salutation in closing the petition, "your obedient ex-soldier," communicates the centrality of this professional identity to his suffering and sense of loss.[30]

The petition of 69-year-old Benjamin Amin was similar. In 1971, he was compelled to take a leave of absence from his position with the border guards to have an appendectomy. At his return, to his surprise, he was "shouted on . . . beaten, and dismissed from his job." More than three decades later, Amin was still perplexed by this turn of events. When he pursued legal aid, he was advised to stay silent. "So long as military regime is concerned," the lawyer bluntly stated, "I cannot help you." "They would arrest me and shoot me." And that was that. His family suffered when he was ejected from the service. "With 90% of my salary off, my children dropped from school" and Amin's relationship with his wife deteriorated. "One day when I found that my wife had become very harsh to me, I asked her why? She said in Akan, shall I stay with you and starve to death?" Eventually, she left. Like many other unfairly dismissed soldiers, Amin eloquently communicated his grief and begged for the commission to step into a context where there was no proper recourse. "Can a person be held responsible for a crime he has not committed?" he asked. "Is it possible that a person accusing you of committing a crime, be the same person who [tries] you, finds you guilty, imposes sentence on you and execute the sentence?" [31] For Ghanaian soldiers, political turbulence thwarted their professional and personal aspirations. This sense of missed opportunity was evident in the petition of Christian Ahadzi, who was prevented from advancing in rank because he freely spoke his mind. "Oh the humble village boy's hopes are shut. What next?" Ahadzi moaned.[32]

As Ghanaian soldiers counted themselves among the victims of national history, their stories shift the conversation about political violence in Ghana. One commissioner, Lt. General Emmanuel Erskine, said as much; "I felt very embarrassed when some of our very Senior Officers appeared before us at the National Reconciliation Commission to share their pain and mental agony with us," he wrote. "I have, since then, strongly felt that we are lucky that we still have the Ghana Armed Forces with us today in Mother Ghana."[33] By joining in the calls for reparation and reform, Ghanaian soldier stories make it plain that committing violence and suffering violence are not fixed, essential identities but are both "temporary states" that a person may enter and exit, based on the circumstances.[34] This version of human rights history does not lend itself to the morally satisfying, but politically volatile victims' justice. Instead, it lays the foundation for understanding postconflict society as populated by survivors—an amalgamation of individuals and groups who have all been affected, however differently, by the violence of the past.

Survivors' justice pays attention not just to who has been damaged, but also to the variety of ways that individuals and communities have lived (retreated, dissembled, erected barriers, strategized) and ultimately survived the past's violence. By recognizing that all in the community are actively *surviving* the manifestations of past violence, survivors' justice eludes the prescriptions of vengeance that, more often than not, simply invert systems of exclusion. Relinquishing the cold comfort of victim status requires that we engage questions of historical injustice, reparation, and national progress without the moral certainty of anointing a particular people as chosen, innocent, good, or worthy.

This survivors' justice is not a valorization of ethical ambivalence. Nor is it the equivalent of shrugging one's shoulders and saying that all have harmed, all have suffered, so let's continue on with the (violent) status quo. Departing from the categories of victims and perpetrators is not a departure from rigorous accountings of history. Indeed, the opposite is true. Beyond the false ease of the victim/perpetrator dichotomy there is an opportunity to apprehend the complexity of historical violence in the world. Individual evil—to the extent that such can be found—plays a minimal role in the genesis and perpetuation of historical injustice. Hannah Arendt's notion of the banality of evil was not only a warning to the citizens who averted their eyes and kept silent at the proclamations of the Fuhrer. It was also a warning to today's citizens in democratic nations who are blissfully unaware that their shoes are made by six-year-olds in Bangladesh or that their daily coffee, wedding ring, or chocolate bar originate in blood. It is better that we give up the moral certitude of victims and perpetrators, the child's narrative of good and evil that isolates us from knowing the violence that is occurring in the world and our place in it.

Ambivalent Heroes

> My lord, in the village, at that time of our history, nobody, no sane person, would want to stay there. They all ran away, leaving me, my mother, and my two sisters. There was not even anybody there to help us carry my brother in the coffin to the cemetery. We had to do it with my mother, and my two sisters. Now, I managed to muster courage to tell [the soldiers] that we will not comply with their orders. I told them that even if one bought a grasscutter, it takes more than thirty minutes to prepare the grasscutter for soup. How much more for a human being? So we were not going to comply. If they like, they can come finish everybody. We will not comply with their orders. So they left.
> —Yaw Fosu Munufie, NRC Hearing, Tamale[35]

The NRC's soldier stories undermine the dichotomy of innocent victim/guilty perpetrator and instead invite us to understand Ghanaian history as populated by survivors: individuals and groups who have all been affected in diverse ways by the history of state violence. There is another collection of records in this archive that challenges the moral bright lines of standard human rights histories. Courage quietly abounds within the NRC archive's narrative of Ghanaian political violence. There are testimonies and petitions remembering citizens who ferried victims of soldier violence to the hospital, who interrupted public assaults on traders, who risked themselves to shield others from harm. This part of the chapter is built around the stories of heroism preserved in the citizen narrative of the Ghanaian past. These hero stories illuminate local efforts, however limited or ambivalent, to resist state violence. These stories map the forced choices, wavering courage, and sorrow through which resistance is actually made: the NRC archive presents heroes of and for troubled times.

Decades ago, Lila Abu-Lughod aptly warned against a tendency to romanticize resistance in ways that cloud the heft and persistence of power.[36] Exploring the limitations and contingency of social and political movements is a way to better apprehend the state's repressive power. The heroes and heroines of the NRC archive do not easily fit romantic narratives of political heroism. Many of these individuals presented themselves to the NRC as victims. Their stories are not particularly triumphant, and for the most part, the NRC bureaucracy did not praise or applaud the actions of these individuals. However, I group them together, using the language of heroism, because these stories display moments when Ghanaians incurred risk in an attempt to rescue, support, or aid a fellow citizen who was suffering. Illuminating how, when, and why Ghanaians stood up against state violence, these stories are pinpoints of light within a bleak landscape. They are also, for the most part, ill-fated and limited attempts to carve out spaces of safety and humanity within a context of pervasive state violence. These glimpses of resistance reveal the exigencies of life within the crucible of state violence. Scrutinizing these images of ambivalent resistance generates an invaluable conversation about where reservoirs of civic accountability and individual responsibility may yet be found in Ghana.

Finding heroes amid the disorder of human history is undeniably political, an effort to knit together past, present, and future for a purpose.[37] Hero stories have frequently been deployed in the cause of nation building to "give the idea of a Nation warmth" and allow its leaders to "command ready human allegiance."[38] Heroes are being invented and reinvented daily, according to the political desires of communities striving for place and power within the nation.[39] Lifting up heroes is always and everywhere a claim about political legitimacy and collective identity. The NRC Report identified an absence of credible and forthright leadership on matters of human rights in Ghanaian history; this is a document of *missing heroes*.

The NRC final report—reflecting on the actions of Ghana's judiciary and bar association, the labor movement, the traditional rulers and chieftaincy,

religious bodies, media, student movements, and professional organizations—was hard-pressed to locate sites of resistance to human rights abuse
in Ghanaian history. In fact, the report described quietude and political
acquiescence as national character traits and a general emotional condition.
"'Might makes right' has been the dominant philosophy of the leaders," reads
the NRC Report. "'Keep yourself out of trouble' has been that of those who
were in a position to make a difference to the victims."[40] In a "Profile of the
Ghanaian" the country's political woes are distilled into individual character
flaws that are then applied to the nation. The third trait in this profile is self-
ishness. "This may be stated as: 'once the problem or the human rights violation or abuse affects somebody else, and not me, it really is not my business.'"[41]
The fourth trait among some individual Ghanaians, cowardice, "allowed the
human rights violations and abuses to occur."[42] Bluntly, the report claimed
that in Ghana, "people generally are afraid to confront officialdom on any
issue. Most people do not openly criticize governments or people in authority
for fear of losing their jobs or being punished."[43] And yet, the NRC archive
includes stories of citizens who did place their jobs, bodies, and lives at risk
and bore the consequences. What is the significance of the NRC bureaucracy's narrative of missing heroes?

Part of the story of Ghana's missing heroes reflects the limitations of
looking for leadership only among Ghana's "big men" and identifying resistance only in articulated, programmatic statements of dissent and not in the
oppositional acts situated in local, interpersonal interactions. "Big men" in
Ghana are persons who have achieving a recognizable success with social,
political, and economic consequences.[44] It is a designation that may be
rooted in a combination of different factors such as educational achieve-
ment, pedigree and heritage, material wealth, public respectability, generos-
ity, and influence. Throughout the postindependence period, conventional
images of Ghanaian heroism have been firmly entrenched within this patriarchal and elitist big-man tradition. In the nationalist iconography, Ghanaian heroes are almost exclusively big men.[45] Accordingly, in the search for
heroes, the NRC officials intuitively looked toward big men, toward political elites, professional organizations, and people with national platform and
voice. This group's silence was translated into a general absence of heroic
leadership and this group's failings became national character traits. There
is, however, another narrative of Ghanaians who stood up to state violence
in order to protect loved ones and strangers. Although the NRC Report
concludes that resistance was a rarity, scarcely found within Ghana, the

citizen stories unearth a multiplicity of heroes: fishermen, traders, shop-keepers, and soldiers who stepped out in courage despite the ubiquity of state violence.

How did Ghanaians respond to the cycles of authoritarian and alienating government? The NRC archive contains reports of soldiers who refused to join in the violence, and of citizens who risked their lives by begging, plead-ing, bribing, and chastising agents of violence. Other Ghanaians, who had silently witnessed atrocities, came to the NRC decades later with haunted eyes, determined this time to speak.

Yaa Anima, one of the many market women detained and tortured during both the AFRC and PNDC years, recalled the other detainees who helped her survive the violence of Gondor Barracks. "Brakatu. Ahinbwe. Asuo Pra." These were the other women who "came to her aid" despite the fact that they too were detained and subject to prison violence.[46] Decades later Anima still remembered and spoke their names. In many cases, the names of the Good Samaritans are not even known. This was the case for Victoria Ain-adjei, another trading woman in Accra who sold cosmetics and linens at the famous Makola Market No. 1. During the AFRC revolution, Ainadjei suf-fered repeated harassment from soldiers who tarred her with the *kalabule* brush. Her petition is itself an homage to a fierce determination to survive. If her stall was demolished, she began to hawk her wares on the open street. When she was beaten within an inch of her life, she took time to recover and rest before returning to trading. A few days after the AFRC takeover, Ainadjei rushed to Makola when she heard soldiers had gathered at her stall. When she arrived, the soldiers corralled all the market women and traders together into a queue in front of Makola's second gate. The soldiers called them all criminals, pronounced them guilty, and declared that they would be executed on the spot. "We, the captives, both men and women, were cry-ing and begging for our dear lives." The soldiers mocked them, taunting that "people were dying like goats and fowls at the 37 Military Hospital" and they had the audacity to cry over the "small death" that they were facing. At that moment, a man working for the town council interrupted this ghastly scene. He asked the soldiers to let the women go free and volunteered to stand in for them. The soldiers agreed, releasing the women and taking the town council member away. The nameless Good Samaritan was never heard from again. "I do not know what happened to this man," Ainadjei explained.[47] Her NRC petition is the only public record of this bystander's largesse—his willingness to risk his life to protect others.

The importance of these records, as incomplete and partial as they are, cannot be underestimated. Philosopher David Crocker calls for transitional justice processes that "profile examples of moral heroism in the face of barbarism." Telling the "tale of the good," particularly "against the backdrop of all the evil that has taken place," is necessary if a different future is to be realized.[48] Collecting and publicizing the stories of Serbs who aided Muslim neighbors (and vice versa) during the Bosnian War strikes a blow against those who would reify religious-ethnic conflict as natural, unavoidable, and eternal. Illuminating the moments, locations, or lives that do not conform to narratives of human depravity, eternal conflict, or unavoidable evil is a way of restoring hope. Tales of good deeds interrupt the pessimist's tendency to reduce communities to pathology and then elevate this pathology to destiny. In this way, the stories of Animah, Ainadjei, and others challenge the narrative of the overly passive and deferential Ghanaian.

Yaw Fosu Munufie's testimony at the NRC Tamale hearing is a tale of heroism amid considerable cruelty. During the PNDC years, an eighteen-month-old infant "was attacked by convulsions" in the town of Busunya around 9 p.m. Despite the curfew imposed by the new military government, her father lifted her convulsing body, called his friend Akyeampong to come along, and ran to the police station. The baby's father begged the police to allow him to bring his daughter to a "native doctor" about a half mile away. The police saw the seizing child, had compassion, and wrote a special permit guaranteeing safe passage for the three of them. On the short journey, the father and child were intercepted by a military truck full of soldiers. The father showed the soldiers his permit and his daughter, who was having a seizure in his arms. "The soldiers said no, the police have no right to give that permit, they have broken the curfew and so they will deal with them." Just like that, they shot the baby's father in the back. "My lord, I have the picture here," Munufie stated. "They shot him at the back." Akyeampong jumped into a gravel pit and hid there, under cover of darkness, while the soldiers fired in his direction; he survived and ran back to the family house to tell all that had occurred. "Curfew was still in force, there was no way anybody could come there, my lord, to see whether [the father] was dead or could be saved." At first light, they sent the message to Yaw Fosu Munufie some miles away about what had befallen his brother and baby niece. "When we got to the scene, my brother had not completely died. . . . This my brother had been covered with plantain leaves, just like you kill an animal, you cover it with plantain leaves. And everybody in the village was afraid to go there. My lord, we carried my brother home. . . . Just as we were about to wash the two dead bodies, the military truck came back with the same group of soldiers. [The soldiers] started giving warning shots in the air." [49]

The soldiers gave the family just thirty minutes to prepare the bodies of the father and daughter for burial or risk further violence.

> My lord, in the village, at that time of our history, nobody, no sane person, would want to stay there. They all ran away, leaving me, my mother, and my two sisters. There was not even anybody there to help us carry my brother in the coffin to the cemetery. We had to do it with my mother, and my two sisters. Now, I managed to muster courage to tell them that we will not comply with their orders. I told them that even if one bought a grasscutter, it takes more than thirty minutes to prepare the grasscutter for soup. How much more for a human being? So we were not going to comply. If they like, they can come finish everybody. We will not comply with their orders. So they left. [50]

This heartrending story nevertheless contains multiple moments of humanity and courage. From the police officers who saw an ill infant and decided to value a human life over the letter of the law, to Yaw Fosu Munufie, who decided to bury his brother and niece despite soldiers' threats, filial attachment, love, and compassion fuel the resistance to military violence.

The story of Bernice Amoni, a trading woman in Kpando, also spoke to the ways in which love and family ties bolstered Ghanaian bravery. During the PNDC years, representatives of the local revolutionary groups accosted Amoni about the price of her *kenkey*, a staple dish. Her boyfriend, William Dusu, challenged these men. A few days later, four soldiers hauled him away to the prison yards at Kpando Todzi. "They asked me why I was challenging their authority," he said; they beat and kicked him, made him roll on the ground, and forced him to stare at the sun. When William Dusu's brother, Daniel, heard this news he rushed to the prison yard to argue for William's release. Daniel was also taken into custody, stripped naked, and beaten. [51]

Sammy Sampson Manu also stepped in to protect a friend from soldier violence and suffered the consequences. When Manu returned to his home town of Bimbilla in 1979, he witnessed soldiers assaulting his friend Yaw Owusu. Manu begged the soldiers to stop and asked to discuss the situation. Instead, the soldiers immediately turned on him; Manu "was beaten mercilessly for pleading on [his] friend's behalf." He specifically remembered that the hook side of a belt was used in the assault. He lost his left eye and contin-ues to suffer related injuries and so he asked the NRC for financial support and assistance.

In 1982, Susana Korletey decided to travel to Nsawam to sell secondhand clothes to raise school fees for her son. "Being so helpful and sympathetic," her son came along to help. The bus they boarded to go to Nsawam Market never arrived at that destination. En route, the bus changed direction on the orders of a soldier seated at the driver's elbow. Upon arriving at El Wak Sta-dium in Accra, the passengers were made to disembark and led to a room full of soldiers. The soldiers informed the passengers that they had all paid more than the controlled price for the bus fare; this was an economic crime and all were going to be whipped. A large table was brought in and the pas-sengers were told to form a queue and one by one, prostrate themselves on the table. "My son felt that I being a woman and not very fit, it would be very dangerous [for me] to go through the ordeal." After receiving his strokes, Korletey's son begged the soldiers to spare his mother, saying that he would "appreciate it if they could permit him to bear her share of the punishment in addition to his [own]." For making this suggestion, her son was nearly killed. Soldiers stripped him down before beating and kicking him about "like a lifeless object." Afterward, the soldiers turned to Susana. She was pushed onto the table and beaten until she cried out the name of Jesus. Susana Korletey remembered the devastation following their ordeal. She spent significant amounts of money and time nursing herself and her son back to health. Too fearful to market her goods, her business collapsed. Eventually, her extended family intervened to support her son's studies.[52]

Military rule and violence challenged the bonds of affection and care cen-tral to family and community life. Part of the horror of the preceding stories is that the violence of soldiers criminalized the affective bonds connecting people together. In the days of soldier rule, fathers were supposed to stand by helpless while their children were taken ill; brothers were expected to leave their dying siblings "covered with plantain leaves" in a ditch. Sons were expected to stand by and watch their mothers beaten; friends and brothers could not even beg for mercy for a loved one without paying the price. All relationships were made subordinate to the arbitrary law of soldiers. In this context, attempts to honor the ties that bind, to preserve and remake "social worlds" were acts of resistance, and even of heroism. [53]

Along with stories heralding the courage of Good Samaritans, the NRC archive includes the stories of Ghanaians who sought to mitigate the hardships of military rule within their local communities. Basil Gbere Yaabere was only twenty-two years old in 1982 when he crafted a plan to respond to the food shortage in his native town Lawra (Upper West). Yaabere arranged for guinea corn from Wa to be transported to Lawra and sold in the local market. Yaabere worked with the local PNDC chapter in the hopes of avoiding accusations of *kalabule* and economic crime. Despite this, on the first day the guinea corn was brought to market, Yaabere was beaten and arrested. Yaabere was brought before the regional branch of the PNDC, the Upper West Peoples' Defence Committee, where he was excoriated and threatened. Marked as an enemy of the PNDC, Yaabere faced roadblocks at every turn in his pursuit of higher education and employment; he faced a life "enslaved under [the] antagonizing umbrella" of the PNDC.[54]

Like Basil Yaabere, Nana Boakye-Agyeman sought to help a local community struggling under PNDC policies. This was among his duties and obligations as a traditional ruler enstooled at the border town of Kofibadukrom in Dorma, Brong-Ahafo. Spanning Ghana and Cote d'Ivoire, Kofibadukrom is one of many communities that have persisted despite colonialism's arbitrary borders. In 1985, Kofibadukrom was becoming militarized because of the weekly market, which was only six hundred meters from the Cote d'Ivoire border. Soldiers and border guards scrutinized and harassed all who came to the market as potential smugglers who might contravene Ghana's strict price controls. In a letter, Nana Boakye-Agyeman officially requested the government curtail the heavy military presence in his town. "There is no security problem at Kofibadukrom or at the market. . . . We aver that both the Ivory Coast section and the Ghana section of the town are under the chief's control and he can cause the arrest of any culprit who runs to the Ivory Coast side." The chief insisted that the people would police themselves; the military was unnecessary because his own people would take up the charge of "stamping out smuggling." He sought to persuade the PNDC to give up its campaign to close down the Kofibadukrom market, noting the existence of markets in other border towns. "If during my reign . . . the market is out of the town, it will be viewed as ill-luck brought to the town by my presence. This will also go down in history as a failure on my part." Despite Nana's efforts, soldiers arrived and used force and fire to close the Kofibadukrom market. Nana's letters continued; he wrote the regional PNDC office and the local press decrying these "wanton acts of destruction" as a "wrong against the gods and people of Kofibadukrom . . . a taboo for which . . . the perpetrators need to be punished."[55] Three times, Nana Boakye-Agyeman wrote an open letter to the *Pioneer* to plead his case; each time, his appeal fell on deaf ears. His petition before the NRC included copies of the various letters he had written to the Committee for Defense of the Revolution District Office and the related *Pioneer* articles. This collection of writings is a testament to the courage and persistence of a local leader who repeatedly raised his voice to defend the independence, economic rights, and security of his town amid from the PNDC's price control and anti-smuggling policies.

In all of these stories, these citizen displays of human courage and connection did not change the course of events. The protests did not deter soldiers from confiscating goods, save a child's life, or prevent the torture of civilians. These visions of resistance were, ultimately, unsuccessful. Likewise, the agents of this resistance are not the heroes of nationalist myth. The individuals who stepped forward to help their family, loved ones, or suffering strangers were not big men whose resistance was publicly noted or praised. For resisting PNDC policies, these Ghanaians were often marked as criminals, enemies of the people, or fools.

The continuing ambivalence surrounding these stories of individual resistance was glaring during the public testimony of Harrison Tetteh Adimeh, a fisherman who regularly plied waters between Ghana and Togo. In 1984, he encountered a group of Ghanaian refugees stranded in Togo after a mass eviction of West Africans from Nigeria. Taking pity on them, Adimeh ferried the refugees to Ghana for free. Upon arrival in Greater Accra, Adimeh delivered them to the chief fisherman according to the standard protocol for unexpected finds at sea. When the chief fisherman contacted the Accra police, all were arrested—Adimeh, his fishing partner, the eight returnees, and even the chief fisherman. Adimeh was taken to the Bureau of National Investigations, beaten terribly, and then transferred to Ussher Fort Prison. He remained in Ussher Fort for two years, spent the next six years in Sekondi Prison, and was finally released in 1992 as Ghana transitioned back to electoral democracy. Eight years of incarceration cost Adimeh dearly. He lost his boat, business, and relationships with family and friends. He emerged from jail impoverished.

When Adimeh told his harrowing story at the Accra public hearings, Commissioner Uborr Dalafu Label II asked the stooped fisherman whether, given all that had happened, he would make the same decision today. After a brief hesitation, Adimeh simply said, "I will help any Ghanaian who is genuinely in distress." At this the listening audience audibly gasped and

Commissioner Labal simply said, "Thank you. Thank you for your response. God bless you."[56] Another commissioner, Lt. Gen. Emmanuel Erskine, was not satisfied with this answer. Erskine scolded Adimeh, reminding him that ferrying refugees from Togolese to Ghanaian waters was breaking the law at that time.[57] Instead of praising Adimeh's compassion, Erskine warned him of the need to respect legal boundaries. His message was clear: in the contest between compassion and law, law must be supreme. Adimeh refused to denounce his own actions, impassive in the face of this suggestion that civil compassion should be subject to the whims of government.

The citizen archive's stories of resistance illuminate those Ghanaians who exhibited courage and conviction in turbulent times. It also exposes that the consequences of speaking out in times of violence are rarely positive. In these stories, resistance is rarely triumphant. It is usually incomplete, partial, ineffective, and limited. This was also the testimony of Kofi Nkrumah-Sian, a Good Samaritan who saw soldiers beating Gifty Adom in Mampong Market in 1979 and ran to get the local police to intervene. Both Gifty Adom and her mother Madam Birago remember Nkrumah-Sian as a Good Samaritan, a "certain man" who prevailed upon the police to arrest the soldiers in question. Years later, when he came to the NRC to talk about his role in the violence, Kofi Nkrumah-Sian remembered his actions with ambivalence. "Due to the fear then in the Ghanaian public because of the behavior of the soldiers, nobody, including me, could rescue the lady. *All that I did* (my emphasis) at that time was to make a report of what was happening."[58] Madam Birago remembers him as a hero; Gifty Adom mentions his role in saving her life. However, Kofi Nkrumah-Sian dwells on the inadequacy of his own response; the brutality of the times and the fear that prevented him from rescuing Gifty Adom as he would have wished. Nkrumah-Sian's ambivalence reflects the images of resistance that appear in the NRC citizen archive. Here, the heroes failed to change state policy or block the wheels of grinding injustice. More often, they were vilified, condemned, and sometimes incarcerated for long years because of their daring. The chief could not protect his people from the predations of the border guards. Basil Yaabere's life was irretrievably limited because he sought to proactively respond to the food insecurity in his town. Yaa Animah could not be protected, but Asuo Pra, Brakatu, and Ahinbwe were there to comfort her. The decade that Harrison Adimeh spent in prison will never be returned to him.

Conclusion

In the NRC archive, Ghanaians thrust these narratives of incomplete and ambivalent resistance into the space usually reserved for producing national heroes. This record of Ghanaian heroism includes the image of Harrison Adimeh being chastised by Commissioner Erskine and urged to "forge ahead and forget the past." It includes the ambivalence of Kofi Nkrumah-Sian, who succeeded in stopping a soldier who was beating a pregnant woman but could not erase the silent witness of atrocity by his community, paralyzed by fear. The heroes are Yaw Fosu Munufie, who insisted on properly burying his murdered brother even as he had not yet mustered the courage to hold a proper funeral. While these glimpses of conviction and courage may seem insignificant, there is political value in marking out these new constellations of resistance within a public history-writing project. Similarly, by describing Ghanaian soldiers as both agents of state violence and targets of state violence, the cacophony of the NRC archive undermines the dichotomy between victim and perpetrator, illuminating instead a Ghanaian population consisting of survivors. Together, both petition collections illuminate a way forward that must relinquish the bright lines and moral certainty of innocent victims, evil perpetrators, and acclaimed heroes and embrace the moral complexity of lives built in the shadow of political violence.

CHAPTER 7

Time for Suffering / Time for Justice

In March 2003, while testifying before the National Reconciliation Commission (NRC), twenty-nine-year-old Kofi Agyepong was overcome with emotion. His voice faltered and broke as he remembered his uncle's death at the hands of soldiers during the Provisional National Defense Council (PNDC) era. Agyepong's mother died when he was eleven years old, and he, along with his six siblings, was entrusted to his uncle's care. Two years later, in 1986, Agyepong heard his uncle's name listed among persons executed by the PNDC for treason. Although Agyepong did not know the details about his uncle's death, a friend filled the void by repeating gruesome rumors about his uncle's demise. Maybe he had been tied to a vehicle and dragged until flesh separated from bone. Perhaps he had been riddled with bullets and then thrown into the sea. Years later, at the NRC public hearings, Kofi Agyepong traced a line from his uncle's death to his own lack of education and employment; without family support, life had become very difficult. In response to this halting testimony, Commissioner Erskine "advised him [Agyepong] to forget the past, to forge ahead, and build a bright future for himself instead of dwelling on the pain."[1]

This was often the advice commissioners offered citizens during the public hearings: relinquish the painful past, focus on the hopeful future. Fixating on what had come before, it seemed, would be detrimental to the NRC participants and the nation at large. And yet, the necessity of revisiting the painful past is the premise of the global truth-and-reconciliation-commission (TRC) phenomenon. Ghana, like the other nations that have embraced the TRC, encounter this dilemma of how to appropriately revisit the past's violence without succumbing to it. How do we plunge into the shadows of citizen memory without being consumed? Where, exactly, should we begin telling the story of our personal and collective catastrophes? When were the seeds planted? How many generations can be held accountable?

Global TRCs wrestle with the conundrum that Walter Benjamin describes in his "Theses on the Philosophy of History." Benjamin describes the Paul Klee painting *Angelus Novus* as depicting an imagined divine being, the angel of history, who is all-seeing but paralyzed in action. Both omniscient and ineffective, this angel contemplates the mounting brokenness of human history but cannot ably mend the damage. With wings caught in a storm that "irresistibly propel" her into the future, the angel's head and heart face the "piling wreckage upon wreckage" of the past. In this image, both the ambivalence of history's power and our trepidation about the entanglement of past and present are evident.[2]

TRCs appeal to diverse communities around the world partially because they offer a formula by which nations and communities may corporately contemplate history's violence without being consumed. The truth commission promise is that individuals and nations can confront the violence of their becoming, as long as they do so from the safety of a neutral present and with an eye firmly fixed on the reconciled future. All the techniques that TRCs employ—public testimony, reparations, amnesty—are rooted in a concept of linear historical time, in which the past is fixed firmly behind and indelibly separated from the present and the future. The commissioners' advice to Agyepong and so many others affirmed this guiding principle: the past is already behind you, believe in how far we have come and turn your heart toward the bright future. But the stories that Ghanaians presented to the NRC did not always reflect this linear concept of historical time. To the contrary, in citizen stories, historical time is layered, co-constituted, and entangled; the violence of the past is indivisible from the present, and it is imbricated with the future. When Kofi Agyepong's voice breaks in the Accra public hearings, he is speaking of losing his mother in 1984, his uncle's death in 1986, and his unemployment in 2003. His suffering encompasses the years during which he could not manage his secondary-school fees, the continuing uncertainty about his uncle's death (did he suffer and how?), and his inability to support himself as a twenty-nine-year-old man. All of these experiences shape his experience of pain and are all included in his story of human rights violations.

These different visions of historical time are part of the NRC archive's productive cacophony. Stories like Ageypong's do not conform to the NRC bureaucracy's time line: they cannot leave the past behind or exculpate the present, much less assume a brighter future. This chapter explores the NRC archive's temporally transgressive petitions as part of an expanded vision of historical justice that does not depend on a linear concept of historical time.

One of the criticisms facing transitional justice initiatives is that they further a type of "retrospective politics" that prefers to review past violence instead of addressing present injustice. It can be alluring, transitional justice scholars like John Torpey astutely note, to mourn the past instead of confront the present.[3] There is a burgeoning "commemorative discourse of victimhood," that is "is very much the opposite of a constructive and dynamic engagement with the present."[4] The past is another country and can often be excoriated, criticized, and condemned without requiring significant political action in the present. The allure of plunging into the past, then, may be as a way of turning away from the failures of the present, and our attendant political responsibilities. This critique of retrospective politics resurrects the anxiety of Benjamin's angel of history and its assumption of linear and progressive notions of historical time. Configuring the past and present as separate and discrete sphere invites this debate about where we should turn our heads and heart; it presupposes that in the matter of addressing injustice, these realms are set apart and in competition with one another.

This is the fear at the foundations of the retrospective politics critique: when there are limited resources for addressing injustice how can we waste time restoring the past when we should be creating the future? However, in the NRC archive there is no scarcity of suffering and many citizens did not place human rights violations into a linear, progressive notion of historical time that quarantines violence in this way. Instead Ghanaians described suffering that erupts in the past and present, and threatens the future. Herein, the work of historical justice is not estranged from contemporary political action; addressing state violence in the past, present, and future are one and the same.

This chapter focuses on a collection of petitions that diverge from the linear progressive notion of historical time central to the NRC bureaucracy. There were citizens who transgressed the NRC's temporal mandate by scrutinizing the colonial past and the current political moment (Ghana's Fourth Republic, 1993–present). By insisting that human rights violations extend back to the colonial era and continue despite the return of electoral democracy, these stories answer Berber Bevernage's call for historical justice models that do "not force us to choose between retrospective justice, on the one hand, and justice in the present or the future, on the other."[5]

The Violence of the Past

At every turn, the sponsoring Kufuor government presented national reconciliation as a way to divide the violent past from the current dispensation. In 2003, at a meeting with Western Region chiefs, Kufuor described national reconciliation was "an exercise to recapture the country's lost soul" and help Ghana recapture its "spirit of showmanship and wealth." [6] In this formulation, the NRC is an antidote for a national existential crisis. Violence, firmly located in the past, has tarnished the country's national essence, and national reconciliation is a finite ritual that will set the country back on course. The NRC's expanded temporal mandate also reflects this linear progressive notion of historical violence. Citizens were invited to submit complaints about state human rights violations from independence in 1957 until the 1992 democratic transition.

However, Ghanaian citizens embraced other notions of historical time in their petitions and testimonies; they did not, collectively, presume that violence was past, that the present was secure, or that the future was unknown. In their stories, the harm produced by political violence is compounded and suffering shifts form and substance as consecutive regimes come to leadership. These stories unearth a state violence that is cyclical and repetitive, battering families in waves over time, eroding confidence and optimism. Moreover, petitions in the NRC archive complain about violence both occurring in the colonial Gold Coast and following the 1992 democratic transition. Marked as nonjurisdictional, these petitions reject the idea that colonial violence ended with independence on March 6, 1957, and eschew the myopia of claiming that a democratic constitution in a neoliberal era banishes human rights abuse to the past.

Despite the capacious temporal mandate of the national reconciliation experiment (1957–1992), some Ghanaians transgressed these boundaries by bringing forward stories about human right violations that occurred in the days of the British Gold Coast colony. Although these petitions were deemed nonjurisdictional because they fell outside the commission's temporal mandate, they are nonetheless preserved in the NRC archive. This dual act of preservation and marginalization reflects an ongoing debate about where pre-independence-era violence fits into contemporary analyses of African human rights abuse.

Increasingly, scholars and practitioners who parse African political dilemmas are reluctant to discuss the years before political independence. No less an authority than the former UN secretary general Kofi Annan has exhorted

Africa to look "beyond its colonial past" in order to understand its current problems.[7] Supposedly "emphasizing the culpability of colonialism in Africa" only serves those who want to maintain the status quo.[8] This is also the refrain of former US president Barack Obama, whose primary message to Africa has been to stop "pinning the blame on the colonial past for the ills of the present."[9] For these leaders, "the colonialism-imperialism paradigm is kaput" as a way of explaining Africa's contemporary struggles,[10] and those who look to the imperial past should more fruitfully speak of the corruption, avarice, or disorganization of postcolonial African leadership.[11] This rhetoric, which supposes that one must criticize *either* European imperialists or postcolonial politicians for Africa's plight, echoes the criticism that we must choose whether to confront historical violence or contemporary injustice. Both these critiques reflect a version of historical time that quarantines violence to a particular era; they ignore the threads connecting European colonialism to postcolonial African politics and the ways present-day injustice builds upon the violence of the past.

This perspective, however, is not the only way to understand the relationship between historical and contemporary violence. In the NRC archive's alternative time lines of harm, the colonial past is not clearly demarcated from neoliberal present. The systems of exclusion created in the British Gold Coast extend to the present, and the violence done in the past reverberates in the lives of families today. These stories describe histories of violence as cyclical and overlaid, draw attention to the continuity between present and past, and indict contemporary African leaders who have been unable or unwilling to transform the colonial states they inherited into a "meaningful democratic institution in the lives of ordinary citizens."[12] The moribund debate about whether to blame external or internal forces for Africa's troubles crumbles under the weight of citizen stories that illuminate the longevity and heft of state violence.

Vivian Tibboh described British colonial land-acquisition policies as the root of her family's poverty. Before Accra's Osu neighborhood was a bustling urban center, it was Ataa Botwe, a neighborhood where Tibboh's grandfather owned approximately three hundred acres of land. Somewhere around 1929, the "colonialists" sought to acquire this land. Under duress, the elder Tibboh agreed to allow the colonial administration to utilize a portion of his plot to build the European Hospital Extension. He was told that he would be compensated. Then, through a series of dishonest dealings, the Gold Coast government acquired ownership of the entire plot without proper compensation.

First, the colonial administration required that the Tibboh family be inoculated against infection. "The colonialists indicated that they could not reside in the area together with the blacks since they would be infected by diseases common among the blacks." The family was carted more than two hundred kilometers away to Jomo and kept there for more than twenty-four hours to receive inoculations. They returned home to find their houses demolished and their land cleared "for the use of the whites."[13] For Vivian Tibboh, the loss of her family's land was inscribed in the landscape of urban central Accra: the area behind Ridge Hospital, just where the West African Examination Council is located, was once her grandfather's cassava farm.

Colonial violence is both implicit and explicit in this petition. Tibboh's mention of the European Hospital highlights the segregation of the Gold Coast colony's public health infrastructure, which until the 1920s was geared toward serving the minority European population.[14] In the post–World War I period, a shift in the methods and goals of British imperialism occurred when the Gold Coast governor Sir Gordon Guggisberg extended to Africans the colonial health, education, and economic development agenda. From the distance of the late twentieth and early twenty-first centuries, this expansion of Gold Coast's health infrastructure is often enveloped in a haze of "colonial nostalgia" that memorializes the technological and biomedical shifts of European rule while erasing the accompanying tyranny and violence.[15] In contrast, Tibboh describes the construction of Accra's Ridge Hospital, not as a high point of colonial humanitarianism, but as a site of colonial disenfranchisement.

For one family, the 1920s and 1930s did not reflect the kinder, gentler colonialism of a benevolent Sir Gordon Guggisberg. This was precisely the time when they lost their fortunes and prospects. Using the blunt language of "colonial masters" and "whites," Tibboh describes the expansion of the Gold Coast health infrastructure as a ruse by which indigenous land was appropriated by the colonial administration. In the image of her grandfather being unceremoniously "carted away" to receive inoculations that would simultaneously safeguard Europeans from African disease and ensure his swift alienation from the land, Tibboh conjures the amalgamated social, economic, and psychological harms of colonial rule. In those days, Tibboh explains, Africans lacked recourse for even the clearest injustices; her grandfather's sons were only "young civil servants" who could not "contend with the colonial masters."[16] Petitions like Tibboh's complicate the scholarship that focuses on colonial nostalgia without also considering colonial antagonism.[17] Recognizing the variety of "colonial re-collections" is a way to understand the complexity of the past as a theater for working out geopolitical and interpersonal tensions while pursuing desired futures.[18] For Tibboh, the pain of the past's injustices continue into and shape the present. "Currently," she writes, "the family do not have any decent place of abode"; furthermore, they suffer "ridicule" at the hands of the persons whose properties they are compelled to rent.[19] Colonial violence remains present with the Tibboh clan in the form of continued economic hardships, social shame, and personal regrets.

The NRC petitions about the 1956 plebiscite, which decided the fate of British Togoland, also mourn events that occurred in the colonial era as a throbbing wound that continues to plague the body politic. When the Honorable Kosi Kedem submitted his NRC petition, he was speaking on "behalf of the people of former Southern British Togoland," a geographical area that, at the time of the NRC, had not existed on any West African map for almost fifty years.[20] For Kedem, the amalgamation of the Trust Territory of Togoland into independent Ghana was as fresh as the day it happened. He painstakingly described all aspects of the plebiscite—from Britain's administration to the referendum's timing, the convoluted questions put to a largely illiterate population, and the restrictions placed on the Togoland Congress party—as a "gross violation and abuse of the sovereignty, liberty, freedom, and self-determination" of the region's people. He laid the blame for all that occurred squarely at the feet of the British government; "this integration was actually CONTRIVED by Britain for reasons best known to herself." According to Kedem, Britain committed the foundational act of violence by sowing the seeds of regional, ethnic, and political discontentment. However, the postindependence Ghana governments compounded the abuse by treating freedom fighters as secessionists and traitors and erasing the history of Togoland independence and unity. He called for Ghana's government and people to "openly acknowledge the historic injustice and wrong done to the people of former Southern Togoland" and then make amends to the persons or heirs of those who had subsequently been exiled, jailed, or killed for seeking independence for Togoland.[21] For Kedem, there was no conflict between condemning British colonial design and requesting that the Ghanaian government be held accountable for its part in the injustice.

In line with these citizen petitions, the NRC Report also acknowledged the importance of the colonial era in assessing Ghana's human rights history. According to the final report, Ghana is "an artificial political entity comprising four distinct components woven together around the time of Independence." The commissioners addressed Kedem and other similar petitioners by acknowledging the distressing "legacies that Ghana inherited" in a chapter about the historical context of human rights abuse in Ghana.[22] In the NRC archive, remembering colonial violence does not exonerate contemporary African leaders from political responsibility. In these records, the past does not precede the present; it continues to live within Ghana's contemporary social, economic, political, and environmental landscapes.

The Violence of the Present

Along with the petitions about the colonial past, Ghanaians transgressed the NRC's temporal limits by submitting statements and petitions about the recent past: the years after the democratic transition of 1992. Some of these petitions went so far as to claim that the Kufuor government—the newly elected sponsor of the national reconciliation exercise—was also presiding over human rights violations. At least three types of petitions about the Kufuor years (2001–2008) found their way into the NRC archive. In the first, citizens complained about the failures of existing Ghanaian bureaucracies. These stories reflect an expectation that government's duty is to fix existing mechanisms regardless of when the broken system was first established. The second type of petition criticized rival political parties for acts of violence and urged more effort by the Kufuor administration to control individuals and organizations that were victimizing Ghanaians. The third group of petitions unabashedly accuse the Kufuor government of complicity and brutality. All of these petitions are unified in insisting on the persistence of human rights abuses. Neither electoral democracy nor the establishment of a truth commission has sufficiently relegated violence to the past. In these petitions, the work of achieving historical justice requires vigilance in the present.

For Victoria Madjoub, when the Ghana Private Road Transport Union (GPRTU) annexed the land adjacent to her home for a transport hub, bringing with it copious filth, noise, and waste, her inability to pursue reasonable strategies of redress caused suffering. In this way, a fairly mundane zoning complaint became a human rights violation: "As a citizen," she wrote, "I am fighting for my social and environmental rights."[23] Over the course of years, Madjoub had sought assistance from GPRTU, the Accra Metropolitan Association, the inspector general of police, and the former first lady of Ghana, Nana Konadu Agyeman Rawlings. When existing governance and justice mechanisms failed, citizens turned to the NRC. This sense that the NRC was a higher authority that could rectify administrative failings was also evident in the petition of Thomas Bona, a former security guard at Ashanti Goldfields who was dismissed from his job after blowing the whistle about workplace corruption. After being warned by the local union leaders to keep quiet about what he had seen because management was threatening to "terminate our appointments and replace us with contract security service providers," Bonah continued to speak out about company theft, was soon declared redundant, and dismissed.[24] The NRC was also a place to turn for labor disputes.

Other citizens brought petitions about the failures of the Ghanaian court system. A number of petitions submitted to the Tamale NRC Office addressed the failures of the Ghanaian courts to equitably address a bitter and long-standing conflict between the Ahlus-Sunnah and the Tijaniyya, two Northern Ghana religious communities. Clashes between the communities date to the 1970s.[25] One of the community leaders in Damonga District, Abubakar Imoro Shishi, an Ahlus-Sunnah leader, turned to the NRC in the hopes of receiving a more equitable outcome for an ongoing dispute that had first erupted in 2002. Shishi complained that the courts had barred him from returning to his home village in Kpaburso, while his counterpart, the Tijaniyya leader for Kpaburso, faced no such injunction. "The right to a fair trial has been denied me," he wrote. "The court could outlaw both leaders but not one."[26] This injustice, according to Shishi, was the result of partisan influence on the courts; he turned to the NRC as a corrective for the ongoing corruption of the Ghanaian judicial system.

The failures of the Ghanaian present were not only a matter of inefficient administration and corrupt courts. Stories of political violence and police brutality were also included in the NRC archive's indictment of the Ghanaian present. Thomas Asare came to the NRC to report that National Democratic Congress (NDC) activists had assaulted him during the 2000 election season. Asare described himself as an active member of the New Patriotic Party organization at the Cape Coast Lepresarium Camp who had helped to arrange transportation for the camp to the voting stations during the elections. During the run-off elections, he was waylaid by "six macho men" who came to the lepresarium with NDC activists. They pushed him into a car and took him to a residence where he was tortured. "The macho men tried to stretch my deformed fingers," he stated. "This caused me deep pain. They hit me several times at the back with wires and it caused me severe bruises." One NDC lawyer saw what was happening and pleaded with the others to take pity because Asare was a leper. Today, Thomas Asare "still experience[s] deep pain in [his] hands."[27]

Anome Klidza came to the NRC to report that in the past year, his thirty-two-year-old son, Agbeko Kodzo, had been killed by Ghanaian police. Klidza and the family had not been told why the police had taken Agbeko Kodzo's life; there was only a rumor that his son had been storing guns in his room. The police told the family to go collect their son's body from the Aflao Mortuary, but Klidza and his relatives refused. They would not bring the body home or accept or participate in the police's narrative of the killing until an investigation was conducted. This method of protest was ineffective; the police simply transferred the remains to an Accra police hospital. Two months later, when the Klidze family traveled to Accra to pick up their son's remains, they were told his body had already been buried by the police. Now the family knew neither why Adbeko Kodzo was shot nor his final resting place.[28]

The NRC became a site where Ghanaians sought justice for the intractable and persistent violence of the present; it was used when all other avenues seemed closed to them. It gathered petitions about political violence manifest in key national institutions, such as the courts, police service, and prisons. Adhering to a linear, progressive notion of the timeline of historical violence, the NRC dismissed these petitions as nonjurisdictional. Officially, the commission insisted that the time of violence was in the past and contained by the seminal national events of independence and the 1992 democratic transition.

Citizens, however, offered a radically different time line of violence. By calling for the work of historical justice to account for atrocities that have already occurred and are still occurring, the expanded NRC archive reflects Berber Bevernage's optimism about a form of retrospective politics that does not trade contemporary political struggle for the diversion of condemning and mourning the past. In these stories, the past and present are interlaced and layered, making demands upon one another. Enshrining human rights today, Ghanaians suggest, must account for the past, even the colonial violence that bleeds into contemporary Ghanaian landscapes. Likewise, we cannot avert our eyes from the current moment, the institutions that today disenfranchise, alienate, and devastate Ghanaian communities. Historical justice, as defined within the nonjurisdictional petitions of the NRC archive, encompasses past, present, and future.

The Brief Afterlife of the Ghana's Truth Commission

"why some people be mad at me sometimes"

they ask me to remember
but they want me to remember
their memories
and I keep on remembering
mine
                    —Lucille Clifton

My story is a gift. If I give you a gift and you accept that
gift; then you don't go and throw that gift in the waste
basket. You do something with it.
                    —Assembly of First Nations 162

Lucille Clifton's brief and poignant verse claims memory as a realm of struggle. She writes in the shadow of an amorphous "they" who seek to control
what is recalled and forgotten, who exhort individuals to remember according to "their" rules and regulations. Here, memory is a double-edged sword.
When co-opted, memory is a means through which power manufactures
hegemony, but independent memory is a renewable site of resistance. There is
a covert power available to those who "keep on remembering mine." Remembering, Clifton suggests, is not an involuntary or subconscious experience;
it is an *action*, a deliberate and chosen way of preserving self, history, and
vision in the face of a repressive "they." This study has shown that Ghanaians

used a truth and reconciliation commission as an opportunity to "remember mine." But to what ends?

All existing accounts declare that Ghana's national reconciliation has had a minimal impact on the national politics. The National Reconciliation Commission (NRC) archive, the subject of this work, exists only in file folders and cardboard boxes; it is not, in the whole, part of the Ghanaian public consciousness. Here, I consider the consequences, both actual and potential, of Ghana's NRC archive. This chapter includes a measure of speculation because the impact of this archive, as with most bodies of historical documents, cannot fully be known in the present. With the benefit of preservation and publicity, these documents will have an afterlife that extends far into the future.

Global truth commissions are not only powerful because they pursue political transformation; they also generate new citizen-directed archives of political violence. In this study, I have gathered together and interrogated a relatively small selection of a much larger body of documents. My hope is that other readers will identify other "collections," other challenges and debates within these and other truth commissions' records. Inevitably, the stories included here, the patterns I have seen (and those yet to be seen), are influenced by my own identity and interests. I have family members who brought stories of soldier violence to the NRC. Other family members were named as alleged perpetrators and compelled to appear before the commission to answer questions about their role in past administrations. My own story of diaspora is intertwined, in ways known and unknown, with the turbulent national history that I have described. Throughout this research, I have sought to use this background as a resource, not a limitation. Still, I have learned that I cannot escape the possibility of bias. Whenever I have presented portions of this study, depending on which selection I use, I am accused of being a supporter of one political tradition or another. When discussing the testimonies of Ghanaian market women, I am accused of being an anti-Rawlings crusader. When presenting the stories of resettlement victims of the Volta River project, I am likewise accused of being an anti-Nkrumah reactionary. This NRC archive does not fit easily into existing nationalist models of Ghanaian history, partially because it is collective production that reflects multiple experiences of the national past.

Some scholars hail TRC testimony as a way to "replace authoritarian partial accounts of times past with the fullness of collective recollection."[1] Others mystify TRC testimony as fragments of an unspeakable, incommensurable, and ultimately, unknowable, suffering.[2] This study diverges from both these paths, claiming that Ghana's truth commission is best understood as a collective history-writing project and the stories within as artful representations of the past.

The narratives and petitions that Ghanaians shared are neither spontaneous eruptions of emotion nor crystalline reflections of the past. These are curated representations of national political history, carefully crafted by a diverse cross section of the nation at the turn of the twenty-first century. Chapter 1, "Making the NRC Archive," describes the effort that many Ghanaians expended—borrowing money for transport, standing in line, gathering together old documents, hiring petition writers, disrobing to publicly display scarred flesh—in order to participate in the national reconciliation exercise. At the NRC, publicly remembering was an act of agency; coming to the commission was an individual (and community) choice. Ghanaians overcame considerable material, emotional, and psychological obstacles to participate and pursue particular goals.

The intention and care of these narratives is most evident in the written petitions where Ghanaians narrate the past at their own leisure and pace, using proverb and analogy, and in their own languages. It is here that Christian Ahadzi, a Ghanaian soldier, can render his life as a tragic bildungsroman. "Should I be a beggar and my children turn wayward? Why? Why? What was my crime? . . . Oh, the humble village boy's hopes are shut. What next? O Lord, have mercy upon me!"[3] Although individual petitioners were often less in control of their stories at the public hearings, the moments when the voices of citizens and commissioners diverge and clash display the intention and strategy with which Ghanaians spoke.

After telling her harrowing story of being beaten by a belt-wielding soldier while nine months pregnant and the resulting injuries to her unborn son, Grace Adom received the sympathies the national reconciliation commissioners. The commissioners then made a series of inquiries, asking Adom why she had not pursued the solder who had so brutalized her. After the birth of her son did she report to the police and try to contact him? Would she be able to recognize the soldier if she saw him? Does she know where he lives? Did she inform him of her son's disabilities? Grace Adom's replies are instructive: "At that time, it was the Rawlings era, it was very difficult for me. I was advised by someone to go see the authorities but I was so terrified that I couldn't go." "After the case had been settled," Adom remembered, "he [the soldier] shook my hands, [but] out of pain, I did not even look at his face, so I would not be able to identify him."[4]

Also instructive is the commissioners' insistence on a community mechanism to hold this soldier to account. "Efforts should be made, not by you, by your relatives, to let the person know the results of that dastardly act. . . . He must made to be aware of the result of the attack." In response, Grace Adom can only sit silently, whisper her affirmation. There is a gap, evident in this exchange, between the commissioners' expectations of redress and Grace Adom's experience of the world. The commissioners suggest that Adom should have pursued this soldier in the past decades; Adom, referencing terror and pain, submits that she could not. Commissioners insist that the soldier lives locally and can be easily found; Adom says that she never looked at her assaulter's face or committed it to her memory. The commissioners insist with indignation that "[the soldier] must be made to know the result of his dastardly act," and that "your relatives must tell him."[5] Adom sits silently. Can a woman who had to work in the market while nine months pregnant depend on a family to speak for her? Is there evidence that the soldier will exhibit remorse? Where should Adom find the courage, or the time, to pursue this course of action? These questions, unasked, linger in the space between the commissioners' high table and the petitioner's seat; it calls to mind Rodney G. S. Carter's exhortation to read silences in the archives also as sites of historical revelation.[6]

I conclude by interrogating the joint political and historical consequences of Ghana's national reconciliation experiment. Each of the previous chapters depends on understanding the NRC archive as the collective result of individual acts of narration. The sum of this archive is greater than its parts. Juxtaposing the different testimonies, petitions, legal opinions, and speeches against one another, as this study has done, creates a polyvocal, intergenerational, and accessible political dialogue that is unusual within Ghanaian public discourse. Many of the stories and voices in the archive are rarely magnified on the national stage, let alone heard together or valorized. Below, I explore a scant few of the challenging conversations that arise from listening closely to the NRC archive's cacophony. Subsequently, I confront the brief afterlife of the national reconciliation experiment. Given the limited release of the NRC final report, and the stultifying media coverage of the public hearings, any discussions of Ghana's truth commission must address its apparent inconsequentiality and rapid disappearance from view.

Contributions

These stories, together, create a nonpartisan, people-focused human rights review that does not quarantine political violence to a particular leader, regime, or political tradition. Informed by the cacophonous NRC archive, Chapter 2 reveals that throughout the course of Ghanaian history, violence has shifted—changed location and form—but it has not disappeared. Rooting out injustice, then, requires relinquishing the partisan obsession with determining which administration is guilty of human rights violations, and which leader is innocent. These stories suggest that we ask, instead, which communities are being marginalized and who is suffering at any given moment and avoid the partisan political analysis which has usually obscured the persistence of suffering among the poor. Here, there is a warning against the politics of demonization and sanctification and the ways it masks the violence that is structural, compounded, and rarely solved by choosing one "big man" over another.

Chapter 3 is built around the stories of Ghanaian market women who described the physical, sexual, and economic violence they suffered during periods of economic crisis. By displaying their physical and emotional scars, these women disrupt the rhetoric of *kalabule*, which frames Ghanaian trading women as predators. At the same time, these women's voices are also part of an international discursive milieu in which the violated African woman's body is overdetermined and overexposed. Encountering the NRC archive requires that we consider the ambivalence—both the risks and the rewards— of human rights testimony. Representational, existential, and political risks accompany claims of victimhood. On the one hand, human rights rhetoric allows individuals to place their oppression into a broader moral and political context.[7] On the other hand, many marginalized communities cannot join the human rights chorus without wrestling with how the language of human rights intersects with histories of colonial exploitation, racial dehumanization, and cultural imperialism.[8] And so Mahmood Mamdani notes that US public opinion treats Iraq's future as a matter of political complexity, while reducing Darfur to a moral test: to save or not to save.[9] Lila Abu-Lughod looks at the lives of rural Muslim women in Egypt and rejects terms like "oppression," "choice," and "freedom" as "blunt instruments" that do not capture these women's lives, their "tireless efforts, songs of loss and longing and their outbursts about rights."[10] Kenyan youth activist Boniface Mwangi questions not only the effectiveness but also the premise of human rights voluntourism in Africa. "Why do you want to help us? Help your own country."[11] Each of these thinkers is insisting that we must consider how claims of victimhood are produced and heard, and account for a world that views and consumes the suffering of various types of victims differently. The stories of market women reveal that there are multiple audiences that simultaneously bear witness to the testimony of a human rights victim.[12] Only by paying attention to how victim status functions in various locales and at different scales can we apprehend the power and the limitation of international human rights.

In the NRC, Ghanaians acted as agents, not only subjects, of human rights rhetoric. By defining "human rights violations" in particular ways and not in others, Ghanaians utilized an expansive human-rights concept according to their own sensibilities and desires. In Chapter 4, Ghanaians described human rights abuses as domestic violence that seeped into the intimate crevices of everyday life, shifting the way people loved, lived, and dreamed of the future. This lesson—that victimization is rarely contained to a single body—requires a response to historical violence that acknowledges the communal and social dimensions of suffering. Incarcerated people are missed; those who have gone into exile leave hungry children behind. When the police assault or "disappear" a person, those left behind are traumatized and may become fearful. Counting the costs of violence requires looking beyond the individual victim and considering the affected families, social networks, and communities.

In this way, these records push against the boundaries of a human rights concept that has traditionally been focused on the individual, but reticent about the private sphere.[13] Although the international human-rights concept has "evolved out of concrete historical conditions and struggles," it need not be trapped by this history.[14] The scope and focus of international human rights is subject to change. As civil-society organizations and the United Nations have sought to "move on from the sterile years" of Cold War–inflected human-rights law and rhetoric to build a more integrated, holistic, and just vision of human rights, people around the world have also been defining and transforming using human rights.[15] We may easily observe Amnesty International's 2001 decision to incorporate economic, social, and cultural rights into its mission statement or the Organization of African Unity's (now African Union) efforts to include a collective subject within human rights law.[16] However, the creativity and tenacity of grassroots organizations and local people's engagement with human rights often goes unnoticed. This study suggests that we perceive truth commissions as sites where local actors may publicly participate in this ongoing effort to stretch, calibrate, and redefine human rights in the world.

The potential of local voices is also evident in two collections of stories mourning the suffering unleashed by national development initiatives. Both the Volta River resettlements and the Ada communities on the Songor Lagoon came to the NRC with petitions and testimonies about ongoing struggles against land alienation. Chapter 5 features individuals and local organizations speaking out against public and private development initiatives that pit national economic growth against local land rights. Here, these marginalized communities publicly stepped into a role usually closed to them—that of the expert. In both global development and international human rights, the authority of "experts" has played a central role in shaping the lives of poor, local, and marginalized communities around the world. Many critiques have been launched of international development's experts, these "one-eyed giants," who peddle knowledge but lack wisdom.[17] In the NRC, the subjects of development insert themselves into this discussion as experts with fulsome critiques and visions. Instead of participating, buying into, and submitting to initiatives that they did not create in order to pursue goals that they did not choose, Ghana's human right victims launched their own critiques of injustice—even when these did not align with the official NRC mandate. In so doing, they show the folly of the prevailing wisdom according to which Africa's most pressing dilemmas will be solved without the creativity, only the obedience, of the continent's people.

Inasmuch as the NRC reveals the power of human rights in the hands of Ghanaian people, this is a limited potential: these petitions detailing the violence of development were officially beyond the NRC's jurisdiction. Nevertheless, in this archive, marginalization is not erasure; the stories, offering eloquent critiques of exploitative public and private development initiatives, are preserved.

International human rights, as manifest in law, according to Balakrishnan Rajagopal, may yet be "capable of aiding the weak and the victims and holding the powerful accountable" or may continue to lubricate the pathways of the powerful throughout the world.[18] Toward these ends, Rajagopal seeks the "radical democratic potential" of human rights, the "pluriverse" vision that does not conform to the categories or the priorities of the dominant political climate.[19] The soldier stories and ambivalent heroes of Chapter 6, perhaps, answer this call. By destabilizing the dichotomy of victim-perpetrator, these stories push past human rights moralism and toward an understanding of the sociology of violence. Today's perpetrator might be tomorrow's sufferer. Simple formulas of blame and innocence do not apprehend the complexity of state violence. The work of historical justice cannot remain in these traditional dichotomies and must, in law and policy, consider the web of harm and responsibility that traverse and bind together a nation. Leaving behind victims and perpetrators is not a reductionist claim that all pain is equal and thus unactionable; it does not hold that those who held the guns and those who ran from them are the same. It is, however, a step toward a survivors' justice that traces the winding and long-term consequences of political violence—the benefits accrued to some, the hardships meted out to others. Acknowledging the complexity of violence is a step toward unraveling its impact.

The NRC stories also transgress another organizing principle in transitional justice: the idea that violence can be quarantined safely in the past. In Chapter 7, Ghanaians described political violence that preceded national independence and continued despite democratic elections. State repression was cyclical and compounded. Human rights violations in the past created vulnerabilities that continued to influence families' fortunes into the future. This alternative time line of harm is a call for a more complex understanding of political violence and its impact on the lives and futures of African people.

Clearly, the NRC was not a "nail Rawlings commission" because Ghanaians did not allow it to be so. Citizens shared stories that focused on their lives and struggles and that collectively, did not reproduce the "big man" bias in political analysis. By placing their own lives and voices at the center of this public history-writing project, Ghanaians intrude into critical debates about Ghana's history and its future. As such, this study of an unruly NRC archive strikes a contrast to the scholarship declaring that the age of human rights is over, or at least, waning. A new wave of scholars criticizes human rights discourse's inefficacy, its inability to transform the prevalence or brutality of violence and injustice around the world. For Eric Posner, the plummeting hope of human rights is nowhere more apparent than in the proliferation of the purposefully toothless instruments of international human-rights law.[20] However, part of the lesson of the NRC archive is that human rights' global reach extends beyond UN instruments and civil-society organizations. The lesson from the African continent's locales is that human rights becomes significant for diverse communities in multiple ways and at different times. The narratives in the NRC archive simply do not fit into Posner's distillation of human rights law as an effort by "Westerners" to discharge a "moral responsibility to help less well-off people living in foreign countries."[21] In Posner's formulation, Africa does not enter the picture except as a site that stubbornly will not be saved by an anemic human-rights regime. Frankly, it is very easy to be disappointed in human rights if we are unable to catch sight of the varied, fruitful ways that people in the world's locales deploying rights talk for diverse ends. This study of the NRC archive stands in stark contrast to this new scholarship sounding the death knell for human rights.

Approaching TRC testimony in this way—as a manifestation of global human rights practice and as a text worthy of sustained historical and political analysis—is rare. Antjie Krog, Kopano Ratele, and Nosisi Mpolweni's *There Was This Goat* is a remarkable study that takes TRC testimony seriously as an act of historical and political creation.[22] Three South Africans—a journalist, a linguist, and a gender studies scholar—attempt to understand the testimony of Mrs. Notrose Nobomvu Konile, who spoke "incomprehensibly" of dreamed goats and destitution before the South African TRC. The result is a journey into the social, political, and linguistic history of South Africa and the racialized memories and identities of the three academics who seek understanding. However, even this remarkable study ends with ambivalence. Mrs. Konile has finally been heard, but the meaning of this gesture (if anything at all) for Konile or the authors is entirely indeterminate.[23]

Consequences

Global truth commissions collect, publicize, and mourn individual testimonies for myriad reasons: to ameliorate the suffering of those who have been harmed; to expand the historical record; to shame perpetrators of political violence; to prevent impunity, and to publicly embrace democracy and human rights. This freight of hopes contributes to the "inflated expectation" that TRCs should be "impossible machines" that make miracles.[24] That these commissions have not served as a panacea for political violence or ably catalyzed sufficiently new beginnings for divided nations is apparent. Perhaps it was wrong to ever expect that a single commission, no matter how grand, could do all this. Nevertheless, two fundamental questions remain. First, what do TRCs actually produce within the societies that embrace them? Second, can TRCs be part of the work of combatting human rights violations on the African continent and around the world?

Prior laudatory assumptions—that public testimony is inevitably cathartic and freeing for victims; that TRCs strike a blow against impunity and combat the silences created by political violence—are being challenged.[25] There are now troubling depictions of TRC public hearings as sites where "perpetrators continue to behave with apparent callousness and disdain for victims."[26] Holly Guthrey parses the possibility that TRC testimony may continue or compound victim trauma in her study of the Timor-Leste and the Solomon Islands TRC. The emotional consequence of TRC testimony for victims, Guthrey suggests, depends on whether they believe their participation has resulted "in substantive outcomes."[27] This possibility of victim healing is inextricable from the question of whether TRCs can deliver on the promise of social, economic, or political transformation. When individuals see that the world is somehow *changed* by their testimony, they are more likely to feel heard and reconciled.

The Transitional Justice Database, created by three political scientists, uses 161 countries to undertake comparative, statistical, and transnational analysis of the consequences of TRCs on human rights practice.[28] Moving away from the conjecture and optimism that have long held sway, these authors advise caution. They warn that TRCs must be part of a "justice balance" that includes other instruments like special courts, trials, or amnesties in order to propel a country toward a better human-rights score (as determined by leading human-rights NGOs and the US State Department).[29] The impact of TRC is a matter of contingencies: given particular economic and social conditions, certain mechanisms must be chosen over others and applied in a specific sequence if TRCs are to improve state human rights practice. Similarly circumspect, Eric Brahm muses that the value of these commissions may emerge only over time and in relation to other factors.[30] In his clarifying discussion about truth commission impact, Onur Bakinur describes two smoking-gun examples that would serve as undeniable evidence of the effectiveness of a particular commission. If a leader claims to be inspired by the TRC in enacting a particular policy, or members of the population claim that their views on human rights have changed because of the TRC, such examples would represent evidence of a particular commission's efficacy.[31] Both of Bakinur's examples approach the truth commissions as an institution external to a country's people and leaders—an outside force that acts upon them. In contrast, this study describes the Ghana NRC not as an

external force, but as an institution co-created by Ghanaian people and leaders. In this people-centric view, truth commissions may have as many goals
as participants, and their consequences must be traced to the individual,
family, community, and national levels. Evaluating a TRC on these terms, as
an institution created by citizens, governments, and civil society (national
and international) together, requires that we leave behind the "toolkit"
approach's search for "positivist mechanisms that engineer outcomes."
Instead we must approach TRCs as "ongoing labor that "extends far beyond
the so-called transition, unfolding slowly over time and space, needing the
healing and repair work of several generations."[32] In this formulation, TRCs
are only ever a mirror and a beginning.

And so a riotous and unruly NRC archive reflects the fault lines within
the body politic. The NRC's primary organizing questions—what constitutes
a human rights abuse in national history, and what should be done—are fundamental in postindependence African historical and political analysis. The
NRC archive is valuable as a public attempt to wade into these debates and is
remarkable for allowing a diverse cross section of Ghanaian citizens to have
their say. The resulting cacophony dashes the hope that TRCs will spin peace
or justice from straw; however, it does reflect the reality of difference. In these
records no unitary experience of Ghanaian history exists; populations travel
different paths through the national history and hold various visions of restoration. This is the unexpected truth of Ghana's NRC: the work of historical
justice will inevitably require wrestling with cacophony.

And yet there is no escaping the disappearance of this archive from Ghana's political sphere. More than a decade after the NRC was established the
final report is "yet to be disseminated, and it might never be."[33] There are
many possible explanations for this disappearance. Audrey Gadzekpo and Jo
Ellen Fair have astutely considered how the NRC's regulations for media coverage buried the public hearings behind dead prose and "dampened public
enthusiasm" for the NRC.[34] This disappearance is also the result of the NRC
report's limited release. When the fifteen-hundred-page, five-volume report
was submitted to the Ghanaian government in 2004, the sponsoring government enthusiastically embraced its findings and expertise, exhorted civil, military, and police establishments to include aspects of the NRC Report in their
curriculum, and promised to furnish the report to all school libraries, public
and private."[35] This was to be required reading for the nation.[36] These things
did not happen.[37] When government control passed to the National Democratic Congress in 2008, the state did not devote resources to an exercise that

was seen as part of the legacy of the Kufuor administration. As a result, the massive NRC Report received little publicity.

These domestic Ghana-specific explanations are not the whole story. For processes that so carefully collect the voices of victims (usually expending considerable resources), TRCs do not always publicize, engage with, or respond to stories that have been shared. By tracing the TRC genealogy to the colonial commission of inquiry, Adam Sitze unearths the historical and legal antecedents of the TRC's maddening capacity to promise so much and deliver so little.

Throughout the British empire, colonial commissions of inquiry were created in the wake of scandal or governmental failure. Much like truth commissions, these bodies collected victim testimony to investigate what had gone wrong in the colonial administration's governances of its subject peoples and land. Using Foucault's notion of governmentality, Sitze describes commissions as "institutions of sovereign power" that allowed empire "to pose questions to themselves about the scope, limits, and aims of governance."[38] Created to preserve and refine colonial power, these commissions were directed (implicitly or explicitly) to restore public confidence in the administration. As such, these commissions were not at all adverse to the notion that they should 'open their ear' to the voices of the victims of colonial administrative violence, but they were highly unlikely to initiate changes that undermined the premises of imperial rule.[39]

The 1865 Jamaica Royal Commission, which held sixty hearings and listened to the testimony of over seven hundred people involved in the Morant Bay uprising, doggedly pursued victim voices and just as easily discounted them; in Sitze's words, the commission "heard almost nothing" submitted by local victims and rebels.[40] According to the commission, the evidence given by "natives," (which was collected in a publication of more than a thousand pages long) was "disorderly, vague, incoherent, venal, unverifiable and mainly without value."[41] Within the colonial exclusionary epistemic lens, "native" testimony might be collected, preserved, and mourned, but it could not be valued equally to the British testimony. Moreover any critique raised of the colonial right to rule was studiously overlooked.[42] Sitze's description of this "strange mechanism of inclusive exclusion" [43] is relevant when considering the brief afterlife of Ghana's NRC and other truth commissions that collect tomes of victim petitions and testimony and then lock them away in archives, only to be seen by scholars.[44]

Sitze suggests that in the wake of scandal, colonial administrators were compelled to *gather* these testimonies, *listening* to them as credible or actionable was beside the point. The Ghana NRC's category of victim and the colonial commission's category of native were in this way similar: for their respective governments, both identities were not sites of credible dissent. Although the testimonies of both groups are carefully collected, mourned, and preserved, they are emptied of their political challenge. Michael Neocosmos warns that victim status has been used to depoliticize Africans, to render them "subjects of their own history" marked by "passivity and not agency."[45] The position of Africa's "human rights victims," Neocosmos argues, has not been a site from which to upend the political order and struggle for something better. Even as global civil society and state leaders encounter the African poor as victims to be rescued and empathized with, not heard, "freedom remains on the agenda" for the excluded themselves.[46] The First Nations epigraph to this chapter communicates the frustration of those who participate in truth commissions only to discover no mechanism to translate this participation into meaningful economic, social, or political power.

The NRC archive suggests that many Ghanaians did not approach the TRC with this limit in mind; petitioners saw the commission as a chance to pursue a measure of justice. Accordingly, they launched rigorous critiques of Ghana's history of violence, asserting themselves as experts on the national past and crafters of a future justice. Their collected testimonies call out for empathy, but more obviously, for action. The democratized historiography of the NRC archive, in all its cacophony, is a conversation that might rouse us from the fugue of postindependence African history, if only it were heard.

As much as the NRC is an example of the prodigious potential of truth commissions, it is also a cautionary tale for those who imagine such public testimony will create healing from the shards of a violent past. As techniques of governmentality, these commissions resist confronting the economic injustices, global political entanglements, and domestic dynamics that constrain the lives of the majority of Africa's people. Nevertheless, by bringing these issues to the fore, Ghanaians have created a record of the complexity of their nation's history and politics at the turn of the twenty-first century. Despite the brief afterlife Ghana's NRC, the thousands of pages of documents are preserved, fixed in the "resin" of the archives. The truths of the Ghana NRC— which do not create reconciliation—are a resource that must be used, marshaled, and debated if they are to contribute to political transformation.

Alice Walker reminds us of the folly of discarding the wisdom that has already been spoken. "A people do not throw their geniuses away," she cautions. "And if they are thrown away, it is our duty as artists and as witnesses for the future to collect them again for the sake of our children and, if necessary, bone by bone."[47] In 2016, almost forty countries around the world have staged TRCs, and more are being proposed. The stories are there, if we only have the courage to listen.

NOTES

Introduction

1. Priscilla B. Hayner, *Unspeakable Truths: Facing the Challenge of Truth Commissions* (New York: Routledge, 2002), 3; The Rule of Law and Transitional Justice in Conflict and Post-conflict Societies, Report of the Secretary-General, UN Doc. S/2004/616, August 23, 2004, https://www .un.org/ruleoflaw/files/2004%20report.pdf.

2. Colin Bundy, "The Beast of the Past: History and the TRC," in *After the TRC:* (Athens, OH: Ohio University Press, 2001), 9; Greg Grandin and Thomas Miller Klubock, "Editors' Introduction," *Radical History Review* 2007, no. 97 (December 21, 2007): 3, https://doi.org/10.1215 /01636545-2006-010; Karina Czyzewski, "The Truth and Reconciliation Commission of Canada: Insights into the Goal of Transformative Education," *International Indigenous Policy Journal* 2, no. 3 (August 2011): 1.

3. Robert Osei and Peter Quartey, "The HIPC Initiative and Poverty Reduction in Ghana: An Assessment," Working Paper (WIDER Discussion Papers // World Institute for Development Economics (UNU-WIDER), 2001), https://www.econstor.eu/handle/10419/52965; Lindsay Whitfield, "Growth without Economic Transformation: Economic Impacts of Ghana's Political Settlement," Working Paper, DIIS Working Paper (Copenhagen, Denmark: Danish Institute for International Studies, DIIS, 2011); Ann M. Oberhauser and Kobena T. Hanson, "Negotiating Livelihoods and Scale in the Context of Neoliberal Globalization: Perspectives from Accra, Ghana," *African Geographical Review* 26, no. 1 (January 1, 2007): 11–36, https://doi.org/10.1080 /19376812.2007.9756200.

4. For competing assessments of this legacy see John L. Adedeji, "The Legacy of J. J. Rawlings in Ghanaian Politics 1979–2000," *African Studies Quarterly* 5, no. 2 (Summer 2001): 1–27; E. Brenya et al., "The Rawlings' Factor in Ghana's Politics: An Appraisal of Some Secondary and Primary Data," *Journal of Political Sciences & Public Affairs* 1, no. 4 (September 2015): 1–14, https:// doi.org/10.4172/2332-0761.1000S1.004; E. Gyimah-Boadi and Donald Rothchild, "Rawlings, Populism, and the Civil Liberties Tradition in Ghana," *Issue: A Journal of Opinion* 12, no. 3/4 (1982): 64–69, https://doi.org/10.2307/1166719; Mike Oquaye, "Human Rights and the Transition to Democracy Under the PNDC in Ghana," *Human Rights Quarterly* 17, no. 3 (1995): 556–73.

5. National Reconciliation Commission Act (2002), Act 611, http://www.icla.up.ac.za /images/un/commissionsofinquiries/files/Ghana%202003%20National%20Reconciliation %20Commission%20TOR.pdf.

6. Erica Bouris, *Complex Political Victims* (Bloomfield, CT: Kumarian Press, 2007), 8.

7. See the following contemporaneous account of the difficulty of locating these records: Kwame Boafo-Arthur, "Draft Report on the Ghana National Reconciliation Commission Submitted to the International Center for Transitional Justice," September 16, 2005, p. 5 Collection

Number RL01304, Box 2, Records of the International Center for Transitional Justice, Human Rights Archive, David M. Rubenstein Rare Book and Manuscript Library, Duke University.

8. Joseph K. Adjaye, "Perspectives on Fifty Years of Ghanaian Historiography," *History in Africa* 35 (2008): 11, 14; Roger Gocking, *The History of Ghana*, Greenwood Histories of the Modern Nations (Greenwood Publishing Group, 2005), 70.

9. Mahmood Mamdani, "Beware Human Rights Fundamentalism!," *Mail & Guardian*, March 20, 2009, https://mg.co.za/article/2009-03-20-beware-human-rights-fundamentalism; David Kinley, "Human Rights Fundamentalism," *Sydney Law Review* 29, no. 4 (December 2007): 547.

10. I use this phrase "rights talk" to describe international human rights as a language of political power in the global sphere. This power is captured well by Conor Gearty's description of human rights as a "strong [phrase], epistemologically confident, ethically assured, carrying with it the promise . . . to cut through the noise of assertion and counter-assertion. . . , and thereby to deliver truth." Conor Gearty, *Can Human Rights Survive?* (Cambridge: Cambridge University Press, 2006), 19.

11. There are different ways to count the world's truth commissions. This text's accounting labels as TRCs those commissions that identify themselves as such and describe themselves as part of a global tradition that extends from the 1983 Argentina Comisíon Nacional sobre la Desaparición de Personas to the 1995 South African Commission of Truth and Reconciliation to the 2008 Truth and Reconciliation Commission of Canada. I do not include the 1974 Uganda Commission of Inquiry into the Disappearance of People, for example, nor the Nigerian Human Rights Violations Investigation Commission, known as the Oputa Panel. My designation includes no comment on the commission's effectiveness or completion; it is based solely on the commission's self-assessment. Under this rubric, the thirteen African countries that have staged truth commissions are Burundi (TRC 2014), Côte d'Ivoire (Commission Dialogue Vérité et Réconciliation, 2011), Democratic Republic of Congo (Commission Verité et Réconciliation, 2005), Ghana (National Reconciliation Commission, 2001), Kenya (Truth, Justice and Reconciliation Commission, 2008), Liberia (Truth and Reconciliation Commission, 2005), Mauritius (Truth and Justice Commission, 2009), Mali (Truth, Justice, and Reconciliation Commission, 2014) Morocco (Instance Equité et Réconciliation, 2004), Nigeria (Rivers State Truth and Reconciliation Commission, 2007; Osun Truth and Reconciliation Commission, 2011), Togo (Truth, Justice and Reconciliation Commission, 2009), Sierra Leone (Truth and Reconciliation Commission, 2000), and South Africa (Commission of Truth and Reconciliation, 1995).

12. Pierre Hazan, *Judging War, Judging History: Behind Truth and Reconciliation* (Stanford, CA: Stanford University Press, 2010), 10.

13. Louise Vella, "Translating Transitional Justice: The Solomon Islands Truth and Reconciliation Commission," 2014, 3, http://ips.cap.anu.edu.au/sites/default/files/DP-2014-02-Vella-ONLINE.pdf; Ismael Muvingi, "Donor-Driven Transitional Justice And Peacebuilding," *Journal of Peacebuilding & Development* 11, no. 1 (January 2, 2016): 10–25, https://doi.org/10.1080/15423166.2016.1146566.

14. Dumisa Ntsebeza, "The Uses of Truth Commissions: Lessons for the World," in *Truth V. Justice: The Morality of Truth Commissions,* eds. Robert I. Rotberg and Dennis Thompson (Princeton, NJ: Princeton University Press, 2000), 158.

15. Desmond Tutu, *No Future Without Forgiveness* (New York: Doubleday, 1999), 281–82.

16. Rajeev Bhargava, "Restoring Decency to Barbaric Societies," in *Truth V. Justice: The Morality of Truth Commissions,* eds. Robert I. Rotberg and Dennis Thompson (Princeton, NJ: Princeton University Press, 2000), 45.

17. Michael Ignatieff, "Articles of Faith," *Index on Censorship* 25, no. 5 (September 1, 1996): 110–22.

18. Paulo Gorjão, "The East Timorese Commission for Reception, Truth and Reconciliation: Chronicle of a Foretold Failure?," *Civil Wars* 4, no. 2 (June 1, 2001): 142–62, https://doi.org /10.1080/13698240108402473; Fiona C. Ross, "An Acknowledged Failure: Women, Voice, Violence and the South African Truth and Reconciliation Commission," in *Localizing Transitional Justice* (Stanford, CA: Stanford University Press, 2010).

19. Rebecca Saunders, "Lost in Translation: Expressions of Human Suffering, the Language of Human Rights, and the South African Truth and Reconciliation Commission," *SUR International Journal on Human Rights* 5, no. 9 (January 2008), 50–69, http://www.conectas.org/en /actions/sur-journal/issue/9/1000083-sobre-o-intraduzivel-sofrimento-humano-a-linguagem -de-direitos-humanos-e-a-comissao-de-verdade-e-reconciliacao-da-africa-do-sul; Fiona Ross, *Bearing Witness: Women and Truth and Reconciliation Commission in South Africa* (London: Pluto Press, 2003).

20. Khulumani Support Group, "How the TRC Failed Women in South Africa," *Khulumani Support Group South Africa* (blog), October 3, 2011, http://www.khulumani.net/truth-memory /item/527-how-the-trc-failed-women-in-south-africa-a-failure-that-has-proved-fertile-ground -for-the-gender-violence-women-in-south-africa-face-today.html.

21. Laplante and Theidon describe the silence created by a Peruvian TRC that reproduced a narrative of rural communities divided between "innocent peasants" and "Shining Path terrorists" instead of recognizing the complexity of rural citizens' political agency during the civil war. Lisa J. Laplante and Kimberly Theidon, "Commissioning Truth, Constructing Silences: The Peruvian Truth Commission and the Other Truths of 'Terrorists,'" in *Mirrors of Justice,* eds. Kamari Maxine Clark and Mark Goodale (Cambridge: Cambridge University Press, 2009), 299–301, http://dx.doi.org/10.1017/CBO9780511657511.016; Rosalind Shaw, "Memory Frictions: Localizing the Truth and Reconciliation Commission in Sierra Leone," *International Journal of Transitional Justice* 1, no. 2 (July 1, 2007): 202, doi:10.1093/ijtj/ijm008.

22. Aaron Weah, "Hopes and Uncertainties: Liberia's Journey to End Impunity," *International Journal of Transitional Justice* 6, no. 2 (July 1, 2012): 335, https://doi.org/10.1093/ijtj/ijs007.

23. Kirsten Weld, *Paper Cadavers: The Archives of Dictatorship in Guatemala* (Durham, NC: Duke University Press, 2014), 3.

24. Annelies Verdoolaege, *Reconciliation Discourse: The Case of the Truth and Reconciliation Commission* (Amsterdam/Philadelphia: John Benjamins Publishing, 2008), 36.

25. Jeff Sahadeo, "'Without the Past There Is No Future': Archives, History, and Authority in Uzbekistan," in *Archive Stories: Facts, Fictions and the Writing of History* (Durham, NC: Duke University Press, 2005), 49.

26. Kirsten Weld, *Paper Cadavers: The Archives of Dictatorship in Guatemala*, 6.

27. New Patriotic Party, *Agenda for Positive Change: Manifesto 2000 of the New Patriotic Party* (Accra, Ghana: N.P.P., 2000), chap. 4.

28. "Nail Rawlings Commission (NRC) and All," *Ghanaian Lens,* July 17, 2004. http://www .ghanaweb.com/GhanaHomePage/NewsArchive/Nail-Rawlings-Commission-NRC-And-All -61916.

29. Hazan, *Judging War, Judging History*, 9.

30. "Woman Loses Voice Through Torture," *Ghana Review*, January 29, 2003.

31. Urvashi Butalia, *The Other Side of Silence: Voices from the Partition of India* (Durham, NC: Duke University Press, 2000), 6.

32. Gyanenedra Pandey, *Remembering Partition: Violence, Nationalism and History in India* (Cambridge: Cambridge University Press, 2001), 152.

33. Pandey, 177.

34. Verdoolaege, *Reconciliation Discourse*, 33.

35. Paul Gready, *The Era of Transitional Justice: The Aftermath of the Truth and Reconciliation in South Africa and Beyond* (New York: Routledge: 2010), 46; Deborah Posel, "History as Confession: The Case of the South African Truth and Reconciliation Commission," *Public Culture* 2008 (1): 119–41.

36. Elazar Barkan, "Historians and Historical Reconciliation," *American Historical Review* 114, no. 4 (October 2009): 903.

37. Grandin and Klubock, "Editors' Introduction," 3.

38. Mahmood Mamdani, "Amnesty or Impunity? A Preliminary Critique of the Report of the Truth and Reconciliation Commission of South Africa (TRC)," *Diacritics* 32, no. 3 (February 21, 2005): 33–34, 56–57, https://doi.org/10.1353/dia.2005.0005.

39. Alejandro Castillejo-Cuéllar, "Knowledge, Experience, and South Africa's Scenarios of Forgiveness," *Radical History Review* 2007, no. 97 (December 21, 2007): 11–42, doi:10.1215/01636545-2006-011; Rafael Verbuyst, "History, Historians and the South African Truth and Reconciliation Commission," *New Contree* 66 (July 2013); Deborah Posel, "The TRC Report: What Kind of History? What Kind of Truth?" (working paper, Wits History Workshop, Johannesburg, University of Witswatersrand, June 11, 1999), http://wiredspace.wits.ac.za/handle/10539/8046.

40. Deborah Posel, "History as Confession: The Case of the South African Truth and Reconciliation Commission," *Public Culture* 20, no. 1 (Winter 2008): 120.

41. Grandin and Klubock, "Editors' Introduction," 3. For an alternative perspective, consider Janet Cherry's description of how truth commissions have a "methodical advantage" in employing strategies that pursue both forensic truth and narrative truth. Janet Cherry "Truth and Transitional Justice," in *Assessing the Impact of Transitional Justice: Challenges for Empirical Research*, ed. Hugo van der Merwe, Victoria Baxter, and Audrey R. Chapman (Washington, DC: United States Institute of Peace, 2009).

42. Matt James, "A Carnival of Truth? Knowledge, Ignorance and the Canadian Truth and Reconciliation Commission," *International Journal of Transitional Justice* 6, no. 2 (2012): 1.

43. Madeleine Fullard and Nicky Rousseau, "Uncertain Borders: The TRC and the (Un)Making of Public Myths," *Kronos*, no. 34 (November 1, 2008): 219.

44. Andrea Cornwall and Vera Schatten Coelho, *Space for Change? The Politics of Citizen Participation in New Democratic Arenas* (London: Zed Books, 2007).

45. Mohamed Ahmed Bennis, "The Equity and Reconciliation Committee and the Transition Process in Morocco," Arab Reform Brief, Arab Reform Initiative (September 2006), 3, www.arab-reform.net/spip.php?article398#ancor1.

46. Luke Wilcox, "Reshaping Civil Society Through a Truth Commission: Human Rights in Morocco's Process of Political Reform," *International Journal of Transitional Justice* 3, no. 1 (2009): 58.

47. Cornwall and Coelho, *Space for Change?*, 2.

48. Ibid., 10–13.

49. Michel-Rolph Trouillot, *Silencing the Past: Power and the Production of History* (Boston: Beacon Press, 1995), 2.

50. Charles A. Beard, "Written History as an Act of Faith," *American Historical Review* 39, no. 2 (1934): 220, doi:10.2307/1838720; Peter Novick, *That Noble Dream: The "Objectivity*

Question" and the American Historical Profession (Cambridge: Cambridge University Press, 1988), 1; Adjaye, "Perspectives on Fifty Years," 5, 7–8.

51. Butalia, *The Other Side of Silence: Voices from the Partition of India*, 10.

52. Paul Nugent, "Living in the Past: Urban, Rural and Ethnic Themes in the 1992 and 1996 Elections in Ghana," *The Journal of Modern African Studies* 37, no. 2 (June 1999): 290; Jesse Weaver Shipley, "The Market Decides If We Are Free," *Africa Is a Country* (blog), January 16, 2017, http://africasacountry.com/2017/01/the-market-decides-if-we-are-free/; Lindsay Whitfield, "'Change for a Better Ghana': Party Competition, Institutionalization and Alternation in Ghana's 2008 Elections," *African Affairs* 108, no. 433 (2009): 627–32.

53. David Peterson del Mar, "A Pragmatic Tradition: The Past in Ghanaian Education," *Africa Today* 59, no. 2 (2012): 28; Jean Allman, "The Disappearing of Hanna Kudjoe: Nationalism, Feminism, and the Tyrannies of History," *Journal of Women's History* 21, no. 3 (2009): 13–35.

54. Patrick Gyimah Danso, File "KS00231," NRC Documents, Balme Library, University of Ghana (hereafter cited as NRC Documents). The citizen petitions and accompanying documents were collected between 2002 and 2004 were arranged into files organized by a zonal office alphabetical code (ACC = Accra zonal office; KS = Kumasi zonal office; TD = Takoradi zonal office; TML = Tamale zonal office; BLG = Bolgatanga zonal office; HVR= Ho zonal office) and a number.

55. Jelena Subotic, *Hijacked Justice: Dealing with the Past in the Balkans* (Ithaca, NY: Cornell University Press, 2009), xii.

56. Rosalind Shaw and Lars Waldorf, eds., *Localizing Transitional Justice: Intervention and Priorities After Mass Violence*, Stanford Studies in Human Rights (Stanford, CA: Stanford University Press, 2010), 3.

57. Ibrahim Gassama, "A World Made of Violence and Misery: Human Rights as a Failed Project of Liberal Internationalism," *Brooklyn Journal of International Law* 37, no. 2 (January 1, 2012), http://brooklynworks.brooklaw.edu/bjil/vol37/iss2/3; Emilie M. Hafner-Burton and Kiyoteru Tsutsui, "Justice Lost! The Failure of International Human Rights Law To Matter Where Needed Most," *Journal of Peace Research* 44, no. 4 (July 1, 2007): 407–25, https://doi.org/10.1177/0022343307078942.

58. Kenneth Cmiel, "The Recent History of Human Rights," *American Historical Review* 109, no. 1 (February 2004): 118.

59. Kathryn Sikkink, *Evidence for Hope: Making Human Rights Work in the 21st Century* (Princeton, NJ: Princeton University Press, 2017); Kathryn Sikkink, *The Justice Cascade: How Human Rights Prosecutions Are Changing World Politics* (New York: W.W. Norton, 2011); Thomas Risse, Stephen C. Ropp, and Kathryn Sikkink, *The Persistent Power of Human Rights: From Commitment to Compliance* (Cambridge: Cambridge University Press, 2013).

60. Adam Branch, *Displacing Human Rights: War and Intervention in Northern Uganda* (Oxford: Oxford University Press, 2011), 23.

61. Chinua Achebe, "Africa Is People," in *The Education of the British-Protected Child: Essays* (New York: Alfred A. Knopf, 2009); Chimamanda Ngozi Adichie, "What Are the Dangers of a Single Story?" Part 4 of "Framing the Story," *Ted Radio Hour*, broadcast on National Public Radio, June 7, 2013, http://www.npr.org/2013/09/20/186303292/what-are-the-dangers-of-a-single-story.

62. Teju Cole, "The White-Savior Industrial Complex," *Atlantic*, March 21, 2012; Binyavanga Wainaina, "How Not to Write About Africa in 2012: A Beginner's Guide," *Guardian*, June 3, 2012.

63. Frederick J. D. Lugard, *The Dual Mandate in British Tropical Africa* (Oxon: Frank Case & Co., 1922), 617; Rudyard Kipling "White Man's Burden," *New York Sun,* February, 1899.

64. Harri Englund, *Prisoners of Freedom: Human Rights and the African Poor* (Berkeley: University of California Press, 2006), 30; Makau Mutua, *Human Rights NGOs in East Africa: Political and Normative Tensions* (Philadelphia: University of Pennsylvania Press, 2009), 18–26.

65. Branch, *Displacing Human Rights*, 23.

66. Michael Neocosmos, *Thinking Freedom in Africa: Toward a Theory of Emancipatory Politics* (Johannesburg: Wits University Press, 2017), 4.

67. Branch, *Displacing Human Rights*, 15.

68. Lucie E. White and Jeremy Perelman, *Stones of Hope: How African Activists Reclaim Human Rights to Challenge Global Poverty* (Stanford, CA: Stanford University Press, 2011), 3.

69. Mark Goodale and Sally Engle-Merry, *The Practice of Human Rights: Tracking Law Between the Global and the Local* (Cambridge: Cambridge University Press, 2007); Shaw and Waldorf, *Localizing Transitional Justice*, 2010.

70. Steve J. Stern and Scott Strauss, eds., *The Human Rights Paradox: Universality and Its Discontents* (Madison: University of Wisconsin, 2014) 12.

71. Emilie Hafner-Burton, *Making Human Rights a Reality* (Princeton, NJ: Princeton University Press, 2013), 152.

72. Branch, *Displacing Human Rights*, 29.

73. Sally Engle Merry, "Transnational Human Rights and Local Activism: Mapping the Middle," *American Anthropologist* 108, no. 1 (2006): 38–39.

74. "I Used Evidence as Toilet Roll—Ex-Sergeant," *Ghana Review*, February 7, 2003, http://www.ghanareview.com/int/nrc.html#b3.

75. Adam Gariba, "ACC00100," NRC Documents.

76. Godfred Odame Kissi, "ACC00016," NRC Documents.

77. Ibid.

78. George Jerry Sefa Dei, *Schooling and Education in Africa: The Case of Ghana* (Trenton, N.J.: Africa World Press, 2004), 35; Ziblim Abukari, Ahmed Bawa Kuyini, and Abdulai Kuyini Mohammed, "Education and Health Care Policies in Ghana: Examining the Prospects and Challenges of Recent Provisions," *SAGE Open* 5, no. 4 (December 23, 2015): 1–2, https://doi.org/10.1177/2158244015611454; Talan B. İşcan, Daniel Rosenblum, and Katie Tinker, "School Fees and Access to Primary Education: Assessing Four Decades of Policy in Sub-Saharan Africa," *Journal of African Economies* 24, no. 4 (August 1, 2015): 564, https://doi.org/10.1093/jae/ejv007.

79. *Abolishing School Fees in Africa: Lessons from Ethiopia, Ghana, Kenya, Malawi and Mozambique* (Washington, DC: World Bank and UNICEF, 2009).

80. William Faulkner, *Requiem for a Nun* (New York: Vintage International, 2011).

81. Moses Chrispus Okello et al., *Where Law Meets Reality: Forging African Transitional Justice* (Nairobi: Pambazuka Press, 2012), xix.

82. Lansine Kaba, "Historical Consciousness and Politics in Africa," in *Black Studies: Theory, Method, and Cultural Perspectives* (Pullman, WA: Washington State University Press, 1990), 48–49.

83. Neocosmos, *Thinking Freedom in Africa*, 20.

84. Ibid., 10.

85. Ibid., 12.

86. Adam Branch and Zachariah Mampilly, *Africa Uprising: Popular Protest and Political Change*, African Arguments (London: Zed Books, 2015), 6, 10.

Chapter 1. Making the NRC Archive

1. Luise White, "Telling More: Lies, Secrets, and History," *History and Theory* 39, no. 4 (December 2000): 12.

2. Annelies Verdoolaege, *Reconciliation Discourse: The Case of the Truth and Reconciliation Commission* (Amsterdam/Philadelphia: John Benjamins Publishing, 2008), 32.

3. "Agenda for Positive Change: Manifesto of the New Patriotic Party," May 1, 2000, http://www.ghanareview.com/NPP.html.

4. Ofeibea Quist-Arcton, "Ghana's Kufuor Defends His Government's Record on Transparency, the Economy," AllAfrica, May 25, 2002, http://allafrica.com/stories/200205240737.html ?page=3.

5. "NRC to Help Nation Regain Lost Soul—Kufuor," *Ghana News Agency*, April 17, 2003.

6. Kenneth Agyemang Attafuah, "An Overview of Ghana's National Reconciliation Commission and Its Relationship with the Courts," *Criminal Law Forum* 15, no. 1/2 (March 2004): 125–34.

7. "White Paper on the NRC," Government of Ghana, April 2005, Box 2, Records of the International Center for Transitional Justice, Human Rights Archive, David M. Rubenstein Rare Book and Manuscript Library, Duke University (hereafter ICTJ Records).

8. Attafuah, "An Overview of Ghana's National Reconciliation Commission," 127.

9. "NRC Is an Illegal Body … They Should Dismantle and Go," *Chronicle*, July 1, 2004, Modern Ghana, https://www.modernghana.com/news/58021/nrc-is-an-illegal-body-they -should-dismantle-and-go.html.

10. Nahla Valji, *Ghana's National Reconciliation Commission: A Comparative Assessment*, Occasional Paper Series (New York: International Center for Transitional Justice, September 2006), 6, https://www.ictj.org/publication/ghanas-national-reconciliation-commission -comparative-assessment.

11. Ibid., 34.

12. Ibid., 29.

13. "White Paper on the NRC."

14. International Center for Transitional Justice, "Time Period Mandate in the NRC Bill," November 26, 2001, Box 2, ICTJ Records.

15. Valji, *Ghana's National Reconciliation Commission*, 6.

16. "Report on the NRC Bill by the Committee on Constitutional, Legal and Parliamentary Affairs," November 2001, Box 2, ICTJ Records.

17. The National Reconciliation Commission Act, 2002, Section 3, http://www.ghanareview .com/reconact.html.

18. Valji, *Ghana's National Reconciliation Commission*, 8.

19. "Report on the NRC Bill."

20. "NRC Zonal Office Received 902 Complaints," GhanaWeb, March 16, 2003, http://www .ghanaweb.com/GhanaHomePage/politics/artikel.php?ID=34110.

21. Benjamin Anim, "ACC01351," NRC Documents, Balme Library, University of Ghana (hereafter cited as NRC Documents).

22. Joseph Karim Asare, "ACC00028," NRC Documents.

23. Joseph Karim Asare to NRC, April 9, 2003, "ACC00028," NRC Documents.

24. The statistics provided in the official NRC report were based on approximately 70 percent of the total number of petitions. The NRC's statistical analysis was based on 3,114 out of a total 4,240 statements.

25. Henrietta J. A. N. Mensa-Bonsu, "Gender, Justice and Reconciliation: Lessons from Ghana's NRC" (paper, workshop of the Center for Democratic Development / Coexistence International, Accra, Ghana, June 7, 2007), 10.

26. Kwame Boafo-Arthur, "Draft Report on the Ghana National Reconciliation Commission Submitted to the International Center for Transitional Justice," September 16, 2005, Box 31, ICTJ Records.

27. Mensa-Bonsu, "Gender, Justice and Reconciliation."

28. Ibid.

29. Sylvia Bawa and Francis Sanyare, "Women' Participation and Representation in Politics: Perspectives from Ghana," *International Journal of Public Administration* 36, no. 4 (2013): 285.

30. National Reconciliation Commission Report, Executive Summary, vol.1, chap. 4, p. 7, October 2004.

31. "NRC Presents Report to Government," Modern Ghana, *Ghana News Agency*, October 12, 2004, https://www.modernghana.com/news/64508/nrc-presents-report-to-government.html.

32. "NRC Report, vol. 2, chap. 2, p. 19, October 2004.

33. The sample of petitions used for this study reveals the broad linguistic base represented in the NRC. In a sample of about a thousand petitions, Ghanaians utilized more than fifty dialects and languages when presenting their stories.

34. Clifford Seth Marko, "ACC00157," NRC Documents.

35. Ibid.

36. "Stakeholders Evaluate Media Coverage of the NRC," GhanaWeb, July 31, 2003, http://www.ghanaweb.com/GhanaHomePage/NewsArchive/Stakeholders-evaluate-media-coverage-of-NRC-40291. There were also "in-camera hearings" provided when the commissioners deemed testimony too sensitive for the Ghanaian public.

37. "NRC Report, vol. 2, chap. 2, p. 14, October 2004.

38. Ibid.

39. "Be Compassionate to Witnesses—Bishop," *Ghana Review*, March 14, 2003, http://www.ghanareview.com/int/nrc2.html#a.

40. Ibid.

41. "Refusal to Appear before NRC Is an Offense," *Ghana Review*, February 4, 2003, http://www.ghanareview.com/int/nrc.html#b3.

42. Valji, *Ghana's National Reconciliation Commission*, 7. Retired Supreme Court judge Kweku Amua-Sakyi was the chairman of the commission. The other members included the retired army general Lt. Emmanuel Erskine, a former UNIFIL commander and a 1972 presidential candidate; the Catholic bishop of Koforidua, Rev. Bishop Charles Palmer-Buckle; the legal scholar and professor Henrietta Mensa-Bonsu; ameer and missionary of the Ahmadiyya Muslim Mission, Maulvi Abdul Wahab bin Adam; Uborr Dalafu Label II, an electrical engineer and paramount chief of Sangulu in northern Ghana; Professor Florence Dolphyne, former pro-vice chancellor of the University of Ghana; Mrs. Sylvia Boye, former head of the West African Examination Council; and Mr. Christian Appiagyei former head of the Trades Union Congress. Dr. Kenneth Agyemang Attafuah of Center for Human Rights and Administrative Justice was the executive secretary of the commission.

43. "Commissioners Descend Heavily on Witness," *Ghana Review*, February 14, 2003, http://www.ghanareview.com/int/nrc.html#b4.

44. "NDC Calls for the Removal of NRC Chairman," *Ghana Review*, March 13, 2003, http://www.ghanareview.com/int/nrc2.html#a; Valji, *Ghana's National Reconciliation Commission*, 9.

45. Valji, *Ghana's National Reconciliation Commission*, 11.

46. "ICTJ Ghana Trip Report Feb. 2003," Box 2, ICTJ Records.

47. "Witness Maintain Stand Against Appentengs," GhanaWeb, June 16, 2004. https://www.ghanaweb.com/GhanaHomePage/NewsArchive/Witness-maintain-stand-against-Appentengs-59874?channel=D1

48. Mark Sanders, "Renegotiating Responsibility After Apartheid: Listening to Perpetrator Testimony," *Journal of Gender, Social Policy and the Law* 10, no. 3 (2002): 589; David Mendeloff, "Trauma and Vengeance: Assessing the Psychological and Emotional Effects of Post-Conflict Justice," *Human Rights Quarterly* 31, no. 3 (2009): 605; Karen Brouneus, "Truth-Telling as Talking Cure? Insecurity and Retraumatization in the Rwandan Gacaca Courts," *Security Dialogues* 39, no. 1 (2008): 55.

49. "Public Tribunals and the NRC—Rejoinder From NRC," GhanaWeb, November 26, 2003, http://www.ghanaweb.com/GhanaHomePage/features/artikel.php?ID=47333.

50. Susan Slyomovics, "The Argument from Silence: Morocco's Truth Commission and Women Political Prisoners," *Journal of Middle East Women's Studies* 1, no. 3 (Fall 2005): 78, 81.

51. "'I Used Evidence as Toilet Roll'—Ex-sergeant," *Ghana Review*, February 7, 2003, http://www.ghanareview.com/int/nrc.html#b3.

52. NRC Report, Executive Summary, vol. 1, chap. 1, p. 4, October 2004.

53. Robert Kwame Ameh, "Uncovering Truth: Ghana's National Reconciliation Commission Excavation of Past Human Rights Abuses," *Contemporary Justice Review* 9, no. 4 (2006): 346.

54. Antjie Krog, *Country of My Skull: Guilt, Sorrow, and the Limits of Forgiveness in the New South Africa* (South Africa: Random House, 1998), 36.

55. White, "Telling More," 11.

56. Ibid., 14.

57. Alessandro Portelli, *The Death of Luigi Trastulli and Other Stories: Form and Meaning in Oral History* (Albany: SUNY Press, 1991), 51.

58. Tammy A. Smith, "Remembering and Forgetting a Contentious Past: Voices From the Italo-Yugoslav Frontier," *American Behavioral Scientist* 51, no. 10 (June 2008): 1541; Antonius C. G. M. Robben, "How Traumatized Societies Remember: The Aftermath of Argentina's Dirty War," *Cultural Critique* 59 (2005): 122.

59. Michael Ignatieff, "Articles of Faith," *Index on Censorship* 25, no. 5 (September 1, 1996): 110–22.

60. Jay A. Vora and Erika Vora, "The Effectiveness of South Africa's Truth and Reconciliation Commission: Perceptions of Xhosa, Afrikaner, and English South Africans," *Journal of Black Studies* 34, no. 3 (January 2004): 301–22, doi:10.2307/3180939; Tim Kelsall, "Truth, Lies, and Ritual: Preliminary Reflections on the Truth and Reconciliation Commission in Sierra Leone," *Human Rights Quarterly* 27, no. 2 (2005).

61. Alfred Marteye, "Rawlings Might Not Have Been Aware—Nana Ahima," *Ghana Review*, February 13, 2003, http://www.ghanareview.com/int/nrc.html#b4.

62. "Rawlings Ordered My Release—Witness," *Ghana Review*, February 20, 2003, www.ghanareview.com/int/nrc.html#b4.

63. In his public testimony, Kwabena Adjei Agyepong, the son of one of the disappeared judges, intimated that Rawlings had been involved in either his father's death or in the cover-up. "We always heard a lot of things. But then in 1999 on this 7th January . . . President Rawlings made certain statements that even people who were close to them when they committed crimes,

they were dealt with swiftly and justly. That was the first time it struck my nerve. I said, this is the time for me to respond." *Ghana NRC01_Agyepong*, digital video, ICTJ Records.

64. US Embassy Accra, "Rawlings at NRC: Big Build-Up, Bigger Let- Down," Wikileaks Cable 4ACCRA301, February 13, 2004, http://wikileaks.org/cable/2004/02/04ACCRA301 .html#, accessed November 20, 2017.

65. Ibid.

66. Ibid.

67. *Ghana NRC07_Rawlings*, digital video, Records of the International Center for Transitional Justice, Human Rights Archive, David M. Rubenstein Rare Book and Manuscript Library, Duke University.

68. Ibid.

69. NRC Report, vol. 1, chap. 8, p. 183.

70. *Ghana NRC07_Rawlings*, digital video, Records of the International Center for Transitional Justice, Human Rights Archive, David M. Rubenstein Rare Book and Manuscript Library, Duke University.

71. *GhanaNRC_Torture Brutality Security Services*, digital video, Records of the International Center for Transitional Justice, Human Rights Archive, David M. Rubenstein Rare Book and Manuscript Library, Duke University.

72. *Ghana NRC08_Munufie*, digital video, Records of the International Center for Transitional Justice, Human Rights Archive, David M. Rubenstein Rare Book and Manuscript Library, Duke University.

73. "Witness Tells NRC: Only One Bullet, That's All!," *Ghana Review*, February 6, 2003, http://www.ghanareview.com/int/nrc.html#b3.

74. Kay Schaffer and Sidonie Smith, "Conjunctions: Life Narratives in the Field of Human Rights," *Biography* 27, no. 1 (2004): 4.

Chapter 2. Human Rights and Ghanaian History

1. In January 1960, in Accra, Ghana, the British prime minister Harold Macmillan made the famous "Winds of Change" speech describing African decolonization as an inevitability.

2. Martin Luther King, Jr. "Birth of a New Nation," sermon at the Dexter Avenue Baptist Church, April 7, 1957.

3. Jeffrey S. Ahlman, "Road to Ghana: Nkrumah, Southern Africa and the Eclipse of a Decolonizing Africa," *Kronos*, no. 37 (2011): 23.

4. Donald Harrington, "Ghana Independence Day," *Africa Today* 4, no. 2 (1957): 3.

5. Frederick Cooper, *Africa Since 1940: The Past of the Present* (Cambridge: Cambridge University Press, 2002), 161.

6. "Ghana—Good Kid in a Really Bad Neighborhood," *New York Times*, April 26, 2005; Vasco Molini and Pierella Paci, "Poverty Reduction in Ghana: Progress and Challenges" (Washington DC: World Bank Group, 2015), http://hdl.handle.net/10986/22732; Alexander Lobrano, "Africa's Capital of Cool," *New York Times*, July 12, 2016, https://www.nytimes.com/2016/07/08 /t-magazine/travel/accra-ghana-travel.html.

7. Zoe Adjonyoh, "'Accra's Jamestown Is Electric—It's Like Hackney Wick on Steroids': Zoe Adjonyoh," interview by Robert Hull, *Guardian*, April 28, 2017, https://www.theguardian.com /travel/2017/apr/28/accra-jamestown-ghana-zoe-adjonyoh-chef-interview.

8. David Kennedy, "The International Human Rights Movement: Part of the Problem?," *Harvard Human Rights Journal* 15, no. 99 (Spring 2002): 111.

9. Elie Weisel, "A Tribute to Human Rights," in *The Universal Declaration of Human Rights: Fifty Years and Beyond*, ed. Y. Daniele et al. (Routledge, 1999), 3.

10. Issa Shivji, *The Concept of Human Rights in Africa* (London, UK: Codesria Book Series, 1989).

11. Samuel Moyn, *The Last Utopia: Human Rights in History* (Cambridge, MA: Harvard University Press, 2010), 1.

12. Bonny Ibhawoh, *Imperialism and Human Rights: Colonial Discourses of Rights and Liberties in African History* (Albany, NY: State University of New York Press, 2007), 134.

13. Jan Eckel, "Human Rights and Decolonization: New Perspectives and Open Questions," review of *Menschenrechte im Schatten kolonialer Gewalt: Die Dekolonisierungskriege in Kenia und Algerien 1945–1962*, by Fabian Klose, and *Decolonization and the Evolution of International Human Rights*, by Roland Burke, *Humanity Journal*, no. 1 (June 10, 2014): 113, http://humanityjournal.org/issue-1/human-rights-and-decolonization-new-perspectives-and-open-questions/.

14. Kwame Nkrumah, "African Prospect," *Foreign Affairs* 37, no.1 (1958): 46.

15. Kofi Abrefa Busia, "Gold Coast Independence," November 30, 1956, http://home.koranteng.com/writings/gold-coast-independence.html#footnote.

16. Kofi Abrefa Busia, "The Prospects for Democracy in Africa" (paper, Eighteenth Christmas Holiday Lectures and Discussion for Tomorrow's Citizens, London, January 4, 1961), http://home.koranteng.com/writings/prospects-democracy-africa-lecture.html.

17. Kofi Abrefa Busia, "Reflections On One-Party Government in Ghana" (talk, Delegates Conference of the Ghana Students' Association of Britain and Ireland, London, February 29, 1964), http://home.koranteng.com/writings/reflections-one-party-rule.html.

18. Kofi Abrefa Busia, "Ghana Will Truly Be Free and Happy" (paper, Ghana Students Association, December 21, 1964), http://home.koranteng.com/writings/ghana-truly-free-happy.html.

19. Samuel Moyn, "Imperialism, Self-Determination, and the Rise of Human Rights," in *The Human Rights Revolution: An International History*, eds. Akira Iriye, Petra Goede, and William I. Hitchcock, (New York: Oxford University Press, 2012).

20. Our Staff Reporter, "Act Violates UN Charter—Railmen," *Ashanti Pioneer*, August 1, 1959.

21. "Richardson Telegraphs Nkrumah," *Ashanti Pioneer*, September 19, 1959.

22. C. L. R. James, *Nkrumah and the Ghana Revolution* (Westport, CT: Lawrence Hill, 1977), 162.

23. Colin Baker, *State of Emergency: Crisis in Central Africa, Nyasaland 1959–1960* (New York: I. B. Tauris, 1997), viii and ix.

24. "Nyasa Crisis Protest," *Ashanti Times*, March 14, 1959.

25. Ghanaian Liberal, "Nyasaland's and Ghana's Political Detainees," *Ashanti Times*, March 14, 1959.

26. Ibid.

27. "Man's Inhumanity," *Ashanti Pioneer*, January 19, 1960.

28. "Ghana Through the World Press," *Nottingham Evening News*, January 14, 1960.

29. Sidi Siraju Ali, "The Group Areas Act of South Africa," *Ghanaian*, July 1960.

30. Katema Yifru et al., "Africa Speaks to the United Nations: A Symposium of Aspirations and Concerns Voiced by Representative Leaders at the UN," *International Organization* 16, no. 2 (Spring 1962): 303–30, doi:10.2307/2705387; "Nkrumah at the United Nations Assembly," September 23, 1960, Osagyefo: Dr. Kwame Nkrumah Infobank, accessed September 25, 2017, http://nkrumahinfobank.org/article.php?id=455&c=51.

31. *The Rebirth of Ghana: The End of Tyranny* (Accra, Ghana: Ghana Ministry of Information on behalf of the National Liberation Council, 1966).

32. Kwame Oduro, "Four Years Ago," *Legon Observer*, 1966.

33. Ibid.

34. "Formal Entrenchment of Human Rights—A Myth?," *Legon Observer*, July 22, 1966.

35. Ibid.

36. Ama Biney, *Political and Social Thought of Kwame Nkrumah* (New York: Palgrave Macmillan, 2011), 2.

37. Yakubu Saaka, "Recurrent Themes in Ghanaian Politics: Kwame Nkrumah's Legacy," *Journal of Black Studies* 24, no. 3 (1994): 263; Michael W. Williams, "Nkrumahism as an Ideological Embodiment of Leftist Thought Within the African World," *Journal of Black Studies* 15, no. 1 (1984): 118–19.

38. Jack Goody, "Consensus and Dissent in Ghana," *Political Science Quarterly,* 83, no. 3 (1968): 337.

39. Christian Agubretu, "Settling on the Truth About Nkrumah," Ghana News Agency, October 2, 2012, http://ghananewsagency.org/features/settling-on-the-truth-about-nkrumah-50010.

40. Kwablah Darquah, "ACC00856," NRC Documents, Balme Library, University of Ghana, (hereafter cited as NRC Documents).

41. Emmanuel Odartey France, "ACC00749," NRC Documents.

42. Ibid.

43. Nicholas Kofi Dompreh, "ACC00659," NRC Documents.

44. Biney, *Political and Social Thought of Kwame Nkrumah*, 4; Kwame Akyeampong, *Educational Expansion and Access in Ghana: A Review of 50 Years of Challenge and Progress*, CREATE Pathways to Access Research, Research Monograph 33 (Brighton: University of Sussex, April 2010) http://www.create-rpc.org/pdf_documents/PTA33.pdf.

Joseph Allen Blankson, "ACC00642," NRC Documents.

45. Ibid.

46. Harcourt Fuller, *Building the Ghanaian Nation-State: Kwame Nkrumah's Symbolic Nationalism* (New York: Palgrave Macmillan, 2014), 151; "Memorandum from the President's Deputy Special Assistant for National Security Affairs (Rostow) to President Kennedy," October 2, 1961, Document 235, in *Africa*, ed. Nina Davis Hownad, vol. 21 of *Foreign Relations of the United States, 1961–1963* (Washington, DC: US Government Printing Office, 1995, https://history.state.gov/historicaldocuments/frus1961-63v21.

47. Chairman of the National Liberation Council Lieutenant General Ankrah to President Johnson, March 24, 1966, Document 261, Johnson Library, National Security File, Special Head of State Correspondence File, Ghana, 3/24/66–10/6/66.

48. U. U. Uche, "Changes in Ghana Law Since the Military Take-Over," *Journal of African Law* 10, no. 2 (1966): 109.

49. Naomi Chazan, "Political Culture and Socialization to Politics: A Ghanaian Case," *Review of Politics* 40, no. 1 (1978): 4.

50. Jean Allman, "Kwame Nkrumah, African Studies, and the Politics of Knowledge Production in the Black Star of Africa," *International Journal of African Historical Studies* 46, no. 2 (2013): 181.

51. Philip Dade Armah, "ACC00308," NRC Documents.

52. Emmanuel Amartey Adjaye, "ACC00001," NRC Documents.

53. Ibid.

54. Samuel Boadi Attafuah Fampang, "ACC00266," NRC Documents.

55. Ibid.

56. Adjaye, "ACC00001," NRC Documents.

57. Former employees of the Nkrumah government could not withdraw funds or remove valuables from banks (Decree No. 7) nor transfer assets, including land, buildings, bonds, stock, motor vehicles, and jewelry (Decree No. 40). Decrees No. 23 and 3 required particular organizations, including the Ghana Farmers Cooperative, the Young Pioneers, the Moslem Council, the National Council of Ghana Women, and the Market Women's Union, to forfeit all their assets to the new regime.

58. William Burnett Harvey, "Post-Nkrumah Ghana: The Legal Profile of a Coup (1966)," Articles by Maurer Faculty, Paper 1187, p. 1104, http://www.repository.law.indiana.edu/facpub /1187?utm_source=www.repository.law.indiana.edu%2Ffacpub%2F1187&utm_medium=PDF &utm_campaign=PDFCoverPages.

59. Adjaye, "ACC00001."

60. Fampang, "ACC00266."

61. Allman, "Kwame Nkrumah," 201.

62. Kwame Nkrumah, "A Letter of Consolation to Dr. Kofi A. Busia: On the Coup in Ghana," *Black Scholar* 3, no. 9 (1972): 23.

63. Victor T. Le Vine, "Autopsy on a Regime: Ghana's Civilian Interregnum 1969–72," *Journal of Modern African Studies* 25, no. 1 (1987): 170.

64. "Borrowing to Repay," *Economic and Political Weekly* 7, no. 4 (1972): 130.

65. Kwame Boafo-Arthur, "Structural Adjustment Programs (SAPS) in Ghana: Interrogating PNDC's Implementation," *West Africa Review* 1, no. 1 (1999).

66. Joseph Broni Amponsah, "ACC00457," NRC Documents.

67. "Victim of 'Apollo-568'—Ex-Graphic Boss," GhanaWeb, July 8, 2004, http://www .ghanaweb.com/GhanaHomePage/NewsArchive/Victim-of-Apollo-568-Ex-Graphic-boss -61301.

68. J. G. Amamoo, *Ghana: 50 Years of Independence* (Accra, Ghana: Jafint Ent., 2007), 159.

69. Ibid.

70. National Reconciliation Commission Report, Executive Summary, vol. 1, chap. 4, p. 48, October 2004.

71. Dora Puplampu, "HVR200282," NRC Documents.

72. Nkrumah, " Letter of Consolation to Dr. Kofi A. Busia," 25.

73. Amamoo, *Ghana: 50 Years of Independence*, 156; Boafo-Arthur, "Structural Adjustment Programs (SAPS) in Ghana"; David Goldsworthy, "Ghana's Second Republic: A Post-Mortem," *African Affairs* 72, no. 286 (January 1973): 8–25, doi:10.2307/720579.

74. Maxwell Owusu, "Economic Nationalism, Pan-Africanism and the Military: Ghana's National Redemption Council," *Africa Today* 22, no. 1 (1975): 31–50; Boafo-Arthur, "Structural Adjustment Programs (SAPS) in Ghana"; J. H. Frimpong-Ansah, *The Vampire State in Africa: The Political Economy of Decline in Ghana* (Trenton, NJ: Africa World Press, 1991), 108.

75. I. K. Acheampong et al., "Notes in Transition: Colonel Acheampong on the First One Hundred Days of the National Redemption Council," *Transition*, no. 41 (1972): 37–49.

76. Owusu, "Economic Nationalism, Pan-Africanism and the Military."

77. Ibid., 39.

78. Emmanuel Kwaku Badasu, "ACC00119," NRC Documents.

79. Ibid.

80. Acheampong et al., "Notes in Transition," 37.

81. Samuel Kwame Adovor, "KS00077," NRC Documents.

82. Ibid.

83. A. Adu Boahen, *The Ghanaian Sphinx: Reflections on the Contemporary History of Ghana, 1972–1987* (Accra, Ghana: Sankofa Educational Publishers, 1989).

84. Emmanuel Hansen and Paul Collins, "The Army, the State, and the 'Rawlings Revolution' in Ghana," *African Affairs* 79, no. 314 (1980): 3.

85. John L. Adedeji, "The Legacy of J. J. Rawlings in Ghanaian Politics, 1979–2000," *African Studies Quarterly* 5, no. 2 (Summer 2001): 1–27.

86. NRC Report, vol. 1, chap. 3, p. 64.

87. NRC Report, vol. 1, chap. 6, p. 167.

88. Seidu Alidu, "Economic and Social Injustices in Ghana's Military Regimes: An Investigation of Price Control Policies," *IOSR Journal of Humanities and Social Sciences* 19, no. 2 (February 2014): 58.

89. Osahene Boakye Gyan, "AFRC Petition Statement by Boakye Djan," October 13, 2003, GhanaWeb, November 18, 2003, http://www.ghanaweb.com/GhanaHomePage/NewsArchive/AFRC-petition-statement-by-Boakye-Djan-46866.

90. Ibid.

91. E. Gyimah-Boadi and Donald Rothchild, "Rawlings, Populism, and the Civil Liberties Tradition in Ghana," *Issue: A Journal of Opinion* 12, no. 3/4 (1982): 64, doi:10.2307/1166719.

92. Ibid.

93. Nicholas Nvidah, "ACC00331," NRC Documents.

94. Donald Rothchild, "The Rawlings Revolution in Ghana: Pragmatism with Populism," *CSIS Africa Notes*, no. 42 (May 2, 1985): 4, https://csis-prod.s3.amazonaws.com/s3fs-public/legacy_files/files/publication/anotes_058501.pdf.

95. Boafo-Arthur, "Structural Adjustment Programs (SAPS) in Ghana."

96. Boahen, *Ghanaian Sphinx*, 51–52.

97. Alidu, "Economic and Social Injustices in Ghana's Miltary Regimes," 57.

98. James Agyapong Addai, "KS00055," NRC Documents.

Chapter 3. *Kalabule* Women

1. "Soldiers Douched Woman with Pepper and Gunpowder," *Ghana Review*, January 17, 2003, http://www.ghanareview.com/int/nrc.html#b3.

2. Jacqueline Acquaye, "ACC00048," NRC Documents, Balme Library, University of Ghana (hereafter cited as NRC Documents).

3. Walter Rodney, *How Europe Underdeveloped Africa* (Washington, D.C: Howard University Press, 1974), 105, 233, 266, http://abahlali.org/files/3295358-walter-rodney.pdf; C. L. R. James, *A History of Pan-African Revolt* (Oakland, CA: PM Press, 2012), 72.

4. Cheryl Johnson, "Grass Roots Organizing: Women in Anticolonial Activity in Southwestern Nigeria," *African Studies Review* 25, no. 2/3 (1982): 139; Claire Robertson, "Economic

Women: Women's Rights and Entrepreneurial Women," in *Ghana in Africa and the World: Essays in Honor of Adu Boahen,* ed. Toyin Falola (Trenton, New Jersey: Africa World Press, Inc., 2003), 611.

5. Gracia Clark, "Gender and Profiteering: Ghana's Market Women as Devoted Mothers and 'Human Vampire Bats,'" in *"Wicked" Women and the Reconfiguration of Gender in Africa,* eds. Dorothy Louise Hodgson and Sheryl McCurdy (Portsmouth, NH: Heinemann, 2001), 295.

6. There are multiple explanations for the origins of this term. According to GhanaWeb ("Ghana Dictionary K," accessed September 27, 2017, http://www.ghanaweb.com/GhanaHome Page/dictionary/dict_k.php):

> This word probably drew its roots from the Hausa sentence, "Kari ka buude", meaning: don't open. This could well have been the commercial jargon as well as the understanding between the "Border Guards" and traders in general at our check points. The trader arrives with his or her well sealed goods. The guard is officially obliged to search the goods for contrabands. The trader knows he or she is carrying contrabands. The trader tells the guard: DON'T OPEN—kari ka buude. Understanding prevails, and the trader rewards the mutual understanding in cash or kind. Both parties are satisfied, but the government loses. Kari ka buude gradually gains wide currency, but is eventually corrupted into "KALABULE." or [the term may also be] derived from Calabar, in Nigeria, supposedly where traders with very tricky trading habits originated.

7. *GhanaNRC04_Manu,* digital video, Records of the International Center for Transitional Justice, Human Rights Archive, David M. Rubenstein Rare Book and Manuscript Library, Duke University. Manu's testimony displays the way the term *kalabule* was used as a weapon against trading women: "My lord, I told them that I wasn't a *kalabule* woman, because before God and man, because of the way I was trading. . . . I try as much as possible to beat down their price."

8. Republic of South Africa, *Debates of the National Assembly,* 1995 cited in Adam Sitze, *The Impossible Machine: A Genealogy of South Africa's Truth and Reconciliation Commission* (Ann Arbor: University of Michigan Press, 2016), 131; Kader Asmal, "Truth, Reconciliation and Justice: The South African Experience in Perspective," *Modern Law Review* 63 no. 1 (2000): 1.

9. Paul Gready, "Novel Truths: Literature and Truth Commissions," *Comparative Literature Studies* 46, no. 1 (2009): 156.

10. Ratna Kapur, "The Tragedy of Victimization Rhetoric: Resurrecting the 'Native' Subject in International/Postcolonial Feminist Legal Politics," *Harvard Human Rights Law Journal* 15, no. 1 (2002): 2; Pamela Scully, "Gender, History and Human Rights," in *Gender and Culture at the Limit of Rights,* ed. Dorothy L. Hodgson (Philadelphia: University of Pennsylvania Press, 2011), 17–18.

11. Saul Friedländer, "History, Memory, and the Historian: Dilemmas and Responsibilities," *New German Critique,* no. 80 (2000): 4, https://doi.org/10.2307/488629.

12. Annette Wieviorka, *The Era of the Witness* (Ithaca, NY: Cornell University Press 2007).

13. Meg McLagan, "Human Rights, Testimony and Transnational Publicity," in *Nongovernmental Politics,* ed. Michel Feher (New York: Zone Books, 2007), 306–7.

14. Tshepo Madlingozi, "On Transitional Justice Entrepreneurs and the Production of Victims," *Journal of Human Rights Practice* 2, no. 2 (July 1, 2010): 212, https://doi.org/10.1093/jhuman/huq005.

15. Margaret McLagan, "Circuits of Suffering," *Political and Legal Anthropology Review* 28, no. 2 (2005): 223.

16. Brigittine M. French, "Comment on Trinch's Risky Subjects: The Limits and Possibilities of Speaking Truth to Power," *Dialectical Anthropology* 34, no. 2 (June 2010): 205–7.

17. Amos Goldberg, "The Victim's Voice and Melodramatic Aesthetics in History," *History & Theory* 48, no. 3 (October 2009): 222.

18. Ibid., 220.

19. Susie Linfield, *The Cruel Radiance: Photography and Political Violence* (Chicago: University of Chicago Press, 2010), 127, 129.

20. Maryse Conde, "Three Female Writers in Modern Africa: Flora Nwapa, Ama Ata Aidoo and Grace Ogot," *Présence Africaine*, no. 82 (1972): 132.

21. Gayatri Chakravorty Spivak, "Can the Subaltern Speak?," in *Colonial Discourse and Post-Colonial Theory: A Reader*, ed. Patrick Williams and Laura Chrisman (Hertfordshire: Harvester Wheatsheaf, 1994), 93.

22. Chandra Talpade Mohanty, "Under Western Eyes: Feminist Scholarship and Colonial Discourses," *Feminist Review*, no. 30 (1988): 66, https://doi.org/10.2307/1395054.

23. Salome C. Nnoromele, "Representing the African Woman: Subjectivity and Self in The Joys of Motherhood," *Critique: Studies in Contemporary Fiction* 43, no. 2 (January 1, 2002): 180, https://doi.org/10.1080/00111610209602179.

24. Admittedly, this chapter's use of such terms as "international community" and "human rights organizations" is inexact and generalizing. Both of these terms are imprecise shorthand for heterogeneous and diverse communities, many of which have raised and noted similar problems about the persistence and refitting of colonial tropes and frameworks in contemporary debates about international law, global activism, and human rights. However, the problems with representation that plague human rights media, law, and practice are profound and transcend the progress of a few individuals or organizations. For further reading, see "Saving Amina Lawal: Human Rights Symbolism and the Dangers of Colonialism," *Harvard Law Review* 117, no. 7 (2004): 2368, doi:10.2307/4093341; Makau Mutua, *Human Rights: A Political and Cultural Critique* (Philadelphia: University of Pennsylvania, 2002), 10–31. Jean Bricmont, *Humanitarian Imperialism: Using Human Rights to Sell War* (New York: Monthly Review Press, 2006).

25. Kapur, "Tragedy of Victimization Rhetoric," 6.

26. "Saving Amina Lawal," *Harvard Law Review*; Rogaia Abusharaf, "Revisiting Feminist Discourses on Infibulation," in *Female "Circumcision" in Africa: Culture, Controversy and Change*, eds. Bettina Shell-Duncan and Ylva Hernlund (Boulder, CO: Lynne Rienner Publishers, 2000), 158.

27. Nnoromele, "Representing the African Woman," 178.

28. The phrase "single story" is a reference to Chimamanda Ngozi Adichie's TED talk, "The Danger of a Single Story," filmed October 7, 2009 at TEDGlobal 2009, https://www.ted.com/talks/chimamanda_adichie_the_danger_of_a_single_story

29. William Branigin and Douglas Farah, "Asylum Seeker is Impostor, INS Says," *Washington Post*, December 20, 2000.

30. "We Are Not Savages—Chief Nana Kwa Bonko V," GhanaWeb, January 19, 2003, http://www.ghanaweb.com/GhanaHomePage/NewsArchive/artikel.php?ID=31766.

31. Email communication Mary Francis Diaz, September 12, 1999, Box 44, Washington, DC Office Files Series, Records of the Women's Commission for Refugee Women and Children, Human rights Archive, David M. Rubenstein Rare Book and Manuscript Library, Duke University.

32. Arthur Kleinman and Joan Kleinman, "The Appeal of Experience; The Dismay of Images: Cultural Appropriations of Suffering in Our Times," *Daedalus* 125, no. 1 (1996): 10.

33. Maivân Clech Lâm, "Feeling Foreign in Feminism," *Signs* 19, no. 4 (1994): 866.

34. Kimberly Theidon, "Histories of Innocence: Postwar Stories in Peru," in *Beyond the Toolkit: Rethinking the Paradigm of Transitional Justice*, eds. Rosalind Shaw, Lars Waldorf, and Pierre Hazan (Palo Alto, CA: Stanford University Press, 2010); Silvia Rodriguez Maeso, "The Politics of Testimony and Recognition in the Guatemalan and Peruvian Truth Commissions: The Figure of the Subversive Indian," *Revista Critica de Ciencias Sociais*, no. 3 (2011).

35. Clark, "Gender and Profiteering," 290.

36. Ibid., 295.

37. C. L. R. James, *Nkrumah and the Ghana Revolution* (Westport, CT: Lawrence Hill, 1978).

38. Robertson, "Economic Women."

39. "Four Sold Bread above Control Price Fined," *Ghanaian Times*, January 5, 1966. Rowena M. Lawson, "The Distributive System in Ghana: A Review Article," *Journal of Development Studies* 3, no. 2 (January 1967): 198.

40. M. N. Tetteh, *Anatomy of Rumour Mongering in Ghana: Factors Contributory to the Overthrow of Dr. Kwame Nkrumah* (Accra, Ghana: Ghana Publicity, 1976), 36.

41. Ibid., 37.

42. Luise White, *Speaking with Vampires: Rumor and History in Colonial Africa* (Berkeley: University of California Press, 2000).

43. William Burnett Harvey, "Post-Nkrumah Ghana: The Legal Profile of a Coup," Articles by Maurer Faculty, Paper 1187 (1966), http://www.repository.law.indiana.edu/facpub/1187 ?utm_source=www.repository.law.indiana.edu%2Ffacpub%2F1187&utm_medium=PDF&utm _campaign=PDFCoverPages.

44. Reginal Herbold Green, "The Triple Challenge Before Ghana," *New African*, May 1966, 93. http://disa.ukzn.ac.za/sites/default/files/pdf_files/nav5n4.may66_11.pdf.

45. Ibid.

46. Gracia Clark, "Price Control of Local Foodstuffs in Kumasi, Ghana, 1979.," in *Traders Versus the State: Anthropological Approaches to Unofficial Economies*, ed. Gracia Clark, (Boulder: Westview Press, 1988).

47. Clark, "Gender and Profiteering," 259.

48. Claire Robertson, "The Death of Makola and Other Tragedies," *Canadian Journal of African Studies / Revue Canadienne des Études Africaines* 17, no. 3 (1983): 469–95.

49. Clark, "Gender and Profiteering."

50. Robertson, "Economic Women."

51. Robertson, "Death of Makola."

52. "Commissioners Descend Heavily on Witness," *Ghana Review*, February 14, 2003, http://www.ghanareview.com/int/nrc.html#b4.

53. Gracia Clark, *African Market Women: Seven Life Stories from Ghana* (Bloomington: Indiana University Press, 2010); Clark, "Gender and Profiteering."

54. John Campbell, "Ideology and Politics in the Markets of Ghana," *Canadian Journal of African Studies / Revue Canadienne des Études Africaines* 19, no. 2 (1985): 423.

55. "Market Women Condemn Rawlings for Naked Flogging Justification," VibeGhana, October 24, 2011, http://vibeghana.com/2011/10/24/market-women-condemn-rawlings-for -naked-flogging-justification.

56. Kate Abban, "ACC00469," NRC Documents.

57. Alfred Marteye, "Now, I Am like a Beggar—Madam Kaitoo," *Ghana Review*, March 4, 2003, http://www.ghanareview.com/int/nrc2.html#a.

58. Ibid.

59. "Commissioners Descend Heavily on Witness," *Ghana Review*, February 14, 2003.

60. Ibid.

61. Acquaye,"ACC00048," NRC Documents.

62. Victoria Lankai Ainadjei, "ACC00919," NRC Documents.

63. Gifty Adom, "KS00224," NRC Documents.

64. *GhanaNRC04_Adom*, digital video, Records of the International Center for Transitional Justice, David M. Rubenstein Rare Book and Manuscript Library, Duke University.

65. Adom, "KS00224."

66. *GhanaNRC04_Adom*, digital video.

67. Catharene Cojoe, "ACC01376," NRC Documents.

68. NRC Report, vol. 1, chap. 8, p. 182.

69. Clark, "Price Control," 62.

70. Ofusuah Komeng, "ACC00287," NRC Documents.

71. Augustina Araba Quansah, "ACC00320," NRC Documents.

Chapter 4. Family Histories of Political Violence

1. Judith Butler, "Violence, Mourning, Politics," *Studies in Gender and Sexuality* 4, no. 1 (2003): 23.

2. Melissa W. Wright, "Epistemological Ignorances and Fighting for the Disappeared: Lessons from Mexico," *Antipode* 49 (2017): 254.

3. Veena Das, "The Act of Witnessing: Violence, Poisonous Knowledge, and Subjectivity," in *Violence and Subjectivity*, eds. Veena Das, Arthur Kleinman, Mamphela Ramphele, and Pamela Reynolds (Berkeley: University of California Press, 2000), 208; Arthur Kleinman, Veena Das, and Margaret Lock, introduction to the issue "Social Suffering," *Daedalus* 125, no. 1 (1996): xi.

4. Butler, "Violence, Mourning, Politics," 10.

5. Ibid., 12.

6. Adam Branch, *Displacing Human Rights: War and Intervention in Northern Uganda* (Oxford: Oxford University Press, 2011), 23.

7. Rowan Cruft, "Human Rights, Individualism, and Cultural Diversity," *Critical Review of International Social and Political Philosophy* 8, no. 3 (2005); Terrence E. Paupp, *Redefining Human Rights in the Struggle for Peace and Development* (Cambridge University Press, 2014), 1.

8. Paul Tiyambe Zeleza, "The Struggle for Human Rights in Africa," *Canadian Journal of African Studies / Revue Canadienne Des Études Africaines* 41, no. 3 (2007): 486.

9. A. Bolaji Akinyemi, "The African Charter on Human and People's Rights: An Overview," *Indian Journal of Political Science* 46, no. 2 (April 1, 1985): 207–38; African Charter on Human and People's Rights, preamble, http://www.achpr.org/instruments/achpr/.

10. Gina Bekker, "The African Court on Human and Peoples' Rights: Safeguarding the Interests of African States," *Journal of African Law* 51, no. 1 (2007): 152.

11. Abdullahi A. An-Na'im, "Human Rights in the Arab World: A Regional Perspective," *Human Rights Quarterly* 23, no. 3 (2001): 702–3; Makau Mutua, "Human Rights in Africa: The Limited Promise of Liberalism," *African Studies Review* 51, no. 1 (2008): 18–19, 24; Nicola Perugini and Neve Gordon, *The Human Right to Dominate*, Oxford Studies in Culture and Politics

(Oxford: Oxford University Press, 2015); Nicola Perugini and Neve Gordon, "Is There a Human Right to Kill?," *Nation*, July 2, 2015, https://www.thenation.com/article/is-there-a-human-right -to-kill/.

12. David Luban, "The War on Terrorism and the End of Human Rights," *Philosophy and Public Policy Quarterly* 22 (2002): 13–14; Perugini and Gordon, "Is There a Human Right to Kill?"

13. William Twining, *Human Rights, Southern Voices: Francis Deng, Abdullahi An-Na'im, Yash Ghai and Upendra Baxi* (Cambridge University Press, 2009), 184.

14. The National Reconciliation Commission Act, 2002, Section 3, http://www.ghanareview .com/reconact.html.

15. National Reconciliation Commission Report, Executive Summary, vol. 1, chap. 2, p. 10, October 2004.

16. Kwesi Yankah, "Narrative in Times of Crisis: AIDS Stories in Ghana," *Journal of Folklore Research* 41, no. 2/3 (December 2004): 182.

17. Veena Das, *Life and Words: Violence and the Descent into the Ordinary* (Berkeley: University of California Press, 2007).

18. Nthabiseng Motsemme, "The Mute Always Speak: On Women's Silences at the Truth and Reconciliation Commission," *Current Sociology* 52, no. 5 (2004): 909–32.

19. Fiona C. Ross, "An Acknowledged Failure: Women, Voice, Violence and the South African Truth and Reconciliation Commission," in *Localizing Transitional Justice*, eds. Rosalind Shaw, Lars Waldorf, and Pierre Hazan (Stanford, CA: Stanford University Press, 2010).

20. Antjie Krog, Nosisi Mpolweni, and Kopano Ratele, *There Was This Goat: Investigating the Truth Commission Testimony of Notrose Nobomvu Konile*, 1st edition (Scottsville, South Africa: University Of KwaZulu-Natal Press, 2009).

21. The statistics provided in the NRC Final Report were based on approximately 70 percent of the total petitions.

22. James William Owu, "ACC00271," NRC Documents, Balme Library, University of Ghana (hereafter cited as NRC Documents).

23. George Kojo Addai, "ACC00558," NRC Documents.

24. Sammy Nasser, "ACC00012," NRC Documents.

25. Ibid.

26. Ibid.

27. Ghana. National Assembly, *Parliamentary Debates: National Assembly Official Report*, vol. 6 (Accra: Government Printing Department, 1957), 1674; "Government to Safeguard African Retailers," *Ashanti Pioneer*, July 5, 1957.

28. Emmanuel Akyeampong, "Race, Identity and Citizenship in Black Africa: The Case of the Lebanese in Ghana," *Africa: Journal of the International African Institute* 76, no. 3 (2006): 297–323; Andrew Arsan, *Interlopers of Empire: The Lebanese Diaspora in Colonial French West Africa* (London: Hurst, 2014); Lina Beydoun, "Obstacles to Work Opportunities and Community Organizing Among Lebanese Women in Sierra Leone," *International Journal of Business and Social Science* 3, no. 5 (2012): 250–60.

29. Nasser, "ACC00012."

30. Mulki Al-Sharmani, "Living Transnationally: Somali Diasporic Women in Cairo," *International Migration* 44, no. 1 (March 1, 2006): 58, https://doi.org/10.1111/j.1468-2435.2006 .00355.x.

31. Pamela Reynolds, *The Ground of All Making: State Violence, the Family, and Political Activists* (Berkeley: University of California Press, 2000), 151.

32. NRC Report, Executive Summary, vol. 1, chap. 3, p. 25.

33. Dennis Austin, "The Uncertain Frontier: Ghana-Togo," *Journal of Modern African Studies* 1, no. 2 (June 1963): 139, 142; Dennis Austin, *Politics in Ghana: 1946–1960* (London: Oxford University Press, 1964), 372.

34. David Brown, "Borderline Politics in Ghana: The National Liberation Movement of Western Togoland," *Journal of Modern African Studies* 18, no. 4 (1980): 575.

35. Robert Kwame Antor, "HVR200043," NRC Documents.

36. Hayford Akumiah, "HVR200170," NRC Documents.

37. Edmund Nukro, "HVR200164," NRC Documents.

38. Daniel Agusa, "HVR200135," NRC Documents.

39. Agusa, "HVR200135," NRC Documents.

40. Japhet Akpakpla, "HVR200140," NRC Documents.

41. Nukro, "HVR200164."

42. Akumiah, "HVR200170."

43. Christian Blukoo, "ACC00514," NRC Documents.

44. Ibid.

45. John Bomo Ackah, "ACC00129," NRC Documents.

46. Mary Anthonia Kumeni, "HVR200049" NRC Documents.

47. Samuel Dwira, "ACC00038," NRC Documents.

48. Kwadwo Owusu-Sekyere, "KS00063," NRC Documents.

49. Ibid.

50. Francis M. Anane, "ACC00017," NRC Documents.

51. Anthony Nicholas Bartz-Minlah, "ACC00210," NRC Documents.

52. Frederick Awwa Affoh, "ACC01256," NRC Documents.

53. Ibid.

54. Grace Tetteh, "ACC00244," NRC Documents.

55. Ibid.

56. Arthur Kleinman and Joan Kleinman, "The Appeal of Experience; The Dismay of Images: Cultural Appropriations of Suffering in Our Times," *Daedalus* 125, no. 1 (1996): 15.

57. Margaret Nimo, "KS00023," NRC Documents.

58. Ibid.

Chapter 5. The Suffering of Being Developed

1. I use the term "Ada" to refer to the indigenous Dangme-speaking community associated with salt harvesting on the Songor Lagoon. This community, however, has been historically known by many names. By most reports, their oldest name is Okor. Important sources on the history of the Ada include Nancy Lawler and Ivor Wilks, "Correspondence of Jacob Dosoo Amenyah of Ada Part Two: 1956–1965," *Transactions of the Historical Society of Ghana*, no. 11 (2008): 1–88; Secretaries Committee of Ada Songor Cooperation, "Who Killed Maggie? The Story of the Songor Lagoon" (Cadier en Keer: Ada Songor Cooperation, 1989), https://opendocs .ids.ac.uk/opendocs/handle/123456789/1200.

2. Jonathan Langdon, Kofi Larweh, and Wilna Quarmyne, "'E Yeo Ngo' (Does S/He Eat Salt?): Learning in Movement from a 5 Year PAR Study of the Ada Songor Advocacy Forum, a Social Movement in Ghana" in *Proceedings of the 33rd Annual Conference of the Canadian Association for the Study of Adult Education (CASAE)*, ed. Donovan Plumb (Ottawa: Canadian

Association for the Study of Adult Education [CASAE], 2014), 167–70, http://journals.msvu.ca/ocs/index.php/casae2014/CASAE14/paper/viewFile/149/4.

3. NRC Report, Executive Summary, vol. 1, chap. 2, p. 10.

4. Claude Ake, *Democracy and Development* (Washington, DC: Brookings Institution, 1996), 7.

5. Katherine M. Weist, "Development Refugees: Indians, Africans, and the Big Dams" (Elisabeth Colson Lecture, Refugee Studies Center, Department of International Development, University of Oxford, March 9, 1994); T. Scudder, "Development-Induced Relocation and Refugee Studies: 37 Years of Change and Continuity Among Zambia's Gwembe Tonga," *Journal of Refugee Studies* 6, no. 2 (January 1, 1993): 123, doi:10.1093/jrs/6.2.123.

6. Paul D. Ocheje, "In the Public Interest: Forced Evictions, Land Rights, and Human Development in Africa," *Journal of African Law* 51, no. 2 (2007): 180–81.

7. George Ebenezer Nartey, "ACC00901," NRC Documents, Balme Library, University of Ghana (hereafter cited as NRC Documents).

8. Ibid.

9. Stephan F. Miescher and Dzodzi Tsikata, "Hydro-Power and the Promise of Modernity and Development in Ghana: Comparing the Akosombo and Bui Dam Projects," *Ghana Studies Journal* 12/13 (2010 2009): 16.

10. Ibid., 19.

11. Chris de Wet, "Economic Development and Population Displacement: Can Everybody Win?," *Economic and Political Weekly* 36, no. 50 (December 15, 2001): 4637.

12. Quoted in D. Paul Lumsden, "The Volta River Project: Village Resettlement and Attempted Rural Animation," *Canadian Journal of African Studies / Revue Canadienne des Études Africaines* 7, no. 1 (January 1, 1973), doi:10.2307/483753, 117.

13. Lumsden, "Volta River Project," 119.

14. As early as 1951, the Convention People's Party, of which Kwame Nkrumah was the founder, made the Volta River Project part of its manifesto. In a speech before Ghana's National Assembly in 1961, Nkrumah made the case that the hydroelectric project was necessary for Ghana's development: "Newer nations, such as ours, which are determined by every possible means to catch up in industrial strength, must have electricity in abundance before they can expect any large-scale industrial advance. That basically is the justification for the Volta River Project" (quoted in Lumsden, "Volta River Project," 117).

15. Dennis Laumann, "Che Guevara's Visit to Ghana," *Transactions of the Historical Society of Ghana*, no. 9 (2005): 70, 71.

16. Volta River Development Act, Forty-Sixth Act of the Parliament of the Republic of Ghana, sec. 29 (1), 1961, http://faolex.fao.org/docs/pdf/gha41043.pdf.

17. "Nkrumah Speech to National Assembly," August 24, 1965, Ref. no. S-2680-005-13, United Nations Archives.

18. In the twenty-first century, a new colloquialism, "dumsor," has been created for Ghana's power-sharing situation. "Dumsor" is an amalgamation of the Twi words for "on" and "off"; Jacob Roberts-Mensah, "'Dealing with Dumsor' Is a Photo Essay About the Ghanaian Approach to Power Cuts," OkayAfrica, June 29, 2016, http://www.okayafrica.com/photos/dealing-with-dumsor-photo-essay-ghana-millennials/.

19. NRC Report, vol. 2, October 2004, 126.

20. "Icelanders Protest Karahnjukar Hydropower Project, 2000–2006," Global Nonviolent Action Database, http://nvdatabase.swarthmore.edu/content/icelanders-protest-karahnjukar-hydropower-project-2000-2006.

21. Nava Thakuria, "Tribals Protest Against Tipaimukh Project Near Burma Border," *Mizzima News,* October 30, 2003, http://www.burmatoday.net/mizzima2003/mizzima/2003/10/031030_border_mizzima.htm.

22. De Wet, "Economic Development and Population Displacement," 4637.

23. Frederick Cooper and Randall Packard, "Introduction," in *International Development and the Social Sciences: Essays on the History and Politics of Knowledge,* eds. Frederick Cooper and Randall Packard (Berkeley: University of California Press, 1997), 3.

24. William Easterly, *The Tyranny of Experts: Economists, Dictators and the Forgotten Rights of the Poor* (New York: Basic Books, 2013).

25. Balakrishnan Rajagopal, "The Violence of Development," *Washington Post,* August 9, 2001, https://www.washingtonpost.com/archive/opinions/2001/08/09/the-violence-of-development/1b169574-3992-44ec-bff9-a1e42857f192/?utm_term=.9d8abd83a98a; Balakrishnan Rajagopal, "International Law and the Development Encounter: Violence and Resistance at the Margins," in *On Violence, Money, Power, and Culture: Reviewing the Internationalist Legacy,* 16–27. Proceedings of the 93rd Annual Meeting of the American Society of International Law (Washington: ASIL, 1999).

26. Easterly, *Tyranny of Experts,* 33.

27. "Nkrumah Speech to National Assembly," August 24, 1965.

28. E. A. K. Kalitsi, "Organisation and Economics of Resettlement," in *Volta River Symposium Papers,* 1965.

29. Lumsden, "Volta River Project," 119.

30. Easterly, *Tyranny of Experts,* 37.

31. L. Raschid-Sally et al., "The Resettlement Experience of Ghana Analyzed via Case Studies of the Akosombo and Kpong Dams" (paper, Exploring Experiences of Resettlement, 9th Annual Symposium on Poverty Research in Sri Lanka, November 2008). This critical review states that "little was known of the people living in the basin, and some were so hidden that they had never paid tax or been counted in census. As a result, the Volta compensation and resettlement operations had to begin by looking for the people and finding out more about them" (9). Similarly, Lumsden notes that "the planners in Accra and Kumasi lacked much information about the actual situation and social structures in the area to be flooded." "Volta River Project," 119.

32. Robert Chambers, "Introduction," *The Volta Resettlement Experience,* ed. Robert Chambers (London: Pall Mall Press, 1970), 23.

33. Ibid., 22.

34. Lumsden, "Volta River Project," 120.

35. Ibid.

36. "NRC Ends Sitting in Ho," GhanaWeb, January 30, 2004, http://www.ghanaweb.com/GhanaHomePage/regional/artikel.php?ID=50929.

37. Enoch Mate, "ACC01408," NRC Documents.

38. Chambers, "Introduction," 21.

39. Ibid., 229.

40. Ibid., 30.

41. Ibid., 230.

42. Letitia Obeng, "Should Dams Be Built? The Volta Lake Example," *Ambio* 6, no. 1 (1977): 46–50.

43. Ocheje, "In the Public Interest," 195.

44. Chambers, "Introduction, 28"; Kalitsi, "Organisation and Economics of Resettlement."

45. E. A. K. Kalitsi, "Organization of Resettlement," in Chambers, *Volta Resettlement Experience*.

46. G. W. Amarteifio, "Social Welfare," in Chambers, *Volta Resettlement Experience* (New York: Praeger Publishers, 1970), 106.

47. Ibid., 111.

48. D. A. P. Butcher, "The Social Survey," in Chambers, *Volta Resettlement Experience*, 79.

49. Ibid.

50. Kalitsi, "Organization of Resettlement," 35.

51. Ibid., 39.

52. Butcher, "Social Survey," 83.

53. Ibid., 85.

54. Amarteifio, "Social Welfare," 115.

55. Ibid., 82.

56. Butcher, "Social Survey," 90.

57. Mate, "ACC01408."

58. Ibid.

59. Nartey, "ACC00901."

60. "NRC Ends Sitting in Ho," GhanaWeb.

61. Kalitsi, "Organization of Resettlement," 55.

62. C. O. C. Amate, *The Making of Ada* (Accra, Ghana: Woeli Publishing Services, 1999), 90.

63. Blane Harvey and Jonathan Langdon, "Re-imagining Capacity and Collective Change: Experiences from Senegal and Ghana," *IDS Bulletin* 41, no. 3 (May 2010): 81; Amate, *Making of Ada*, 87.

64. Takyiwaa Manuh, "Survival in Rural Africa: The Salt Cooperatives in Ada District, Ghana," in *Development from Within: Survival in Rural Africa,* eds. D. R. Fraser-Taylor and Fiona Mackenzie (New York: Routledge, 1992), 112; Jonathan Langdon, "Social Movement Learning in Ghana: Communal Defense of Resources in Neoliberal Time," in *Critical Perspectives in Neoliberal Globalization, Development and Education in Africa and Asia,* ed. Dip Kapoor (Rotterdam: Sense Publishers, 2011), 153–70.

65. Darko Kwabena Opoku, *The Politics of Government-Business Relations in Ghana, 1982–2008* (New York: Palgrave Macmillan, 2010), 94.

66. Secretaries Committee of Ada Songor Cooperation, "Who Killed Maggie?," 26.

67. Harvey and Langdon, "Re-Imagining Capacity and Collective Change: Experiences from Senegal and Ghana," 81.

68. "Who Killed Maggie?," 6.

69. Ibid.

70. Ibid., 35.

71. Ibid., 52.

72. Langdon, "Social Movement Learning in Ghana," 161.

73. Ibid., 153, 159.

74. Benjamin Apronti-Ofotsu, "HVR200288," NRC Documents.

75. Opoku, *Politics of Government-Business Relations*, 40.

76. Secretaries Committee of Ada Songor Cooperation, "Who Killed Maggie?"

77. Ibid., 70.

78. Amakwor Anim, "HVR200300," NRC Documents.

79. Awoyo Puplampu, "HVR200281," NRC Documents.

80. Mamle Mansa Sebi, "HVR200301," NRC Documents.

81. "Woman Says Appenteng Forced Her to Chew Salt," GhanaWeb, January 29, 2004.

82. Moses Ayornu, "HVR200303," NRC Documents.

83. Soti Abdulai, "HVR200293," NRC Documents.

84. Jonathan Langdon, Kofi Larweh, and Sheena Cameron, "The Thumbless Hand, the Dog and the Chameleon: Enriching Social Movement Learning Theory Through Epistemically Grounded Narratives Emerging from a Participatory Action Research Case Study in Ghana," *Interface: A Journal for and about Social Movements* 6, no. 1 (May 2014): 29.

85. Apronti-Ofotsu, "HVR200288."

86. Puplampu, "HVR200281."

87. Daniel Akli, "HVR200284," NRC Documents.

88. Ibid.

89. Tetteh Puplampu, "HVR200290," NRC Documents.

90. Teye Bosumprah, "HVR200296," NRC Documents.

91. "Witness Maintain Stand Against Appentengs," GhanaWeb, June 16, 2004, http://www.ghanaweb.com/GhanaHomePage/NewsArchive/Witness-maintain-stand-against-Appentengs-59874.

92. Rita Abrahamsen, "Discourses of Democracy, Practices of Autocracy: Shifting Meanings of Democracy in the Aid-Authoritarianism Nexus," in *Aid and Authoritarianism in Africa: Development Without Democracy*, eds. Tobias Hagmann and Filip Reyntjens (London: Zed Books, 2016), 25.

93. NRC Report, vol. 2, chap. 5, p. 126.

94. NRC Report, vol. 2, chap. 5, p. 127.

95. Apronti- Ofotsu, "HVR200288."

96. "Witness Maintain Stand Against Appentengs," GhanaWeb.

Chapter 6. Soldier, Victim, Hero, Survivor

1. Priscilla B. Hayner, *Unspeakable Truths: Transitional Justice and the Challenge of Truth Commissions* (New York: Routledge, 2001), 28; Michael Humphrey, "From Victim to Victimhood: Truth Commissions and Trials as Rituals of Political Transition and Individual Healing," *Australian Journal of Anthropology* 14, no. 2 (2003): 173.

2. Holly L. Guthrey, *Victim Healing and Truth Commission—Transforming Pain Through Voice in Solomon Islands and Timor-Leste*, vol. 11 of Springer Series in Transitional Justice (Cham, Switzerland: Springer, 2015), 4, 132.

3. "Public Tribunals and the NRC—Rejoinder from NRC," GhanaWeb, November 26, 2003, http://www.ghanaweb.com/GhanaHomePage/features/artikel.php?ID=47333.

4. "NRC Is Biased," *Graphic*, June 30, 2003, https://www.modernghana.com/news/36648/nrc-is-biased-cpp.html; "Public Tribunals and the NRC," GhanaWeb; "Ghana: Tsatsu Drags NRC Chairman to Court," *Ghanaian Chronicle*, July 2, 2004, http://allafrica.com/stories/200407020647.html.

5. Kimberly Theidon, "Histories of Innocence: Postwar Stories in Peru," in *Beyond the Toolkit: Rethinking the Paradigm of Transitional Justice*, eds. Rosalind Shaw, Lars Waldorf, and Pierre Hazan (Palo Alto, CA: Stanford University Press, 2010), 100.

6. Nneoma V. Nwogu, "When and Why It Started: Deconstructing Victim-Centered Truth Commissions in the Context of Ethnicity-Based Conflict," *International Journal of Transitional Justice* 4 (2010): 281.

7. Mahmood Mamdani, "The Logic of Nuremberg," *London Review of Books*, November 7, 2013, 33, 34.

8. Ofeibea Quist-Arcton, "Ghana's Kufuor Defends His Government's Record on Transparency, the Economy," AllAfrica, May 25, 2002, http://allafrica.com/stories/200205240737.html?page=3.

9. Adrienne M. Israel, "Ex-servicemen at the Crossroads: Protest and Politics in Post-War Ghana," *Journal of Modern African Studies* 30, no. 2 (June 1992): 359, 362.

10. Eugene P. Schleh, "Post-Service Careers of World War Two Veterans: The Cases of Gold Coast and Uganda" (paper, *Annual Meeting of the African Studies Association*, New York, November 1967), 3: 7.

11. Julius Nyerere, "Protecting the Gains of Freedom," reprinted in *Joburg Post Online*, April 7, 2017, https://www.joburgpost.co.za/2017/04/07/julius-nyerere-protecting-the-gains-of-freedom/.

12. Ali A. Mazrui, "The Lumpen Proletariat and the Lumpen Militariat: African Soldiers as a New Political Class," *Political Studies* 21, no. 1 (March 1, 1973): 1, https://doi.org/10.1111/j.1467-9248.1973.tb01413.x.

13. Maria Eriksson Baaz and Maria Stern, "Making Sense of Violence: Voices of Soldiers in the Congo (DRC)," *Journal of Modern African Studies* 46, no. 1 (2008): 58, 59; Michael Chege, "The Military in the Transition to Democracy in Africa: Some Preliminary Observations," *CODESRIA Bulletin* 3 (1995):13–16.

14. David Okyere, "KS00160," NRC Documents, Balme Library, University of Ghana. (hereafter NRC Documents).

15. James Owusu-Ansah, "KS00403," NRC Documents.

16. Samuel Boadi Attafuah Fampang, "ACC00266," NRC Documents.

17. Alhaji Osei Kwame Mohammed, "ACC00008," NRC Documents.

18. Martin Kwesi Budu-Kwatiah, "ACC01273," NRC Documents.

19. Leigh A. Payne, *Unsettling Accounts: Neither Truth nor Reconciliation in Confessions of State Violence* (Durham, NC: Duke University Press, 2008), 2.

20. Kofi Appiah, "Microscopic View of the Ghana Police (Part 1)," January 4, 2012, https://www.modernghana.com/news/370220/microscopic-view-of-the-ghana-polic-part-1.html

21. Ghana News Agency, "Ex-soldier Names Nanfuri, Bebli and Others as Torturers, Modern Ghana, February 4, 2003, http://www.modernghana.com/news/30818/1/ex-soldier-names-nanfuri-bebli-and-others-as-tortu.html.

22. "Baako Says 31 December Coup Betrayed 4 June," *Ghana Review*, March 12, 2003, http://www.ghanareview.com/int/nrc2.html#a; George Agyekum, *The Treason Trial of 1986: Torture and Revolutionary Justice* (Cantonments Accra, Ghana: Justice Trust Publications, 2001).

23. "Where are They Now" *GhanaWeb,* December 26, 2012, https://www.ghanaweb.com/GhanaHomePage/NewsArchive/Where-Are-They-Now-260511.

24. Nwogu, "When and Why It Started," 279.

25. "Jack Bebli Denies Shooting Witness' Legs," *Ghana Review*, February 26, 2003, http://www.ghanareview.com/int/nrc.html#b3.

26. Payne, *Unsettling Accounts*, 3.

27. "Bebli Denies Torturing Goka, Others," *Ghana Review*, March 12, 2003, http://www.ghanareview.com/int/nrc2.html#a.

28. Michael Boafo-Ntifo, "ACC00004," NRC Documents.

29. Paul King Asimeng, "ACC00039," NRC Documents.

30. Kofi Akwandoh Akorful, "ACC00104," NRC Documents.

31. Benjamin Anim, "ACC01351," NRC Documents.

32. Christian Kofi Ahadzi, "ACC00231," NRC Documents.

33. Foreward by Lt. General Emmanuel Erskine in S. K. Ofosu-Appiah, *Allegiance Versus Indiscipline: A Ghanaian Soldier's Story* (U.S.A.: Xlibris Corporation, 2010).

34. Nwogu, "When and Why It Started," 286.

35. *Ghana NRC08_Munufie*, digital video, International Center for Transitional Justice records, Human Rights Archive, David M. Rubenstein Rare Book and Manuscript Library, Duke University (hereafter ICTJ Records).

36. Lila Abu-Lughod, "The Romance of Resistance: Tracing Transformations of Power Through Bedouin Women," *American Ethnologist* 17, no. 1 (1990): 41.

37. Thomas Carlyle, *On Heroes, Hero-Worship and the Heroic in History*, Lecture 1, (London: James Fraser, 1841), https://www.gutenberg.org/files/1091/1091-h/1091-h.htm#link2H_4_0007.

38. Ali A. Mazrui, "On Heroes and Uhuru-Worship," *Transition* 11 (1963): 25.

39. Wale Adebanwi, "Death, National Memory, and the Construction of Heroism," *Journal of African History* 49 (2008): 440.

40. NRC Report, Executive Summary, vol. 1, chap. 8, p. 182.

41. NRC Report, vol. 1, chap. 4, p. 87.

42. Ibid., p. 87.

43. Ibid.

44. Stephan F. Miescher, *Making Men in Ghana* (Bloomington: Indiana University Press, 2005), 153.

45. Jean Allman, "The Disappearing of Hanna Kudjoe: Nationalism, Feminism, and the Tyrannies of History," *Journal of Women's History* 21, no. 3 (2009): 13–35; Harcourt Fuller, "Commemorating an African Queen: Ghanaian Nationalism, the African Diaspora, and the Public Memory of Nana Yaa Asantewaa 1952–2009," *African Arts* 47, no. 4 (Winter 2014): 58–71.

46. Yaa Animah, "ACC00007," NRC Documents.

47. Victoria Lankai Ainadjei, "ACC00919," NRC Documents.

48. David A. Crocker, "Truth Commissions, Transitional Justice, and Civil Society," in *Truth v. Justice : The Morality of Truth Commissions*, eds. Robert I. Rotberg and Dennis Thompson (Princeton, NJ: Princeton University Press, 2000), 4.

49. *Ghana NRC08_Munufie*, digital video, ICTJ Records.

50. *Ghana NRC08_Munufie*, digital video, ICTJ Records.

51. William Dusu, "HVR200167," NRC Documents.

52. Susana Korletey, "ACC00194," NRC Documents.

53. Vincent Brown, "Social Death and Political Life in the Study of Slavery," *American Historical Review* (December 2009): 1231–49. Veena Das, "Violence, Gender, and Subjectivity," *Annual Review of Anthropology* 37: 293–99; Michael Humphrey, "From Terror to Trauma: Commissioning Truth for National Reconciliation," *Social Identities: Journal for the Study of Race, Nation, and Culture* 6, no. 1 (2000): 7–27

54. Basil Gbere Yaabere, "ACC00296," September 17, 2007, NRC Documents, African Studies Library, University of Ghana Balme Library.

55. Nana Boakye Agyeman, "TML00069," NRC Documents.

56. Harrison Tetteh Adimeh, "ACC00067," NRC Documents.

57. "I will repeat what led to my detention for eight years," *Ghana Review*, March 24, 2003. http://www.ghanareview.com/int/nrc2.html#d

58. Gifty Adom, "KS00224," NRC Documents.

Chapter 7. Time for Suffering / Time for Justice

1. "Be Compassionate to Witnesses—Bishop," *Ghana Review*, March 14, 2003, http://www
.ghanareview.com/int/nrc2.html#a.

2. "Where we perceive a chain of events, he sees one single catastrophe which keeps piling
wreckage and hurls it in front of his feet. The angel would like to stay, awaken the dead, and
make whole what has been smashed. But a storm is blowing in from Paradise; it has got caught
in his wings with such a violence that the angel can no longer close them. The storm irresistibly
propels him into the future to which his back is turned, while the pile of debris before him
grows skyward. This storm is what we call progress." Walter Benjamin, *Illuminations,* ed. Hannah Arendt, translated by Harry Zohn (New York: Schocken) 1969: 257–58.

3. John Torpey, *Politics and the Past: On Repairing Historical Injustices*, World Social Change
(New York: Rowman and Littlefield Publishers, 2003), 1.

4. Pieter Lagrou, "Europe as a Place for Common Memories? Some Thoughts on Victimhood, Identity and Emancipation from the Past," in *Clashes in European Memory: The Case
of Communist Repression and the Holocaust* eds. Muriel Blaive, Christian Gerbel, and Thomas
Lindenberger (Innsbruck: Studien Verlag, 2011), 283.

5. Berber Bevernage, "The Past Is Evil/Evil Is Past: On Retrospective Politics, Philosophy of History, and Temporal Manichaeism," *History & Theory* 54, no. 3 (October 2015): 351,
doi:10.1111/hith.10763.

6. "NRC to Help Nation Regain Lost Soul—Kufuor," *Ghana News Agency*, April 17, 2003,
https://www.ghanaweb.com/GhanaHomePage/NewsArchive/NRC-To-Help-Nation-Regain
-Lost-Soul-Kufuor-35417?channel=D1

7. "Kofi Annan: It's Time to Look Beyond Our Colonial Past," *New African,* November
29, 2012, http://newafricanmagazine.com/kofi-annan-its-time-to-look-beyond-our-colonial
-past/.

8. Ibid.

9. Alex Spillius, "Barack Obama Tells Africa to Stop Blaming Colonialism for Problems,"
Telegraph, July 9, 2009, http://www.telegraph.co.uk/news/worldnews/africaandindianocean
/5778804/Barack-Obama-tells-Africa-to-stop-blaming-colonialism-for-problems.html;
Michael Scherer, "Barack Obama's Speech to Africa," *Time Magazine*, July 11, 2009, http://
swampland.time.com/2009/07/11/barack-obamas-speech-to-africa/.

10. George Ayittey, "The Colonialism-Imperialism Paradigm Is Kaput (1 of 2)," June 26,
2005, Emergent Africa, http://africaunchained.blogspot.com/2005/06/colonialism-imperialism
-paradigm-is_26.html.

11. Jephias Mapuva and Freeman Chari, "Colonialism No Longer an Excuse for Africa's
Failure," *Journal of Sustainable Development in Africa* 12, no. 5 (2010): 5.

12. Ama Biney, *Political and Social Thought of Kwame Nkrumah* (New York: Palgrave Macmillan, 2011), 7.

13. Vivian Tibboh, "ACC00791," NRC Documents, Balme Library, University of Ghana
(hereafter cited as NRC Documents).

14. Samuel Agyei-Mensah and Ama de-Graft Aikins, "Epidemiological Transition and the
Double Burden of Disease in Accra, Ghana," *Journal of Urban Health* 87, no. 5 (September 2010):
884, doi:10.1007/s11524-010-9492-y; Ryan Johnson, "'An All-White Institution': Defending Private Practice and the Formation of the West African Medical Staff," *Medical History* 54, no. 2
(April 2010): 245.

15. Richard Werbner, *Memory and the Postcolony: African Anthropology and the Critique of Power* (London: Zed Books, 1998), 1; Jonathan Roberts, "Remembering Korle Bu Hospital: Biomedical Heritage and Colonial Nostalgia in the *Golden Jubilee Souvenir*," *History in Africa* 38 (January 1, 2011): 201.

16. Tibboh, "ACC00791," NRC Documents.

17. William Cunningham Bissell, "Engaging Colonial Nostalgia," *Cultural Anthropology* 20, no. 2 (May 1, 2005): 218.

18. Ana Dragojlovic, Marieke Bloembergen, and Hen Schulte Nordholt, "Colonial Recollections: Memories, Objects, Performances," *Journal of the Humanities and Social Sciences of Southeast Asia and Oceania* 170, no. 4 (2014): 439.

19. Tibboh, "ACC00791," NRC Documents.

20. Hon. Kosi Kedem, "ACC01170," NRC Documents.

21. Ibid.

22. NRC Final Report, vol. 1, chap. 3, p. 23.

23. Victoria Mansa Madjoub, "ACC00161," NRC Documents.

24. Ibid.

25. Mohammad Hafiz, "*Takfir* as a Tool for Instigating Jihad Among Muslims: The Ghanaian Example," in *Political Islam from Muhammad to Ahmadinejad: Defenders, Detractors, and Definitions*, ed. Joseph Morrison Skelly (Praeger Security International, 2010), 147–60.

26. Abubakar Imoro Shishi, "TML00134," NRC Documents.

27. Thomas Oppong Asare, "ACC01321," NRC Documents.

28. Anome Klidza, "HVR200354," NRC Documents.

Conclusion. The Brief Afterlife of Ghana's Truth Commission

Note to second epigraph: Gillian Whitlock, "In the Second Person: Narrative Transactions in Stolen Generations Testimony," *Biography* 24, no. 1 (February 1, 2001): 197, doi:10.1353/bio.2001.0026.

1. Jean Comaroff and John L. Comaroff, *Theory from the South* (New York: Routledge, 2012), 138.

2. Annalisa Oboe, "The TRC Women's Hearings as Performance and Protest in the New South Africa," *Research in African Literatures* 38, no. 3 (2007): 66; Antjie Krog, *Country of My Skull: Guilt, Sorrow, and the Limits of Forgiveness in the New South Africa* (repr., New York: Broadway Books, 2000), 66.

3. Christian Kofi Ahadzi, "ACC00231," NRC Documents, African Studies Library, Balme Library, University of Ghana (hereafter NRC Document).

4. *GhanaNRC04_Adom*, digital video, Records of the International Center for Transitional Justice, David M. Rubenstein Rare Book and Manuscript Library, Duke University.

5. Ibid.

6. Rodney G. S. Carter, "Of Things Said and Unsaid: Power, Archival Silences, and Power in Silence," *Archivaria* 61 (September 25, 2006): 217. http://archivaria.ca/index.php/archivaria/article/view/12541.

7. Lucie E. White and Jeremy Perelman, *Stones of Hope: How African Activists Reclaim Human Rights to Challenge Global Poverty* (Palo Alto, CA: Stanford University Press, 2011), xiii.

8. José-Manuel Barretto, "Decolonial Strategies and Dialogue in the Human Rights Field," in *Human Rights from a Third World Perspective*, ed. José-Manuel Barretto (Newcastle: Cambridge Scholars Publishing, 2013), 4.

9. Mahmood Mamdani, "The Politics of Naming: Genocide, Civil War, Insurgency," *London Review of Books* 25, no. 5 (March 8, 2007).

10. Lila Abu-Lughod, *Do Muslim Women Need Saving?* (Cambridge, MA: Harvard University Press, 2013), 25.

11. Cassandra Hermann, "An African's Message for America," *New York Times*, January 5, 2015, http://www.nytimes.com/2015/01/06/opinion/an-africans-message-for-america.html?smid=fb-share.

12. Whitlock's discussion ("In the Second Person," 206) of the Stolen Generation testimonies as a discursive event with particular consequences on those who listened in the "second person," the nonindigenous Australian audience, also highlights the importance of disaggregating the multiple audiences of human rights testimony).

13. Ivana Radačić, "Human Rights of Women and the Public/Private Divide in International Human Rights Law," *Croatian Yearbook of European Law and Policy* 3, no. 3 (March 18, 2008): 443.

14. Paul Tiyambe Zeleza, "The Struggle for Human Rights in Africa," *Canadian Journal of African Studies / Revue Canadienne des Études Africaines* 41, no. 3 (2007): 486.

15. Mary Robinson, "Advancing Economic, Social, and Cultural Rights: The Way Forward," *Human Rights Quarterly* 26, no. 4 (November 5, 2004): 866, doi:10.1353/hrq.2004.0054; Amnesty International, "Economic, Social and Cultural Rights: Questions and Answers," accessed October 2, 2017, http://www.amnestyusa.org/pdfs/escr_qa.pdf.

16. Frans Viljoen, *International Human Rights Law in Africa* (Oxford: Oxford University Press, 2012), 284.

17. Denis Goulet, "Development Experts: The One-Eyed Giants," *World Development* 8, no. 7 (July 1, 1980): 481, doi:10.1016/0305-750X(80)90033-9; Adam Branch, *Displacing Human Rights: War and Intervention in Northern Uganda* (Oxford: Oxford University Press, 2011), 29.

18. Balakrishnan Rajagopal, "International Law and the Development Encounter: Violence and Resistance at the Margins," in *On Violence, Money, Power, and Culture: Reviewing the Internationalist Legacy*, Proceedings of the 93rd Annual Meeting of the American Society of International Law (Washington, DC: ASIL, 1999), 780.

19. Ibid., 768.

20. Eric A. Posner, *Twilight of Human Rights Law* (Oxford: Oxford University Press, 2014), 7.

21. Ibid., 7.

22. Antjie Krog, Nosisi Mpolweni, and Kopano Ratele, *There Was This Goat: Investigating the Truth Commission Testimony of Notrose Nobomvu Konile* (Scottsville, South Africa: University of KwaZulu-Natal Press, 2009).

23. Ibid., 198, 213, 214.

24. Adam Sitze, *The Impossible Machine: A Genealogy of South Africa's Truth and Reconciliation Commission* (Ann Arbor: University of Michigan Press, 2016), 251.

25. Catherine C. Byrne, "Benefit or Burden: Victims' Reflections on TRC Participation," *Peace and Conflict: Journal of Peace Psychology* 10, no. 3 (2004): 237–56; Carlos Martín-Beristain et al., "Psychosocial Effects of Participation in Rituals of Transitional Justice: A Collective-Level Analysis and Review of the Literature of the Effects of TRCs and Trials on Human Rights Violations in Latin America," *Revista de Psicología Social* 25, no. 1 (January 1, 2010): 47–60, doi:10.1174/021347410790193450.

26. Aaron Weah, "Hopes and Uncertainties: Liberia's Journey to End Impunity," *International Journal of Transitional Justice* 6, no. 2 (July 1, 2012): 332, doi:10.1093/ijtj/ijs007.

27. Holly Guthrey, *Victim Healing and Truth Commissions: Transforming Pain through Voice in Solomon Islands and Timor-Leste*, vol. 11 of Springer Series in Transitional Justice (Cham, Switzerland: Springer, 2015), 6.

28. Tricia D. Olsen et al., "When Truth Commissions Improve Human Rights," *International Journal of Transitional Justice* 4 (2010): 463. The database's evaluation of human rights practice is based on Amnesty International and US State Department reports.

29. Ibid., 462.

30. Eric Brahm, "What Is a Truth Commission and Why does It Matter?" *Peace and Conflict Review* 3, no. 2 (Spring 2009): 138–42.

31. Onur Bakiner, "Truth Commission Impact: An Assessment of How Commissions Influence Politics and Society," *International Journal of Transitional Justice* 8, no. 1 (March 1, 2014): 13, doi:10.1093/ijtj/ijt025.

32. Rosalind Shaw and Lars Waldorf, eds., *Localizing Transitional Justice: Intervention and Priorities After Mass Violence*, Stanford Studies in Human Rights (Palo Alto, CA: Stanford University Press, 2010), 3; Moses Chrispus Okello et al., *Where Law Meets Reality: Forging African Transitional Justice* (Nairobi: Pambazuka Press, 2012), xix.

33. Felix Odartey-Wellington and Amin Alhassan, "Disseminating the National Reconciliation Report: A Critical Step in Ghana's Democratic Consolidation," *African Journal of Political Science and International Relations* 10, no. 4 (April 2016): 34.

34. Jo Ellen Fair and Audrey Gadzekpo, "Reconciling a Nation: Ghanaian Journalist and the Reporting of Human Rights," in *Communication, Culture and Human Rights in Africa*, vol. 1 of Communication, Society, and Change (Lanham, MD: University Press of America, 2011), 62.

35. "White Paper on the NRC" (Government of Ghana, April 2005), 2009-0193 International Center for Transitional Justice records, Human Rights Archive, David M. Rubenstein Rare Book and Manuscript Library.

36. Ibid.

37. Odartey-Wellington and Alhassan, "Disseminating the National Reconciliation Report."

38. Sitze, *Impossible Machine*, 132.

39. Ibid., 139.

40. Ibid., 142.

41. Ibid., 141.

42. Ibid., 142.

43. Ibid., 143.

44. Piers Pigou, "Accessing the Records of the Truth and Reconciliation Commission," in *Paper Wars: Access to Information in South Africa*, ed. Kate Allan (Johannesburg: Witswatersrand University Press, 2009), 18.

45. Michael Neocosmos, *Thinking Freedom in Africa: Toward a Theory of Emancipatory Politics* (Johannesburg: Wits University Press, 2017), 4.

46. Ibid., 10.

47. Alice Walker, *In Search of Our Mothers' Gardens* (New York: Mariner: 2003).

BIBLIOGRAPHY

Abolishing School Fees in Africa: Lessons from Ethiopia, Ghana, Kenya, Malawi, and Mozambique. Washington, DC: World Bank and UNICEF, 2009. https://www.unicef.org/publications /files/Aboloshing_School_Fees_in_Africa.pdf.

Abrahamsen, Rita. "Discourses of Democracy, Practices of Autocracy: Shifting Meanings of Democracy in the Aid-Authoritarianism Nexus." In *Aid and Authoritarianism in Africa: Development Without Democracy*, edited by Tobias Hagmann and Filip Reyntjens, 21–43. London: Zed Books, 2016.

Abu-Lughod, Lila. *Do Muslim Women Need Saving?* Cambridge, MA: Harvard University Press, 2013.

———. "The Romance of Resistance: Tracing Transformations of Power Through Bedouin Women." *American Ethnologist* 17, no. 1 (1990): 41–55.

Abukari, Ziblim, Ahmed Bawa Kuyini, and Abdulai Kuyini Mohammed. "Education and Health Care Policies in Ghana: Examining the Prospects and Challenges of Recent Provisions." *SAGE Open* 5, no. 4 (December 23, 2015). doi:10.1177/2158244015611454.

Abusharaf, Rogaia. "Revisiting Feminist Discourses on Infibulation." In *Female "Circumcision" in Africa: Culture, Controversy and Change*, edited by Bettina Shell-Duncan and Ylva Hernlund, 151–66. Boulder, CO: Lynne Rienner Publishers, 2000.

Acheampong, I. K., Issac Osei, Kofi Awoonor, and John Goldblatt. "Notes in Transition: Colonel Acheampong on the First One Hundred Days of the National Redemption Council." *Transition*, no. 41 (1972): 37–49.

Achebe, Chinua. "Africa Is People." In *The Education of the British-Protected Child: Essays*, 155–66. New York: Alfred A. Knopf, 2009.

Adamafio, Tawia. *By Nkrumah's Side: The Labour and the Wounds*. Accra, Ghana: Westcoast Publishing House, 1982.

Adebanwi, Wale. "Death, National Memory, and the Construction of Heroism." *Journal of African History* 49 (2008): 419–44.

Adedeji, John L. "The Legacy of J. J. Rawlings in Ghanaian Politics, 1979–2000." *African Studies Quarterly* 5, no. 2 (Summer 2001): 1–27.

Adjaye, Joseph K. "Perspectives on Fifty Years of Ghanaian Historiography." *History in Africa* 35 (2008): 1–24.

Adu, Kwame Kesse. "Liberty?" *Ashanti Pioneer*, September 26, 1959.

Agawu, Kofi. "The Amu Legacy: Ephraim Amu 1899–1995." *Africa: Journal of the International African Institute* 66, no. 2 (1996): 274–79.

Agubretu, Christian. "Settling on the Truth About Nkrumah." Ghana News Agency, October 2, 2012. http://ghananewsagency.org/features/settling-on-the-truth-about-nkrumah-50010.

Agüero, Felipe. "Dictatorship and Human Rights: The Politics of Memory." *Radical History Review* 2007, no. 97 (December 21, 2007): 123–33. doi:10.1215/01636545-2006-018.

Agyei-Mensah, Samuel, and Ama de-Graft Aikins. "Epidemiological Transition and the Double Burden of Disease in Accra, Ghana." *Journal of Urban Health* 87, no. 5 (September 2010): 879–97. doi:10.1007/s11524-010-9492-y.

Agyekum, George. *The Treason Trial of 1986: Torture and Revolutionary Justice.* Cantonments Accra, Ghana: Justice Trust Publications, 2001.

Ahlman, Jeffrey S. "Road to Ghana: Nkrumah, Southern Africa and the Eclipse of a Decolonizing Africa." *Kronos*, no. 37 (2011): 23–40.

Akashah, Mey, and Stephen P. Marks. "Accountability for the Health Consequences of Human Rights Violations: Methodological Issues in Determining Compensation." *Health and Human Rights* 9, no. 2 (2006): 256–79.

Ake, Claude. *Democracy and Development.* Washington, DC: Brookings Institution, 1996.

Akinyemi, A. Bolaji. "The African Charter on Human and Peoples' Rights: An Overview." *Indian Journal of Political Science* 46, no. 2 (April 1, 1985): 207–38.

Akokpari, John, and Daniel Shea Zimbler, eds. *Africa's Human Rights Architecture.* Aukland Park, South Africa: Fanele, 2008.

Akyeampong, Emmanuel. "Sexuality and Prostitution Among the Akan of the Gold Coast c. 1650–1950." *Past and Present*, no. 156 (August 1997): 144–73.

———. "What's in a Drink? Class Struggle, Popular Culture and the Politics of Akpeteshie (Local Gin) in Ghana, 1930–67." *Journal of African History* 37, no. 2 (1996): 215–36.

Akyeampong, Emmanuel. "Race, Identity and Citizenship in Black Africa: The Case of the Lebanese in Ghana." *Africa: Journal of the International African Institute* 76, no. 3 (2006): 297–323.

Akyeampong, Emmanuel, and Ama de-Graft Aikins. "Ghana at Fifty: Reflections on Independence and After." *Transition* no. 98 (2008): 24–34.

Aldana, Raquel. "A Victim-Centered Reflection on Truth Commissions and Prosecution as a Response to Mass Atrocities." *Journal of Human Rights* 5, no. 1 (2006): 107–26.

Ali, Sidi Siraju. "The Group Areas Act of South Africa," *Ghanaian*, July 1960.

Alidu, Seidu. "Economic and Social Injustices in Ghana's Miltary Regimes: An Investigation of Price Control Policies." *IOSR Journal of Humanities and Social Sciences* 19, no. 2 (February 2014): 57–65.

Allah-Mensah, Beatrix. *Women in Politics and Public Life in Ghana.* Accra, Ghana: Friedrich Ebert Foundation, 2005. http://library.fes.de/pdf-files/bueros/ghana/02989.pdf.

Allais, Lucy. "Restorative Justice, Retributive Justice, and the South African Truth and Reconciliation Commission." *Philosophy & Public Affairs* 39, no. 4 (September 1, 2011): 331–63. doi:10.1111/j.1088-4963.2012.01211.x.

Allen, Amy. "Power and the Politics of Difference: Oppression, Empowerment, and Transnational Justice." *Hypatia* 23, no. 3 (2008): 156–72.

Allman, Jean. "The Disappearing of Hanna Kudjoe : Nationalism, Feminism, and the Tyrannies of History." *Journal of Women's History* 21, no. 3 (2009): 13–35.

———. "Kwame Nkrumah, African Studies, and the Politics of Knowledge Production in the Black Star of Africa." *International Journal of African Historical Studies* 46, no. 2 (2013): 181–203.

———. "Rounding up Spinsters: Gender Chaos and Unmarried Women in Colonial Asante." *Journal of African History* 37, no. 2 (1996): 195–214.

Al-Sharmani, Mulki. "Living Transnationally: Somali Diasporic Women in Cairo." *International Migration* 44, no. 1 (March 1, 2006): 55–77. doi:10.1111/j.1468-2435.2006.00355.x.

Aluko, Olajide. "After Nkrumah: Continuity and Change in Ghana's Foreign Policy." *Issue: A Journal of Opinion* 5, no. 1 (1975): 55–62. doi:10.2307/1166794.

Amamoo, J. G. *Ghana: 50 Years of Independence.* Accra, Ghana: Jafint Ent., 2007.

Amarteifio, G. W. "Social Welfare." In *The Volta Resettlement Experience*, edited by Robert Chambers, 103–47. New York: Praeger Publishers, 1970.

Amate, C. O. C. *The Making of Ada.* Accra, Ghana: Woeli Publishing Services, 1999.

Ameh, Robert Kwame. "Uncovering Truth: Ghana's National Reconciliation Commission Excavation of Past Human Rights Abuses." *Contemporary Justice Review* 9, no. 4 (2006): 345–68.

Ampofo, Akosua Adomako. "Controlling and Punishing Women: Violence against Ghanaian Women." *Review of African Political Economy*, no. 56 (March 1993): 102–11.

An-Na'im, Abdullahi A. "Human Rights in the Arab World: A Regional Perspective." *Human Rights Quarterly* 23, no. 3 (2001): 701–32.

Anane, M.T. Agyeman. "Letters-Drivers Strike." *Ashanti Pioneer*, July 26, 1957.

Andoh, A. S. Y. "Epitaph to Nkrumah's Regime: The Lessons of the Past 15 Years." *Legon Observer*, July 22, 1966, Vol. 1, 2nd ed.

Ansa-Asare, K. "Legislative History of the Legal Regime of Price Control in Ghana." *Journal of African Law* 29, no. 2 (October 1, 1985): 103–17.

Appiah, Joseph. *Joe Appiah: The Autobiography of an African Patriot.* New York: Praeger Publishers, 1990.

Apter, David E. "Nkrumah, Charisma, and the Coup." *Daedalus* 97, no. 3 (Summer 1968): 757–92.

Apusigah, A. Atia. "Promoting Citizen-Government Engagement for Good Governance in Ghana: The Place of Rights-Based Approaches." *European Journal of Social Sciences* 11, no. 4 (2009): 551–64.

Arsan, Andrew. *Interlopers of Empire: The Lebanese Diaspora in Colonial French West Africa.* London: Hurst, 2014.

Asante, Clement E. *The Press in Ghana: Problems and Prospects.* Lanham, MD: University Press of America, 1996.

Asmal, Kader. "Truth, Reconciliation and Justice: The South African Experience in Perspective," *Modern Law Review* 63 no. 1 (2000): 1–24.

Asthana, Roli. "Involuntary Resettlement: Survey of International Experience." *Economic and Political Weekly* 31, no. 24 (June 15, 1996): 1468–75.

Atibil, Christiana. "Democratic Governance and Actors' Conceptualization of 'Civil Society' in Africa: State-Civil Society Relations in Ghana from 1982–2000." *Voluntas: International Journal of Voluntary and Nonprofit Organizations* 23, no. 1 (2012): 43–62.

Attafuah, Kenneth Agyemang. "An Overview of Ghana's National Reconciliation Commission and Its Relationship with the Courts." *Criminal Law Forum* 15, no. 1/2 (March 2004): 125–34.

Austin, Dennis. "Elections in an African Rural Area." *Africa: Journal of the International African Institute* 31, no. 1 (January 1, 1961): 1–18. doi:10.2307/1157816.

———. "The Uncertain Frontier: Ghana-Togo." *Journal of Modern African Studies* 1, no. 2 (June 1963):139–45.

———. *Politics in Ghana: 1946–1960.* London: Oxford University Press, 1964.

Auyero, Javier. "Protest in Contemporary Argentina: A Contentious Repertoire in the Making." In *Out of the Shadows: Political Action and the Informal Economy in Latin America*. University Park: Pennsylvania State University Press, 2006.

Awuah, Emmanuel. "Mobilizing for Change: A Case Study of Market Trader Activism in Ghana." *Canadian Journal of African Studies / Revue Canadienne des Études Africaines* 31, no. 3 (1997): 401–23. doi:10.2307/486193.

Ayee, Joseph. "The 2000 Elections and the Presidential Run-Off in Ghana: An Overview." *Democratization* 9, no. 2 (2002): 148–74.

Ayelazuno, Jasper Abembia. "Neoliberalism and Growth without Development in Ghana: A Case for State-Led Industrialization." *Journal of Asian and African Studies* 49, no. 1 (February 1, 2014): 80–99. doi:10.1177/0021909613478787.

Ayittey, George. "The Colonialism-Imperialism Paradigm Is Kaput (1 of 2)." Emergent Africa. June 26, 2005. http://africaunchained.blogspot.com/2005/06/colonialism-imperialism -paradigm-is_26.html.

Azarya, Victor, and Naomi Chazan. "Disengagement from the State in Africa: Reflections on the Experience of Ghana and Guinea." *Comparative Studies in Society and History* 29, no. 1 (January 1, 1987): 106–31.

Baaz, Maria Eriksson, and Maria Stern. "Making Sense of Violence: Voices of Soldiers in the Congo (DRC)." *Journal of Modern African Studies* 46, no. 1 (2008): 57–86.

Baines, Gary. "The Master Narrative of South Africa's Liberation Struggle: Remembering and Forgetting June 16, 1976." *International Journal of African Historical Studies* 40, no. 2 (2007): 283–302.

Baker, Colin. *State of Emergency: Crisis in Central Africa, Nyasaland 1959–1960*. New York: I. B. Tauris, 1997.

Bakiner, Onur. "One Truth Among Others? Truth Commissions' Struggle for Truth and Memory." *Memory Studies* 8, no. 3 (July 1, 2015): 345–60. doi:10.1177/1750698014568245.

———. "Truth Commission Impact: An Assessment of How Commissions Influence Politics and Society." *International Journal of Transitional Justice* 8, no. 1 (March 1, 2014): 6–30. doi:10.1093/ijtj/ijt025.

Balfour, Lawrie. "Reparations after Identity Politics." *Political Theory* 33, no. 6 (2005): 786–811.

Barkan, Elazar. "Engaging History: Managing Conflict and Reconciliation." *History Workshop Journal*, no. 59 (2005): 229–36.

———. "Historians and Historical Reconciliation." *American Historical Review* 114, no. 4 (October 2009): 899–913.

Barretto, José-Manuel. "Decolonial Strategies and Dialogue in the Human Rights Field." In *Human Rights from a Third World Perspective*, edited by José-Manuel Barretto, 1–43. Newcastle: Cambridge Scholars Publishing, 2013.

Bawa, Sylvia, and Francis Sanyare. "Women's Participation and Representation in Politics: Perspectives from Ghana." *International Journal of Public Administration* 36, no. 4 (March 1, 2013): 282–91. doi:10.1080/01900692.2012.757620.

Baxi, Upendra. "From Human Rights to the Right to Be Human: Some Heresies." *India International Centre Quarterly* 13, no. 3/4 (1986): 185–200.

———. *Human Rights in a Post-Human World: Critical Essays*. New Delhi: Oxford University Press, 2007.

Baynham, Simon. "Quis Custodiet Ipsos Custodes?: The Case of Nkrumah's National Security Service." *Journal of Modern African Studies* 23, no. 1 (March 1, 1985): 87–103.

Beard, Charles A. "Written History as an Act of Faith." *American Historical Review* 39, no. 2 (1934): 219–31. doi:10.2307/1838720.

Bekker, Gina. "The African Court on Human and Peoples' Rights: Safeguarding the Interests of African States." *Journal of African Law* 51, no. 1 (2007): 151–72.

Bennis, Mohamed Ahmed. "The Equity and Reconciliation Committee and the Transition Process in Morocco." Arab Reform Brief. Arab Reform Initiative. September 2006. http://www.arab-reform.net/en/node/347.

Bermanzohn, Sally Avery. "A Massacre Survivor Reflects on the Greensboro Truth and Reconciliation Commission." *Radical History Review* 2007, no. 97 (December 21, 2007): 102–9. doi:10.1215/01636545-2006-015.

Berry, Sara. "Tomatoes, Land, and Hearsay: Property and History in Asante in the Time of Structural Adjustment." *World Development* 25, no. 8 (1997): 1225–41.

Bevernage, Berber. *History, Memory and State-Sponsored Violence: Time and Justice.* New York: Routledge, 2012.

———. "The Past Is Evil/Evil Is Past: On Retrospective Politics, Philosophy of History, and Temporal Manichaeism." *History & Theory* 54, no. 3 (October 2015): 333–52. doi:10.1111/hith.10763.

Beydoun, Lina. "Obstacles to Work Opportunities and Community Organizing Among Lebanese Women in Sierra Leone." *International Journal of Business and Social Science* 3, no. 5 (2012): 250–60.

Bhargava, Rajeev. "Restoring Decency to Barbaric Societies." In *Truth v. Justice: The Morality of Truth Commissions,* edited by Robert I. Rotberg and Dennis Thompson, 45–67. Princeton, NJ: Princeton University Press, 2000.

Bickford, Louis. "The Archival Imperative: Human Rights and Historical Memory in Latin America's Southern Cone." *Human Rights Quarterly* 21, no. 4 (1999): 1097–1122.

Biney, Ama. *Political and Social Thought of Kwame Nkrumah.* New York: Palgrave Macmillan, 2011.

Bing, Geoffrey. *Reap the Whirlwind: An Account of Kwame Nkrumah's Ghana from 1950 to 1966.* London: MacGibbon and Kee, 1968.

Bissell, William Cunningham. "Engaging Colonial Nostalgia." *Cultural Anthropology* 20, no. 2 (May 1, 2005): 215–48.

Boafo-Arthur, Kwame. "Structural Adjustment Programs (SAPS) in Ghana: Interrogating PNDC's Implementation." *Journal of African Policy Studies* 4, no. 2–3 (1998): 1–24.

Boahen, A. Adu. *The Ghanaian Sphinx: Reflections on the Contemporary History of Ghana, 1972–1987.* Accra, Ghana: Sankofa Educational Publishers, 1989.

Boakye, Kofi E. "Attitudes Toward Rape and Victims of Rape: A Test of the Feminist Theory in Ghana." *Journal of Interpersonal Violence* 24, no. 10 (October 2009): 1633–51.

Boni, Stefano. "Twentieth-Century Transformations in Notions of Gender, Parenthood, and Marriage in Southern Ghana: A Critique of the Hypothesis of Retrogade Steps for Akan Women." *History in Africa* 28 (2001): 15–41.

Borer, Tristan Anne. "A Taxonomy of Victims and Perpetrators: Human Rights and Reconciliation in South Africa." *Human Rights Quarterly* 25, no. 4 (November 2003): 1088–116.

Bosire, Lydiah. "Overpromised, Underdelivered: Transitional Justice in Sub-Saharan Africa." International Center for Transitional Justice, July 2006. https://www.ictj.org/publication/overpromised-underdelivered-transitional-justice-sub-saharan-africa.

Botchway, Karl. "Are Development Planners Afraid of History and Contextualization? Notes on Reading a Development Report on Northern Ghana." *Canadian Journal of African Studies* 35, no. 1 (2001): 32–66.

Bouris, Erica. *Complex Political Victims*. Bloomfield, CT: Kumarian Press, 2007.

Boyefio, Gilbert. "NRC Secretariat to Request More Funds." *Statesman*, March 9, 2007. http://www.thestatesmanonline.com/pages/news_detail.php?newsid=4624&section=1.

Bradley, Mark Philip, and Patrice Petro. *Truth Claims: Representation and Human Rights*. New Brunswick, NJ: Rutgers University Press, 2002.

Brahm, Eric. "What Is a Truth Commission and Why Does It Matter?" *Peace and Conflict Review* 3, no. 2 (Spring 2009): 1–14.

Branch, Adam. *Displacing Human Rights: War and Intervention in Northern Uganda*. Oxford: Oxford University Press, 2011.

Branch, Adam, and Zachariah Mampilly. *Africa Uprising: Popular Protest and Political Change*. African Arguments. London: Zed Books, 2015.

Bratton, Michael, Peter Lewis, and E. Gyimah-Boadi. "Constituencies for Reform in Ghana." *Journal of Modern African Studies* 39, no. 2 (June 2001): 231–59.

Brenya, E., S. Adu-Gyamfi, I. Afful, B. Darkwa, M. B. Richmond, S. O. Korkor, E. S. Boakye, and G. K. Turkson. "The Rawlings' Factor in Ghana's Politics: An Appraisal of Some Secondary and Primary Data." *Journal of Political Sciences & Public Affairs* 1, no. 4 (September 2015): 1–14. doi:10.4172/2332-0761.S1.004.

Brouneus, Karen. "Truth-Telling as Talking Cure? Insecurity and Retraumatization in the Rwandan Gacaca Courts." *Security Dialogues* 39, no. 1 (2008): 55–76.

Brown, Alison, Michal Lyons, and Ibrahima Dankoco. "Street Traders and the Emerging Spaces for Urban Voice and Citizenship in African Cities." *Urban Studies* 47, no. 3 (March 2010): 666–83.

Brown, David. "Borderline Politics in Ghana: The National Liberation Movement of Western Togoland." *Journal of Modern African Studies* 18, no. 4 (1980): 575–609.

Brown, Vincent. "Social Death and Political Life in the Study of Slavery." *American Historical Review* (December 2009): 1231–49.

Brown, Wendy. "Morality as Anti-Politics." In *Materializing Democracy: Toward a Revitalized Cultural Politics,* edited by Dana D. Nelson and Russ Castronovo. Durham, NC: Duke University Press, 2002.

Brukum, N. J. K. "Sir Gordon Guggisberg and Socio-Economic Development of Northern Ghana, 1919–1927." *Transactions of the Historical Society of Ghana*, n.s., no. 9 (January 1, 2005): 1–15.

Brydon, Lynne. "Women at Work: Some Changes in Family Structure in Amedzofe-Avatime, Ghana." *Africa: Journal of the International African Institute* 49, no. 2 (1979): 97–111.

Buford Warren and Hugo van der Merwe. "Reparations in Southern Africa." *Cahiers d'études africaines* 44, no. 1–2 (2004): 33–41.

Bundy, Colin. "The Beast of the Past: History and the TRC." In *After the TRC: Reflection on Truth and Reconciliation in South Africa,* edited by Wilmot James and Linda van de Vijver, 9–20. Athens, OH: Ohio University Press, 2001.

Burke, Roland. "'The Compelling Dialogue of Freedom': Human Rights at the Bandung Conference." *Human Rights Quarterly* 28, no. 4 (2006): 947–65.

Bush, Raymond. "What Future for Ghana?" *Review of African Political Economy*, no. 19 (1980): 86–91.

Busia, Kofi Abrefa. "Ghana Will Truly Be Free and Happy." Paper presented at the Ghana Students Association, December 21, 1964. http://home.koranteng.com/writings/ghana-truly
-free-happy.html.

———. "The Prospects for Democracy in Africa." Paper presented at the Eighteenth Christmas
Holiday Lectures and Discussion for Tomorrow's Citizens, London, January 4, 1961. http://
home.koranteng.com/writings/prospects-democracy-africa-lecture.html.

———. "Gold Coast Independence," Memorandum. November 30, 1956. http://home.koranteng
.com/writings/gold-coast-independence.html#footnote.

Butalia, Urvashi. The Other Side of Silence: Voices from the Partition of India. Durham, NC: Duke
University Press, 2000.

Butcher, D. A. P. "The Social Survey." In The Volta Resettlement Experience, edited by Robert
Chambers, 78–102. New York: Praeger Publishers, 1970.

Butler, Judith. "Violence, Mourning, Politics," Studies in Gender and Sexuality 4, no. 1 (2003):
9–37.

Byrne, Catherine C. "Benefit or Burden: Victims' Reflections on TRC Participation." Peace and
Conflict: Journal of Peace Psychology 10, no. 3 (2004): 237–56.

Caldwell, J. C. "The Erosion of the Family: A Study of the Fate of the Family in Ghana." Population Studies 20, no. 1 (July 1966): 5–26.

Campbell, John. "Ideology and Politics in the Markets of Ghana." Canadian Journal of African
Studies / Revue Canadienne des Études Africaines 19, no. 2 (1985): 423–30.

Cantulpo, Nancy Chi, Lisa Vollendorf Martin, Kay Pak, and Sue Shin. "Domestic Violence in
Ghana: The Open Secret." Georgetown Journal of Gender and Law 7 (2006): 531–97.

Carlyle, Thomas. On Heroes, Hero-Worship and the Heroic in History, Lecture 1. London: James
Fraser, 1841.

Carter, Rodney G. S. "Of Things Said and Unsaid: Power, Archival Silences, and Power in
Silence." Archivaria 61 (September 25, 2006). http://archivaria.ca/index.php/archivaria
/article/view/12541.

Castells, Manuel, and Alejandro Portes. "World Underneath: The Origins, Dynamics and Effects
of the Informal Economy." In The Informal Economy: Studies in Advanced and Less Developed Countries, edited by Alejandro Portes, Manuel Castells and Lauren A. Benton, 11–40.
Baltimore, MD: Johns Hopkins University Press, 1989.

Castillejo-Cuéllar, Alejandro. "Knowledge, Experience, and South Africa's Scenarios of Forgiveness." Radical History Review 2007, no. 97 (December 21, 2007): 11–42. doi:10.1215/
01636545-2006-011.

Centeno, Miguel Angel, and Alejandro Portes. "The Informal Economy in the Shadow of the
State." In Out of the Shadows: Political Action and the Informal Economy in Latin America,
edited by Patricia Fernández-Kelly and Jon Shefner, 23–48. University Park: Pennsylvania
State University Press, 2006.

Cervenka, Zdenek. "The Effects of Militarization of Africa on Human Rights." Africa Today 34,
no. 1/2 (1987): 69–84.

Chalfin, Brenda. "Risky Business: Economic Uncertainty, Market Reforms and Female Livelihoods in Northeast Ghana." Development and Change 31, no. 5 (November 1, 2000): 987–
1008. doi:10.1111/1467-7660.00186.

Chambers, Robert. The Volta Resettlement Experience. London: Pall Mall Press, 1970.

Chanock, Martin. Law, Custom, and Social Order: The Colonial Experience in Malawi and Zambia. Cambridge: Cambridge University Press, 1985.

Chazan, Naomi. "Political Culture and Socialization to Politics: A Ghanaian Case." *Review of Politics* 40, no. 1 (1978): 3–31.

Chege, Michael. "The Military in the Transition to Democracy in Africa: Some Preliminary Observations." *CODESRIA Bulletin* 3 (1995): 13–16.

Cherry, Janet. "Truth and Transitional Justice in South Africa." In *Assessing the Impact of Transitional Justice: Challenges for Empirical Research*, edited by Hugo van der Merwe, Victoria Baxter, and Audrey R. Chapman, 249–64. Washington, DC: United States Institute of Peace, 2009.

Chick, John. "Cecil King, the Press, and Politics in West Africa." *Journal of Modern African Studies* 34, no. 3 (September 1996): 375–93. doi:10.2307/161377.

Christian Afaglo Togbui Wiping His Tears at the NRC. Photograph. GhanaWeb News. February 1, 2003. www.ghanaweb.com/GhanaHomePage/NewsArchive/photo.day.php?ID =32228.

Clark, Gracia C. *African Market Women: Seven Life Stories from Ghana*. Bloomington: Indiana University Press, 2010.

———. "Gender and Profiteering: Ghana's Market Women as Devoted Mothers and 'Human Vampire Bats.'" In *"Wicked" Women and the Reconfiguration of Gender in Africa*, edited by Dorothy L. Hodgson and Sheryl A. McCurdy. Social History of Africa. Portsmouth, NH: Heinemann, 2001.

———. "Negotiating Asante Family Survival in Kumasi, Ghana." *Africa: Journal of the International African Institute* 69, no. 1 (1999): 66–86.

———. "Price Control of Local Foodstuffs in Kumasi, Ghana, 1979." In *Traders Versus the State: Anthropological Approaches to Unofficial Economies*, edited by Gracia Clark, 57–79. Boulder: Westview Press, 1988.

Clarke, Kamari Maxine, and Mark Goodale. *Mirrors of Justice: Law and Power in the Post-Cold War Era*. Cambridge, NY: Cambridge University Press, 2009.

Cmiel, Kenneth. "The Recent History of Human Rights." *American Historical Review* 109, no. 1 (February 2004): 117–35.

Coker-Appiah, Dorcas, and Kathy Cusack. *Breaking the Silence and Challenging the Myths of Violence Against Women and Children in Ghana, Report of a National Study on Violence*. Accra, Ghana: Gender Studies and Human Rights Documentation Centre, 1999.

Colvin, Christopher J. "Overview of the Reparations Program in South Africa." In *The Handbook of Reparations*, edited by Pablo De Greiff, 176–214. Oxford: Oxford University Press, 2006.

Comaroff, Jean, and John L. Comaroff. *Civil Society and the Political Imagination in Africa*. Chicago: University of Chicago Press, 1999.

———. *Law and Disorder in the Postcolony*. Chicago: University of Chicago Press, 2006.

———. *Theory from the South*. New York: Routledge, 2012.

Conde, Maryse. "Three Female Writers in Modern Africa: Flora Nwapa, Ama Ata Aidoo and Grace Ogot." *Présence Africaine*, no. 82 (1972): 132–43.

Cooper, Allan D. "From Slavery to Genocide: The Fallacy of Debt in Reparations Discourse." *Journal of Black Studies* 43, no. 2 (March 1, 2012): 107–26.

Cooper, Frederick, and Randall Packard. Introduction to *International Development and the Social Sciences: Essays on the History and Politics of Knowledge*, edited by Frederick Cooper and Randall M. Packard, 1–43. Berkeley: University of California Press, 1997.

Cornwall, Andrea, and Vera Schatten Coelho. *Space for Change? The Politics of Citizen Participation in New Democratic Arenas.* London: Zed Books, 2007.

Crocker, David A. "Truth Commissions, Transitional Justice, and Civil Society." In *Truth V. Justice: The Morality of Truth Commissions,* edited by Robert I. Rotberg and Dennis Thompson, 99–121. Princeton, NJ: Princeton University Press, 2000.

Cruft, Rowan. "Human Rights, Individualism, and Cultural Diversity." *Critical Review of International Social and Political Philosophy* 8, no. 3 (2005): 265–87.

Czyzewski, Karina. "The Truth and Reconciliation Commission of Canada: Insights into the Goal of Transformative Education." *International Indigenous Policy Journal* 2, no. 3 (August 2011): 1–12.

Daniels, W. C. Ekow. "The Impact of the 1992 Constitution on Family Rights in Ghana." *Journal of African Law* 40, no. 2 (1996): 183–93.

Danquah, J. B. "Lights of Freedom Are Going Out: Message to Chiefs and People." *Ashanti Pioneer,* August 1, 1959.

Das, Veena. "The Act of Witnessing: Violence, Poisonous Knowledge, and Subjectivity." In *Violence and Subjectivity,* edited by Veena Das, Arthur Kleinman, Mamphela Ramphele, and Pamela Reynolds, 205–25. Berkeley: University of California Press, 2000.

———. *Life and Words: Violence and the Descent into the Ordinary.* Berkeley: University of California Press, 2007.

———. "Violence, Gender, and Subjectivity." *Annual Review of Anthropology* 37 (2008): 293–99.

David, Roman, and Susanne Choi Yuk-ping. "Victims on Transitional Justice: Lessons from the Reparation of Human Rights Abuses." *Human Rights Quarterly* 27, no. 2 (May 2005): 392–435.

Dean, Carolyn J. "Minimalism and Victim Testimony." *History & Theory* 49, no. 4 (December 2010): 85–99. doi:10.1111/j.1468-2303.2010.00561.x.

De Greiff, Pablo. "Justice and Reparations." In *The Handbook of Reparations,* edited by Pablo De Greiff, 451–77. Oxford: Oxford University Press, 2006

Dei, George J. Sefa. "Social Difference and the Politics of Schooling in Africa: A Ghanaian Case Study." *Compare: A Journal of Comparative and International Education* 35, no. 3 (September 1, 2005): 227–45. doi:10.1080/03057920500212522.

Del Mar, David Peterson. "A Pragmatic Tradition: The Past in Ghanaian Education." *Africa Today* 59, no. 2 (2012): 23–38.

Destombes, Jerome. "From Long-Term Patterns of Seasonal Hunger to Changing Experiences of Everyday Poverty: Northeastern Ghana c. 1930–2000." *Journal of African History* 47 (2006): 181–205.

De Wet, Chris. "Economic Development and Population Displacement: Can Everybody Win?" *Economic and Political Weekly* 36, no. 50 (December 15, 2001): 4637–46.

Dicklitch, Susan, and Doreen Lwanga. "The Politics of Being Non-political: Human Rights Organizations and the Creation of a Positive Human Rights Culture in Uganda." *Human Rights Quarterly* 25, no. 2 (May 2003): 482–509. doi:10.2307/20069673.

Dong-Choon, Kim. "The Long Road Toward Truth and Reconciliation." *Critical Asian Studies* 42, no. 4 (December 2010): 525–52. doi:10.1080/14672715.2010.515387.

Donnelly, Jack. "Cultural Relativism and Universal Human Rights." *Human Rights Quarterly* 6, no. 4 (November 1, 1984): 400–419. doi:10.2307/762182.

Dragojlovic, Ana, Marieke Bloembergen, and Hen Schulte Nordholt. "Colonial Re-collections: Memories, Objects, Performances." *Journal of the Humanities and Social Sciences of Southeast Asia and Oceania* 170, no. 4 (2014): 435–41.

Du Pisani, Jacobus, and Kwang-Su Kim. "Establishing the Truth About the Apartheid Past: Historians and the South African Truth and Reconciliation Commission." *African Studies Quarterly* 8, no. 1 (Fall 2004): 77–95.

Easterly, William. *The Tyranny of Experts: Economists, Dictators and the Forgotten Rights of the Poor*. New York: Basic Books, 2013.

Eckel, Jan. "Human Rights and Decolonization: New Perspectives and Open Questions." Review of *Menschenrechte im Schatten kolonialer Gewalt: Die Dekolonisierungskriege in Kenia und Algerien 1945–1962*, by Fabian Klose, and *Decolonization and the Evolution of International Human Rights*, by Roland Burke. *Humanity Journal*, no. 1 (June 10, 2014). http://humanityjournal.org/issue-1/human-rights-and-decolonization-new-perspectives-and-open-questions/.

Eley, Geoff. "Historicizing the Global, Politicizing Capital: Giving the Present a Name." *History Workshop Journal*, no. 63 (Spring 2007): 154–88.

Elischer, Sebastian. "Do African Parties Contribute to Democracy? Some Findings from Kenya, Ghana and Nigeria." *Africa Spectrum* 43, no. 2 (January 1, 2008): 175–201.

Ellingston, John R. "The Right to Work." *Annals of the American Academy of Political and Social Science* 243 (January 1946): 27–39.

Elliott, Michael A. "Human Rights and the Triumph of the Individual in World Culture." *Cultural Sociology* 1, no. 3 (March 2007): 343–63.

Emerson, Rupert. "The Fate of Human Rights in the Third World." *World Politics* 27, no. 2 (January 1975): 201–26. doi:10.2307/2009881.

Emewu, Ikenna. "Disregard of Oputa Panel Report, Cause of Political Violence." AllAfrica. March 5, 2003. http://allafrica.com/stories/200303050539.html.

Englund, Harri. "The Dead Hand of Human Rights: Contrasting Christianities in Post-Transition Malawi." *Journal of Modern African Studies* 38, no. 4 (2000): 579–603.

———. *Prisoners of Freedom: Human Rights and the African Poor*. Berkeley: University of California Press, 2006.

Erskine, Emmanuel. "Foreword." In *Allegiance Versus Indiscipline: A Ghanaian Soldier's Story*, by S. K. Ofosu-Appiah, 12–20. Bloomington: Xlibris Corporation, 2010.

Eze, Emmanuel C. "Between History and the Gods: Reason, Morality, and Politics in Today's Africa." *Africa Today* 55, no. 2 (2008): 77–94.

Fair, Jo Ellen, and Audrey Gadzekpo. "Reconciling a Nation: Ghanaian Journalist and the Reporting of Human Rights." In *Communication, Culture and Human Rights in Africa*, edited by Bala A. Musa, 51–68. Vol. 1 of Communication, Society, and Change. Lanham, MD: University Press of America, 2011.

Fallon, Kathleen M. *Democracy and the Rise of Women's Movements in Sub-Saharan Africa*. Baltimore: Johns Hopkins University Press, 2008.

———. "Transforming Women's Citizenship Rights Within an Emerging Democratic State: The Case of Ghana." *Gender and Society* 17, no. 4 (August 2003): 525–43.

Farmer, Paul. "On Suffering and Structural Violence: A View from Below." *Daedalus* 125, no. 1 (January 1, 1996): 261–83.

Farred, Grant. "Many Are Guilty, Few Are Indicted; In My Country." *Radical History Review* 2007, no. 97 (December 21, 2007): 155–62. doi:10.1215/01636545-2006-021.

Feldman, Allen. "Violence and Vision: The Prosthetics and Aesthetics of Terror." In *Violence and Subjectivity*, edited by Veena Das, Arthur Kleinman, Mamphela Ramphele, and Pamela Reynolds, 46–78. Berkeley: University of California Press, 2000.

Ferguson, James. *Global Shadows: Africa in the Neoliberal World Order*. Durham, NC: Duke University Press, 2006.

Ferme, Mariane. "Staging Pylitsi: The Dialogics of Publicity and Secrecy in Sierra Leone." In *Civil Society and the Political Imagination in Africa,* edited by John L. Comaroff and Jean Comaroff, 160–91. Chicago: University of Chicago Press, 1999.

Fernandez-Kelly, Patricia, and Jon Shefner. *Out of the Shadows: Political Action and the Informal Economy in Latin America*. University Park: Pennsylvania State University Press, 2006.

Field, Sean. "Beyond 'Healing': Trauma, Oral History and Regeneration." *Oral History* 34, no. 1 (Spring 2006): 31–42.

Fitch, Bob, and Mary Oppenheimer. *Ghana: End of an Illusion*. New York: Monthly Review Press, 1966.

Fitzgerald, John J. "The Winter Soldier Hearings." *Radical History Review* 2007, no. 97 (December 21, 2007): 118–22. doi:10.1215/01636545-2006-017.

Fombad, Charles Manga. "Update: Transitional Justice in Africa: The Experience with Truth Commissions." New York University School of Law. 2012. about:reader?url=http%3A%2F%2Fwww.nyulawglobal.org%2Fglobalex%2FAfrica_Truth_Commissions1.html.

Francis, Sanusi. "The Ugly Face of Unemployment in Ghana." ModernGhana. August 10, 2009. http://www.modernghana.com/news/232182/1/the-ugly-face-of-unemployment-in-ghana.html.

Franck, Thomas M. "Out of Lagos Shall Go Forth the Law." *Africa Today* 8, no. 2 (February 1, 1961): 4–11.

French, Brigittine M. "Comment on Trinch's Risky Subjects: The Limits and Possibilities of Speaking Truth to Power." *Dialectical Anthropology* 34, no. 2 (June 2010): 205–7.

Fridy, Kevin S. "The Elephant, Umbrella, and Quarrelling Cocks: Disaggregating Partisanship in Ghana's Fourth Republic." *African Affairs* 106, no. 423 (April 1, 2007): 281–305. doi:10.1093/afraf/adl040.

Fridy, Kevin S., and Victor Brobbey. "Win the Match and Vote for Me: The Politicisation of Ghana's Accra Hearts of Oak and Kumasi Asante Kotoko Football Clubs." *Journal of Modern African Studies* 47, no. 1 (2009): 19–39.

Friedlander, Saul. "History, Memory, and the Historian: Dilemmas and Responsibilities." *New German Critique*, no. 80 (2000): 3–15. doi:10.2307/488629.

———. *When Memory Comes*. New York: Farrar, Straus and Giroux, 1978.

———. *The Years of Extermination: Nazi Germany and the Jews, 1939–1945*. New York: HarperCollins, 2007.

Friedrichs, David O. "On Resisting State Crime: Conceptual and Contextual Issues." *Social Justice* 36, no. 3 (117) (2009): 4–27.

Frimpong-Ansah, J. H. *The Vampire State in Africa: The Political Economy of Decline in Ghana*. Trenton, NJ: Africa World Press, 1991.

Fujii, Lee Ann. "Shades of Truth and Lies: Interpreting Testimonies of War and Violence." *Journal of Peace Research* 47, no. 2 (March 2010): 231–41.

Fullard, Madeleine, and Nicky Rousseau. "Uncertain Borders: The TRC and the (Un)Making of Public Myths." *Kronos*, no. 34 (November 1, 2008): 215–39.

Fuller, Harcourt. *Building the Ghanaian Nation-State: Kwame Nkrumah's Symbolic Nationalism.* New York: Palgrave Macmillan, 2014.

———. "Commemorating an African Queen: Ghanaian Nationalism, the African Diaspora, and the Public Memory of Nana Yaa Asantewaa 1952–2009." *African Arts* 47, no. 4 (Winter 2014): 58–71.

Gadzekpo, Audrey. "Reflections of Ghana's Recent Elections." *Review of African Political Economy* 28, no. 88 (June 2001): 267–73.

Garland, Elizabeth. "Developing Bushmen: Building Civil(ized) Society in the Kalahari and Beyond." In *Civil Society and the Political Imagination in Africa,* edited by John L. Comaroff and Jean Comaroff, 72–103. Chicago: University of Chicago Press, 1999.

Gassama, Ibrahim. "A World Made of Violence and Misery: Human Rights as a Failed Project of Liberal Internationalism." *Brooklyn Journal of International Law* 37, no. 2 (January 1, 2012). http://brooklynworks.brooklaw.edu/bjil/vol37/iss2/3.

Gearey, Adam. "'Tell All the Truth, but Tell It Slant': A Poetics of Truth and Reconciliation." *Journal of Law and Society* 31, no. 1 (March 1, 2004): 38–59.

Gearty, Conor. *Can Human Rights Survive?* Cambridge: Cambridge University Press, 2006.

Geest, Sjaak van der. "Money and Respect: The Changing Value of Old Age in Rural Ghana." *Africa: Journal of the International African Institute* 67, no. 4 (1997): 534–59.

Ghana News Agency. "NRC Hears Four Cases in Its Maiden Hearing." GhanaWeb. January 14, 2003. http://www.ghanaweb.com/GhanaHomePage/NewsArchive/artikel.php?ID=31542.

Ghanaian Liberal. "Nyasaland's and Ghana's Political Detainees." *Ashanti Times,* March 14, 1959.

Gillard, Emanuela-Chiara. "Reparation for Violations of International Humanitarian Law." *International Review of the Red Cross* 85, no. 851 (September 2003): 529–52.

Gitelson, Susan Aurelia. "Major Shifts in Recent Ugandan Foreign Policy." *African Affairs* 76, no. 304 (July 1977): 359–80.

Glendon, Mary Ann. *Rights Talk: The Impoverishment of Political Discourse.* New York: Free Press, 1991.

Gocking, Roger. "Colonial Rule and the 'Legal Factor' in Ghana and Lesotho." *Africa: Journal of the International African Institute* 67, no. 1 (1997): 61–85. doi:10.2307/1161270.

———. *The History of Ghana.* Westport, CT: Greenwood Publishing Group, 2005.

Goldberg, Amos. "The Victim's Voice and Melodramatic Aesthetics in History." *History & Theory* 48, no. 3 (October 2009): 220–37.

Goldberg, Elizabeth Swanson. *Beyond Terror: Gender, Narrative and Human Rights.* New Directions in International Studies. New Brunswick, NJ: Rutgers University Press, 2007.

Goldsworthy, David. "Ghana's Second Republic: A Post-Mortem." *African Affairs* 72, no. 286 (January 1973): 8–25.

Gonzo, Webster. *Unemployment in an African Country: A Psychological Perspective.* Windhoek: University of Namibia Press, 2003.

Goodale, Mark, and Sally Engle-Merry. *The Practice of Human Rights: Tracking Law Between the Global and the Local.* Cambridge: Cambridge University Press, 2007.

Goodman, James, and Paul James. *Nationalism and Global Solidarities: Alternative Projections to Neoliberal Globalisation.* Florence, KY: Routledge, 2011.

Goody, Jack. "Consensus and Dissent in Ghana." *Political Science Quarterly* 83, no. 3 (September 1968): 337–52. doi:10.2307/2147503.

Gorjão, Paulo. "The East Timorese Commission for Reception, Truth and Reconciliation: Chronicle of a Foretold Failure?" *Civil Wars* 4, no. 2 (June 1, 2001): 142–62. doi:10.1080/13698240108402473.

Goulet, Denis. "Development Experts: The One-Eyed Giants." *World Development* 8, no. 7 (July 1, 1980): 481–89. doi:10.1016/0305-750X(80)90033-9.

Grandin, Greg. "The Instruction of Great Catastrophe: Truth Commissions, National History, and State Formation in Argentina, Chile, and Guatemala." *American Historical Review* 110, no. 1 (2005): 46–67. doi:10.1086/531121.

———. "Introduction: A U.S. Truth Commission?" *Radical History Review* 2007, no. 97 (December 21, 2007): 99–101. doi:10.1215/01636545-2006-014.

Grandin, Greg, and Thomas Miller Klubock. Editors' Introduction to *Radical History Review* 2007, no. 97 (December 21, 2007): 1–10. doi:10.1215/01636545-2006-010.

Graubard, Stephen R. Preface to the issue "Social Suffering." *Daedalus* 125, no. 1 (1996): v–x.

Gready, Paul. "Novel Truths: Literature and Truth Commissions." *Comparative Literature Studies* 46, no. 1 (2009): 156–76.

———. *The Era of Transitional Justice: The Aftermath of the Truth and Reconciliation in South Africa and Beyond*. New York: Routledge, 2010.

Green, Reginal Herbold. "The Triple Challenge Before Ghana." *New African*, May 1966, 93–96. http://disa.ukzn.ac.za/sites/default/files/pdf_files/nav5n4.may66_11.pdf.

Grischow, Jeff D. "Kwame Nkrumah, Disability, and Rehabilitation in Ghana, 1957–66." *Journal of African History* 52, no. 2 (2011): 179–99. doi:10.1017/S0021853711000260.

Gupta, Akhil. *Postcolonial Developments: Agriculture in the Making of Modern India*. Durham, NC: Duke University Press, 1998.

Guthrey, Holly L. *Victim Healing and Truth Commissions—Transforming Pain Through Voice in Solomon Islands and Timor-Leste*. Vol. 11 of Springer Series in Transitional Justice. Cham, Switzerland: Springer, 2015. http://www.springer.com/us/book/9783319124865.

Gyimah-Boadi, E., and Donald Rothchild. "Rawlings, Populism, and the Civil Liberties Tradition in Ghana." *Issue: A Journal of Opinion* 12, no. 3/4 (1982): 64–69. doi:10.2307/1166719.

Hafiz, Mohammed. "*Takfir* as a Tool for Instigating Jihad Among Muslims: The Ghanaian Example." In *Political Islam from Muhammad to Ahmadinejad: Defenders, Detractors, and Definitions*, edited by Joseph Morrison Skelly, 147–60. Santa Barbara, CA: Prageer Security International, 2010.

Hafner-Burton, Emilie. *Making Human Rights a Reality*. Princeton, NJ: Princeton University Press, 2013.

Hafner-Burton, Emilie M., and Kiyoteru Tsutsui. "Justice Lost! The Failure of International Human Rights Law to Matter Where Needed Most." *Journal of Peace Research* 44, no. 4 (July 1, 2007): 407–25. doi:10.1177/0022343307078942.

Hansen, Emmanuel, and Paul Collins. "The Army, the State, and the 'Rawlings Revolution' in Ghana." *African Affairs* 79, no. 314 (1980): 3–23.

Hanson, Kobena. "Rethinking the Akan Household: Acknowledging the Importance of Culturally and Linguistically Meaningful Images." *Africa Today* 51, no. 1 (2004): 27–45.

Harrington, Donald. "Ghana Independence Day." *Africa Today* 4, no. 2 (1957): 3.

Harris, Richard L. "The Effects of Political Change on the Role Set of the Senior Bureaucrats in Ghana and Nigeria." *Administrative Science Quarterly* 13, no. 3 (December 1968): 386–401. doi:10.2307/2391049.

Hart, Jennifer. "'One Man, No Chop': Licit Wealth, Good Citizens, and the Criminalization of Drivers in Postcolonial Ghana." *International Journal of African Historical Studies* 46, no. 3 (October 2013): 373–96.

Hart, Keith. "Informal Income Opportunities and Urban Employment in Ghana." *Journal of Modern African Studies* 11, no. 1 (March 1973): 61–89.

———. "The Politics of Unemployment in Ghana." *African Affairs* 75, no. 301 (October 1976): 488–97.

Haruna, Peter Fuseini. "Reflective Public Administration Reform: Building Relationships, Bridging Gaps in Ghana." *African Studies Review* 44, no. 1 (April 2001): 37–57.

Harvey, Blane, and Jonathan Langdon. "Re-imagining Capacity and Collective Change: Experiences from Senegal and Ghana." *IDS Bulletin* 41, no. 3 (May 2010): 79–86.

Harvey, William Burnett. "Post-Nkrumah Ghana: The Legal Profile of a Coup." Articles by Maurer Faculty. Paper 1187 (1966). http://www.repository.law.indiana.edu/facpub/1187?utm_source=www.repository.law.indiana.edu%2Ffacpub%2F1187&utm_medium=PDF&utm_campaign=PDFCoverPages.

Hasty, Jennifer. "The Pleasures of Corruption: Desire and Discipline in Ghanaian Political Culture." *Cultural Anthropology* 20, no. 2 (May 2005): 271–301.

———. *The Press and Political Culture in Ghana*. Bloomington: Indiana University Press, 2005.

Hayner, Priscilla B. "Fifteen Truth Commissions—1974 to 1994: A Comparative Study." *Human Rights Quarterly* 16, no. 4 (November 1994): 597–655.

———. *Unspeakable Truths: Transitional Justice and the Challenge of Truth Commissions*. New York: Routledge, 2002.

Haynes, Jeffrey. "Railway Workers and the P.N.D.C. Government in Ghana, 1982–90." *Journal of Modern African Studies* 29, no. 1 (March 1, 1991): 137–54.

———. "Sustainable Democracy in Ghana? Problems and Prospects." *Third World Quarterly* 14, no. 3 (1993): 451–67.

Hazan, Pierre. *Judging War, Judging History: Behind Truth and Reconciliation*. Stanford, CA: Stanford University Press, 2010.

Hesford, Wendy S. "Documenting Violations: Rhetorical Witnessing and the Spectacle of Distant Suffering." *Biography* 27, no. 1 (2004): 104–44.

Hess, Janet. "Exhibiting Ghana: Display, Documentary, and 'National' Art in the Nkrumah Era." *African Studies Review* 44, no. 1 (April 2001): 59–77.

Hodge, Peter. "The Ghana Workers Brigade: A Project for Unemployed Youth." *British Journal of Sociology* 15, no. 2 (June 1964): 113–28.

Hodgson, Dorothy L., and Sheryl A. McCurdy. "Introduction: 'Wicked' Women and the Reconfiguration of Gender in Africa." In *"Wicked" Women and the Reconfiguration of Gender in Africa*, edited by Dorothy L. Hodgson and Sheryl A. McCurdy, 13–48. Social History of Africa. Portsmouth, NH: Heinemann, 2001.

Højbjerg, Christian K. "Victims and Heroes: Manding Historical Imagination in a Conflict-Ridden Border Region (Liberia-Guinea)." In *The Powerful Presence of the Past*, edited by Jacqueline Knörr and Wilson Trajano Filho, 273–94. Leiden, The Netherlands: Koninklijke Brill NV, 2010.

Hollander, Jocelyn A., and Rachel L. Einwohner. "Conceptualizing Resistance." *Sociological Forum* 19, no. 4 (2004): 533–54.

Howard, Rhoda. "Evaluating Human Rights in Africa: Some Problems of Implicit Comparisons." *Human Rights Quarterly* 6, no. 2 (May 1984): 160–79.

Howard-Hassmann, Rhoda E. "A Truth Commission for Africa?" *International Journal* 60, no. 4 (2005): 999–1016. doi:10.2307/40204095.

Howard-Hassmann, Rhoda E., and Anthony Lombardo. "Framing Reparations Claims." *African Studies Review* 50, no. 1 (2007): 27–48.

Howe, Russell Warren. "Did Nkrumah Favour Pan-Africanism?" *Transition*, no. 27 (1966): 13–15. doi:10.2307/2934195.

Humphrey, Michael. "From Victim to Victimhood: Truth Commissions and Trials as Rituals of Political Transition and Individual Healing." *Australian Journal of Anthropology* 14, no. 2 (2003): 171–87.

———. "From Terror to Trauma: Commissioning Truth for National Reconciliation." *Social Identities: Journal for the Study of Race, Nation, and Culture* 6, no. 1 (2000): 7–27.

Hyden, Goran. "The Failure of Africa's First Intellectuals." *Transition*, no. 28 (January 1967): 14–18. doi:10.2307/2934471.

Ibhawoh, Bonny. *Imperialism and Human Rights: Colonial Discourses of Rights and Liberties in African History*. SUNY Series on Human Rights. Albany: State University of New York Press, 2008.

Ignatieff, Michael. "Articles of Faith." *Index on Censorship* 25, no. 5 (September 1, 1996): 110–22.

Imbleau, Martin. "Initial Truth Establishment by Transitional Bodies and the Fight Against Denial." *Criminal Law Forum* 15, no. 1/2 (March 2004): 159–92.

Ingrao, Charles. "Confronting the Yugoslav Controversies: The Scholars' Initiative." *American Historical Review* 114, no. 4 (October 2009): 947–62.

İşcan, Talan B., Daniel Rosenblum, and Katie Tinker. "School Fees and Access to Primary Education: Assessing Four Decades of Policy in Sub-Saharan Africa." *Journal of African Economies* 24, no. 4 (August 1, 2015): 559–92. doi:10.1093/jae/ejv007.

Israel, Adrienne M. "Ex-servicemen at the Crossroads: Protest and Politics in Post-War Ghana." *Journal of Modern African Studies* 30, no. 2 (June 1992): 359–68.

James, C. L. R. *Nkrumah and the Ghana Revolution*. Westport, CT: Lawrence Hill, 1977.

———. *A History of Pan-African Revolt*. Oakland, CA: PM Press, 2012.

James, Matt. "A Carnival of Truth? Knowledge, Ignorance and the Canadian Truth and Reconciliation Commission." *International Journal of Transitional Justice* 6, no. 2 (2012): 182–204.

———. "Uncomfortable Comparisons: The Canadian Truth and Reconciliation Commission in International Context." *Les Ateliers de l'ethique* 5, no. 2 (2010).

Jeffries, Richard. "The Labour Aristocracy? Ghana Case Study." *Review of African Political Economy*, no. 3 (October 1975): 59–70. doi:10.2307/3997824.

Jeong, Ho-Won. "Liberal Economic Reform in Ghana: A Contested Political Agenda." *Africa Today* 42, no. 4 (December 1, 1995): 82–104.

Jockers, Heinz, Dirk Kohnert, and Paul Nugent. "The Successful Ghana Election of 2008: A Convenient Myth?" *Journal of Modern African Studies* 48, no. 1 (2010): 95–115. doi:10.1017/S0022278X09990231.

Johnson, Cheryl. "Women in Anticolonial Activity." *African Studies Review* 25, no. 2/3 (1982): 137–57.

Johnson, Ryan. "'An All-White Institution': Defending Private Practice and the Formation of the West African Medical Staff." *Medical History* 54, no. 2 (April 2010): 237–54.

Jones, Tim. "The Fall and Rise of Ghana's Debt: How a New Debt Trap Has Been Set." London: Jubilee Debt Campaign UK, October 9, 2016.

Joyce, James Avery. *Human Rights: International Documents*. Vol. 3. Alphen aan den Rijn, The Netherlands: Sijthoff and Noordhoff International Publishers, 1978.

Julius, Chrischene. "'Digging Deeper than the Eye Approves': Oral Histories and Their Use in the 'Digging Deeper' Exhibition of the District Six Museum." *Kronos* 34 (November 2008): 106–38.

Kalitsi, E. A. K. "Issues on Compensation for Affected Persons," n.d. http://ghanadamsdialogue .iwmi.org/Data/Sites/2/media/projectdocuments/issuepaper-compensention.pdf.

———. "Organisation and Economics of Resettlement." In *Volta River Symposium Papers*, 1965.

———. "Organization of Resettlement." In *The Volta Resettlement Experience*, edited by Robert Chambers, 34–57. New York: Praeger Publishers, 1970.

Kamara-Umunna, Agnes, and Emily Holland. *And Still Peace Did Not Come: A Memoir of Reconciliation*. New York: Hyperion Books, 2011.

Kapoor, Dip, ed. *Critical Perspectives on Neoliberal Globalization, Development and Education in Africa and Asia*. Rotterdam: Sense Publishers, 2011.

Kapur, Ratna. "The Tragedy of Victimization Rhetoric: Resurrecting the 'Native' Subject in International/Postcolonial Feminist Legal Politics." *Harvard Human Rights Law Journal* 15, no. 1 (2002): 1–38.

Kelsall, Tim. "Truth, Lies, and Ritual: Preliminary Reflections on the Truth and Reconciliation Commission in Sierra Leone." *Human Rights Quarterly* 27, no. 2 (2005): 361–91.

Kennedy, David. "The International Human Rights Movement: Part of the Problem?" *Harvard Human Rights Journal* 15, no. 99 (Spring 2002): 101–26.

Khulumani Support Group. "How the TRC Failed Women in South Africa." Khulumani Support Group South Africa, October 3, 2011. http://www.khulumani.net/truth-memory/item/527 -how-the-trc-failed-women-in-south-africa-a-failure-that-has-proved-fertile-ground-for -the-gender-violence-women-in-south-africa-face-today.html.

Kinley, David. "Human Rights Fundamentalism." *Sydney Law Review* 29, no. 4 (December 2007): 545–75.

Kipling, Rudyard. "White Man's Burden." *New York Sun,* February, 1899.

Kleinman, Arthur. "The Violences of Everyday Life: The Multiple Forms and Dynamics of Social Violence." In *Violence and Subjectivity,* edited by Veena Das, Arthur Kleinman, Mamphele Ramphele, and Pamela Reynolds, 226–41. Berkeley: University of California Press, 2000.

Kleinman, Arthur, Veena Das, and Margaret Lock. Introduction to the issue "Social Suffering." *Daedalus* 125, no. 1 (1996): xi–xx.

Kleinman, Arthur, and Joan Kleinman. "The Appeal of Experience; The Dismay of Images: Cultural Appropriations of Suffering in Our Times." *Daedalus* 125, no. 1 (1996): 1–23.

Kobo, Ousman. "'We Are Citizens Too': The Politics of Citizenship in Independent Ghana." *Journal of Modern African Studies* 48, no. 1 (2010): 67–94.

Kofi, Tetteh A. "The Elites and Underdevelopment in Africa: The Case of Ghana." *Berkeley Journal of Sociology* 17 (January 1, 1972): 97–115.

Kraus, Jon. "Capital, Power and Business Associations in the African Political Economy: A Tale of Two Countries, Ghana and Nigeria." *Journal of Modern African Studies* 40, no. 3 (2002): 395–436.

———. "On the Politics of Nationalism and Social Change in Ghana." *Journal of Modern African Studies* 7, no. 1 (April 1969): 107–30.

Krog, Antjie. *Country of My Skull: Guilt, Sorrow, and the Limits of Forgiveness in the New South Africa*. South Africa: Random House, 1998.

Krog, Antjie, Nosisi Mpolweni, and Kopano Ratele. *There Was This Goat: Investigating the Truth Commission Testimony of Notrose Nobomvu Konile*. Scottsville, South Africa: University Of KwaZulu-Natal Press, 2009.

Kube, Kwame. "Article on Religious Criticism of Human Rights Situation." *Ashanti Pioneer*, March 29, 1960.

Kusafuka, Ayumi. "Truth Commissions and Gender: A South African Case Study." *African Journal on Conflict Resolution* 9, no. 2 (2009): 45–68. http://www.ajol.info/index.php/ajcr /article/viewFile/52172/40798.

Kwarteng, Francis. "J. B. Danquah and Co.: The Case for the Preventive Detention Act." *GhanaWeb*. March 5, 2015. http://www.ghanaweb.com/GhanaHomePage/features/artikel .php?ID=348937.

Lagrou, Pieter. "Europe as a Place for Common Memories? Some Thoughts on Victimhood, Identity and Emancipation from the Past." In *Clashes in European Memory: The Case of Communist Repression and the Holocaust*, edited by Muriel Blaive, Christian Gerbel, and Thomas Lindenberger, 281–88. Innsbruck: Studien Verlag, 2011.

Lâm, Maivân Clech. "Feeling Foreign in Feminism." *Signs* 19, no. 4 (1994): 865–93.

Lambrose, R. J. "The Abusable Past." *Radical History Review* 2007, no. 97 (December 21, 2007): 171–75. doi:10.1215/01636545-2006-023.

Lanegran, Kimberly Rae. "Truth Commissions, Human Rights Trials, and the Politics of Memory." *Comparative Studies of South Asia, Africa and the Middle East* 25, no. 1 (2005): 111–21.

Langdon, Jonathan. "Contesting Globalization in Ghana: Communal Resource Defense and Social Movement Learning." *Journal of Alternative Perspectives in Social Sciences* 2, no. 1 (2010): 309–39.

———. "Moving with the Movement: Collaborative Building of Social Movement Learning Participatory Action Research (PAR) Spaces in Ada, Ghana." In *Proceedings of the 31st Annual Conference of the Canadian Association for the Study of Adult Education (CASAE)*, edited by Susan Brigham, 216–22. Ottawa: Canadian Association for the Study of Adult Education (CASAE), 2012. http://www.casae-aceea.ca/sites/casae/files/2012_CASAE_Proceedings .pdf.

———. "Social Movement Learning in Ghana: Communal Defense of Resources in Neoliberal Time." In *Critical Perspectives in Neoliberal Globalization, Development and Education in Africa and Asia*, edited by Dip Kapoor, 153–70. Rotterdam: Sense Publishers, 2011.

Langdon, Jonathan, Kofi Larweh, and Sheena Cameron. "The Thumbless Hand, the Dog and the Chameleon: Enriching Social Movement Learning Theory Through Epistemically Grounded Narratives Emerging from a Participatory Action Research Case Study in Ghana." *Interface: A Journal for and About Social Movements* 6, no. 1 (May 2014): 27–44.

Langdon, Jonathan, Kofi Larweh, and Wilna Quarmyne. "'E Yeo Ngo' (Does S/He Eat Salt?): Learning in Movement from a 5 Year PAR Study of the Ada Songor Advocacy Forum, a Social Movement in Ghana." In *Proceedings of the 33rd Annual Conference of the Canadian Association for the Study of Adult Education (CASAE)*, edited by Donovan Plumb, 167–70. Ottawa: Canadian Association for the Study of Adult Education (CASAE), 2014. http:// journals.msvu.ca/ocs/index.php/casae2014/CASAE14/paper/view/89

Laplante, Lisa J., and Kimberly Theidon. "Commissioning Truth, Constructing Silences: The Peruvian Truth Commission and the Other Truths of 'Terrorists.'" In *Mirrors of Justice: Law and Power in the Post-Cold War Era*, edited by Kamari Maxine Clark and Mark Goodale, 291–315. Cambridge: Cambridge University Press, 2009.

————. "Truth with Consequences: Justice and Reparations in Post-Truth Commission Peru." *Human Rights Quarterly* 29, no. 1 (February 1, 2007): 228–50.

Last, Murray. "Reconciliation and Memory in Postwar Nigeria." In *Violence and Subjectivity*, edited by Veena Das, Arthur Kleinman, Mamphele Ramphela, and Pamela Reynolds, 315–32. Berkeley: University of California Press, 2000.

Laumann, Dennis. "Che Guevara's Visit to Ghana." *Transactions of the Historical Society of Ghana*, no. 9 (2005): 61–74.

Lauren, Paul Gordon. *The Evolution of International Human Rights: Visions Seen*. 2nd ed. Philadelphia: University of Pennsylvania Press, 2003.

Lawler, Nancy, and Ivor Wilks. "Correspondence of Jacob Dosoo Amenyah of Ada Part Two: 1956–1965." *Transactions of the Historical Society of Ghana*, no. 11 (2008): 1–88.

Lawson, Rowena M. "The Distributive System in Ghana: A Review Article." *Journal of Development Studies* 3, no. 2 (January 1967): 195–205.

Lee, Alec M. "Past Futures." *Operational Research Quarterly (1970–1977)* 27, no. 1 (January 1, 1976): 147–53. doi:10.2307/3009133.

Legon Committee on National Reconstruction. *The Legon Observer*," July 8, 1966.

Lentz, Carola. "The Chief, the Mine Captain and the Politician: Legitimating Power in Northern Ghana." *Africa: Journal of the International African Institute* 68, no. 1 (1998): 46–67. doi:10.2307/1161147.

Lentz, Carola, and Veit Erlmann. "A Working Class in Formation? Economic Crisis and Strategies of Survival Among Dagara Mine Workers in Ghana." *Cahiers d'Études africaines* 29, no. 113 (1989): 69–111.

Le Vine, Victor T. "Autopsy on a Regime: Ghana's Civilian Interregnum 1969–72." *Journal of Modern African Studies* 25, no. 1 (1987): 169–78.

Libby, Ronald T. "External Co-Optation of a Less Developed Country's Policy Making: The Case of Ghana, 1969–1972." *World Politics* 29, no. 1 (October 1976): 67–89.

Lindsay, Charlotte. "The Impact of Armed Conflict on Women." In *Listening to the Silences: Women and War*, edited by Helen Durham and Tracey Gurd, 21–35. Vol. 8 of International Humanitarian Law Series. Leiden, The Netherlands: Martinus Nijhoff Publishers, 2005.

Lindsay, Lisa. *Working with Gender: Wage Labor and Social Change in Southwestern Nigeria*. London: Heinemann, 2003.

Linfield, Susie. *The Cruel Radiance: Photography and Political Violence*. Chicago: University of Chicago Press, 2010.

Lloyd, Cynthia B., and Anastasia J. Gage-Brandon. "Women's Role in Maintaining Households: Family Welfare and Sexual Inequality in Ghana." *Population Studies* 47, no. 1 (March 1993): 115–31.

Lonsdale, John. "African Pasts in Africa's Future." *Canadian Journal of African Studies / Revue Canadienne des Études Africaines* 23, no. 1 (January 1, 1989): 126–46. doi:10.2307/485378.

————, John. "Editorial: Agency in Tight Corners: Narrative and Initiative in African History." *Journal of African Cultural Studies* 13, no. 1 (June 2000): 5–16.

Loveman, Brian, and Elizabeth Lira. "Truth, Justice, Reconciliation, and Impunity as Historical Themes: Chile, 1814–2006." *Radical History Review* 2007, no. 97 (December 21, 2007): 43–76. doi:10.1215/01636545-2006-012.

Low, D. A. "Uganda Unhinged." *International Affairs (Royal Institute of International Affairs 1944–)* 49, no. 2 (April 1973): 219–28.

Luban, David. "The War on Terrorism and the End of Human Rights." *Philosophy and Public Policy Quarterly* 22 (2002): 9–14.

Ludi, Regula. "The Vectors of Postwar Victim Reparations: Relief, Redress and Memory Politics." *Journal of Contemporary History* 41, no. 3 (2006): 421–50.

Lugard, Frederick J.D. *The Dual Mandate in British Tropical Africa.* Abingdon, UK: Frank Cass & Co., 1922.

Lumsden, D. Paul. "The Volta River Project: Village Resettlement and Attempted Rural Animation." *Canadian Journal of African Studies / Revue Canadienne des Études Africaines* 7, no. 1 (January 1, 1973): 115–32. doi:10.2307/483753.

Lund, Christian. "'Bawku Is Still Volatile': Ethno-Political Conflict and State Recognition in Northern Ghana." *Journal of Modern African Studies* 41, no. 4 (December 1, 2003): 587–610.

Lyon, Fergus. "Trust, Networks and Norms: The Creation of Social Capital in Agricultural Economies in Ghana." *World Development* 28, no. 4 (April 2000): 663–81. doi:10.1016/ S0305-750X(99)00146-1.

MacGaffey, Wyatt. "The Blacksmiths of Tamale: The Dynamics of Space and Time in a Ghanaian Industry." *Africa: The Journal of the International African Institute* 79, no. 2 (2009): 169–85.

Mackey, Allison. "Troubling Humanitarian Consumption: Reframing Relationality in African Child Soldier Narratives." *Research in African Literatures* 44, no. 4 (2013): 99–122.

Madison, D. Soyini. *Acts of Activism: Human Rights as Radical Performance.* Cambridge: Cambridge University Press, 2010.

Madlingozi, Tshepo. "On Transitional Justice Entrepreneurs and the Production of Victims." *Journal of Human Rights Practice* 2, no. 2 (2010): 208–28.

Maeso, Silvia Rodriguez. "The Politics of Testimony and Recognition in the Guatemalan and Peruvian Truth Commissions: The Figure of the 'Subversive Indian.'" *Revista Crítica de Ciências Sociais*, no. 3 (2011). doi:10.4000/rccsar.280.

Maier, Charles S. "Doing History, Doing Justice: The Narrative of the Historian and of the Truth Commission." In *Truth v. Justice: The Morality of Truth Commissions*, edited by Robert Rotberg, and Dennis Thompson, 261–78. Princeton, NJ: Princeton University Press, 2000.

Mamdani, Mahmood. "Amnesty or Impunity? A Preliminary Critique of the Report of the Truth and Reconciliation Commission of South Africa (TRC)." *Diacritics* 32, no. 3 (February 21, 2005): 33–59. doi:10.1353/dia.2005.0005.

———. "Beware Human Rights Fundamentalism!" *Mail & Guardian*, March 20, 2009. https:// mg.co.za/article/2009-03-20-beware-human-rights-fundamentalism.

———. "The Logic of Nuremberg." *London Review of Books* 35, no. 21 (November 7, 2013): 33–34.

———. "The Politics of Naming: Genocide, Civil War, Insurgency." *London Review of Books* 25, no. 5 (March 2007): 5–8.

———. "The Uganda Asian Expulsion Twenty Years After." *Economic and Political Weekly* 28, no. 3/4 (January 16, 1993): 93–96.

———. *Citizen and Subject: Contemporary Africa and the Legacy of Late Colonialism.* Princeton, NJ: Princeton University Press, 1996.

Manby, Bronwen. "The African Union, NEPAD, and Human Rights: The Missing Agenda." *Human Rights Quarterly* 26, no. 4 (2004): 983–1027.

Manuh, Takyiwaa. "Survival in Rural Africa: The Salt Cooperatives in Ada District, Ghana." In *Development from Within: Survival in Rural Africa*, edited by D. R. Fraser Taylor and Fiona Mackenzie, 102–24. New York: Routledge, 1992.

Mapuva, Jephias, and Freeman Chari. "Colonialism No Longer an Excuse for Africa's Failure." *Journal of Sustainable Development in Africa* 12, no. 5 (2010): 22–36.

Marteye, Alfred. "Now, I Am Like a Beggar—Madam Kaitoo." *Ghana Review*, March 4, 2003. http://www.ghanareview.com/int/nrc2.html#a.

———. "Rawlings Might Not Have Been Aware—Nana Ahima." *Ghana Review*, February 13, 2003. http://www.ghanareview.com/int/nrc.html#b4.

Martín-Beristain, Carlos, Darío Páez, Bernard Rimé, and Patrick Kanyangara. "Psychosocial Effects of Participation in Rituals of Transitional Justice: A Collective-Level Analysis and Review of the Literature of the Effects of TRCs and Trials on Human Rights Violations in Latin America." *Revista de Psicología Social* 25, no. 1 (January 1, 2010): 47–60. doi:10.1174/021347410790193450.

Matera, Marc, Misty L. Bastian, and S. Kingsley Kent. *The Women's War of 1929: Gender and Violence in Colonial Nigeria.* New York: Palgrave Macmillan, 2012.

Mazrui, Ali A. "The Lumpen Proletariat and the Lumpen Militariat: African Soldiers as a New Political Class." *Political Studies* 21, no. 1 (March 1, 1973): 1–12. doi:10.1111/j.1467-9248.1973.tb01413.x.

———. "Nkrumah: The Leninist Czar." *Transition*, no. 75/76 (1997): 106–26. doi:10.2307/2935397.

———. "On Heroes and Uhuru-Worship." *Transition* 11 (1963): 23–28.

Mbaku, John Mukum. "Corruption in Africa: Causes, Consequences and Cleanups." In *Ghana in Africa and the World: Essays in Honor of Adu Boahen*, edited by Toyin Falola, 569–99. Trenton, NJ: Africa World Press, Inc., 2003.

McCain, James A. "Higher Education in Ghana: Implications for the Future." *Journal of Black Studies* 10, no. 1 (September 1979): 60–68. doi:10.2307/2784051.

McCalpin, Jermaine O. "Truth and Freedom in Haiti: An Examination of the Haitian Truth Commission." *Global South* 6, no. 1 (2012): 138–55. doi:10.2979/globalsouth.6.1.138.

McLagan, Margaret. "Circuits of Suffering." *Political and Legal Anthropology Review* 28, no. 2 (2005): 223–39.

———. "Human Rights, Testimony and Transnational Publicity." In *Nongovernmental Politics*, edited by Michel Feher, 304–17. New York: Zone Books, 2007.

Mendeloff, David. "Truth-Seeking, Truth-Telling, and Postconflict Peacebuilding: Curb the Enthusiasm?" *International Studies Review* 6, no. 3 (2004): 355–80.

Menkel-Meadow, Carrie. "Remembrance of Things Past? The Relationship of Past to Future in Pursuing Justice in Mediation." *Cardozo Journal of Conflict Resolution* 5 (2004): 97–115.

Mensa-Bonsu, Henrietta J. A. N. "Gender, Justice and Reconciliation: Lessons from Ghana's NRC." Paper presented at the workshop of the Center for Democratic Development / Coexistence International. Accra, Ghana, June 7, 2007.

Merry, Sally Engle. "Transnational Human Rights and Local Activism: Mapping the Middle." *American Anthropologist* 108, no. 1 (2006): 38–51.

Miescher, Stephan F. "Building the City of the Future: Visions and Experiences of Modernity in Ghana's Akosombo Township." *Journal of African History* 53, no. 3 (2012): 367–90. doi:10.1017/S0021853712000679.

———. "The Life Histories of Boakye Yiadom : Exploring the Subjectivity and 'Voices' of a Teacher-Catechist in Colonial Ghana." In *African Words, African Voices: Critical Practices in Oral History*, edited by Luise White, Stephan F. Miescher, and David William Cohen, 162–93. Bloomington: Indiana University Press, 2001.

————. "'Nkrumah's Baby': The Akosombo Dam and the Dream of Development in Ghana, 1952–1966." *Water History* 6, no. 4 (December 1, 2014): 341–66. doi:10.1007/s12685-014-0112-8.

————. *Making Men in Ghana*. Bloomington: Indiana University Press, 2005.

Miescher, Stephan F., and Dzodzi Tsikata. "Hydro-Power and the Promise of Modernity and Development in Ghana: Comparing the Akosombo and Bui Dam Projects." *Ghana Studies Journal* 12/13 (2010 2009): 15–53.

Mignolo, Walter. "Who Speaks for the Human in Human Rights?" *Human Rights in Latin American and Iberian Cultures* 5, no. 1 (2009).

Millar, Gearoid. "Assessing Local Experiences of Truth-Telling in Sierra Leone: Getting to 'Why' Through a Qualitative Case Study Analysis." *International Journal of Transitional Justice* 4, no. 3 (November 1, 2010): 477–96. doi:10.1093/ijtj/ijq017.

Miller, Hayli. "Facilitating Women's Voices in Truth Recovery: An Assessment of Women's Participation and the Integration of a Gender Perspective in Truth Commissions." In *Listening to the Silences: Women and War,* edited by Helen Durham and Tracey Gurd, 171–222. Vol. 8 of International Humanitarian Law. Leiden, The Netherlands: Martinus Nijhoff Publishers, 2005.

Miller, Zinaida. "Effects of Invisibility: In Search of the 'Economic' in Transitional Justice." *International Journal of Transitional Justice* 2, no. 3 (2008): 266–91.

Minow, Martha. *Between Vengeance and Forgiveness*. Boston: Beacon Press, 1998.

Mitchell, Matthew I. "Ghana's Offshore Oil: Resource Curse or Blessing?" Africa Portal: A Project of the Africa Initiative. No. 44, November 2012. https://www.africaportal.org/publications/ghanas-offshore-oil-resource-curse-or-blessing/.

Mohanty, Chandra Talpade. "Under Western Eyes: Feminist Scholarship and Colonial Discourses." *Feminist Review*, no. 30 (1988): 61–88. doi:10.2307/1395054.

————. "'Under Western Eyes' Revisited: Feminist Solidarity through Anticapitalist Struggles." *Signs* 28, no. 2 (2003): 499–535. doi:10.1086/342914.

Molini, Vasco and Pieralla Paci. *Poverty Reduction in Ghana: Progress and Challenges.* Washington DC: World Bank Group, 2015. http://hdl.handle.net/10986/22732.

Morrison, Minion K. C. "Political Parties in Ghana through Four Republics: A Path to Democratic Consolidation." *Comparative Politics* 36, no. 4 (2004): 421–42. doi:10.2307/4150169.

Morrison, Minion K. C., and Jae Woo Hong. "Ghana's Political Parties: How Ethno/Regional Variations Sustain the National Two-Party System." *Journal of Modern African Studies* 44, no. 4 (2006): 623–47.

Morsink, Johannes. "The Philosophy of the Universal Declaration." *Human Rights Quarterly* 6, no. 3 (August 1984): 309–34.

Motsemme, Nthabiseng. "The Mute Always Speak: On Women's Silences at the Truth and Reconciliation Commission." *Current Sociology* 52, no. 5 (2004): 909–32.

Moyn, Samuel. *The Last Utopia: Human Rights in History.* Cambridge, MA: Harvard University Press, 2010.

————. "Empathy in History, Empathizing with Humanity." *History and Theory* 45, no. 3 (2006): 397–415.

————. "Imperialism, Self-Determination, and the Rise of Human Rights." In *The Human Rights Revolution: An International History*, edited by Akira Iriye, Petra Goedde, and William I. Hitchcock, 158–79. New York: Oxford University Press, 2012.

Muriuki, Godfrey. Review of *"African Futures." International Journal of African Historical Studies* 23, no. 2 (January 1, 1990): 367–69. doi:10.2307/219376.

Mutongi, Kenda. *Worries of the Heart: Widows, Family, and Community in Kenya*. Chicago: University of Chicago Press, 2007.

Mutua, Makau. "Human Rights in Africa: The Limited Promise of Liberalism." *African Studies Review* 51, no. 1 (2008): 17–39.

———. *Human Rights NGOs in East Africa: Political and Normative Tensions*. Philadelphia: University of Pennsylvania Press, 2009.

———. "Savages, Victims, and Saviors: The Metaphor of Human Rights." *Harvard International Law Journal* 42, no. 1 (2001): 201–45.

———. *Human Rights: A Political and Cultural Critique*. Philadelphia: University of Pennsylvania, 2002.

Muvingi, Ismael. "Donor-Driven Transitional Justice and Peacebuilding." *Journal of Peacebuilding & Development* 11, no. 1 (January 2, 2016): 10–25. doi:10.1080/15423166.2016.1146566.

———. "Sitting on Powder Kegs: Socioeconomic Rights in Transitional Societies." *International Journal of Transitional Justice* 3, no. 2 (2009): 163–82.

Nauriya, Anil. "Securing the Right to Work: Some Constitutional and Economic Aspects." *Economic and Political Weekly* 25, no. 2 (January 13, 1990): 77–80.

Neocosmos, Michael. *Thinking Freedom in Africa: Toward a Theory of Emancipatory Politics*. Johannesburg: Wits University Press, 2017.

Nesiah, Vasuki. "Truth Commissions and Gender: Principles, Policies and Procedures." Report of the International Center for Transitional Justice. July, 2006. https://www.ictj.org/publication/truth-commissions-and-gender-principles-policies-and-procedures.

New African Magazine. "Kofi Annan: 'It's Time to Look Beyond Our Colonial Past.'" November 29, 2012. http://newafricanmagazine.com/kofi-annan-its-time-to-look-beyond-our-colonial-past/.

Nigam, Aditya. "'Right to Work': Reading 'Rights' Through Discourse on 'Work.'" *Economic and Political Weekly* 33, no. 5 (February 31, 1998): PE16-PE24.

Nkrumah, Kwame. "Kwame on Rhodesia." *Daily Graphic*, February 23, 1966.

———. "A Letter of Consolation to Dr. Kofi A. Busia: On the Coup in Ghana." *Black Scholar* 3, no. 9 (1972): 23–26.

———. *Voice from Conakry*. London: PANAF Books, 1967.

———. "African Prospect," *Foreign Affairs* 37, no. 1 (1958): 45–53.

Nnoromele, Salome C. "Representing the African Woman: Subjectivity and Self in the Joys of Motherhood." *Critique: Studies in Contemporary Fiction* 43, no. 2 (January 1, 2002): 178–90. doi:10.1080/00111610209602179.

Normand, Roger, and Sarah Zaidi. *Human Rights at the UN: The Political History of Universal Justice*. Bloomington: Indiana University Press, 2008.

Norval, Aletta J. "Truth and Reconciliation: The Birth of the Present and the Reworking of History." *Journal of Southern African Studies* 25, no. 3 (September 1, 1999): 499–519.

Novick, Peter. *That Noble Dream: The "Objectivity Question" and the American Historical Profession*. Cambridge University Press, 1988.

Ntsebeza, Dumisa. "The Uses of Truth Commissions: Lessons for the World." In *Truth V. Justice: The Morality of Truth Commissions*, edited by Robert I. Rotberg and Dennis Thompson, 158–69. Princeton, NJ: Princeton University Press, 2000.

Nugent, Paul. "Ethnicity as an Explanatory Factor in the Ghana 2000 Elections." *African Issues* 29, no. 1/2 (2001): 2–7. doi:10.2307/1167102.

———. "Living in the Past: Urban, Rural and Ethnic Themes in the 1992 and 1996 Elections in Ghana." *Journal of Modern African Studies* 37, no. 2 (June 1999): 287–319.

Nwogu, Nneoma V. *Shaping Truth, Reshaping Justice: Sectarian Politics and the Nigerian Truth Commission*. Lanham, MD: Lexington Books, 2007.

———. "When and Why It Started: Deconstructing Victim-Centered Truth Commissions in the Context of Ethnicity-Based Conflict." *International Journal of Transitional Justice* 4 (2010): 275–89.

Nzongola-Ntalaja, Georges. "Citizenship, Political Violence, and Democratization in Africa." *Global Governance* 10, no. 4 (2004): 403–9.

Obeng, Letitia. "Should Dams Be Built? The Volta Lake Example." *Ambio* 6, no. 1 (1977): 46–50.

Oberhauser, Ann M., and Kobena T. Hanson. "Negotiating Livelihoods and Scale in the Context of Neoliberal Globalization: Perspectives from Accra, Ghana." *African Geographical Review* 26, no. 1 (January 1, 2007): 11–36. doi:10.1080/19376812.2007.9756200.

Oboe, Annalisa. "The TRC Women's Hearings as Performance and Protest in the New South Africa." *Research in African Literatures* 38, no. 3 (2007): 60–76.

Ocheje, Paul D. "In the Public Interest: Forced Evictions, Land Rights, and Human Development in Africa." *Journal of African Law* 51, no. 2 (2007): 173–214.

Odartey-Wellington, Felix, and Amin Alhassan. "Disseminating the National Reconciliation Report: A Critical Step in Ghana's Democratic Consolidation." *African Journal of Political Science and International Relations* 10, no. 4 (April 2016): 34–46.

Odinkalu, Chidi Anselm. "Analysis of Paralysis or Paralysis by Analysis? Implementing Economic, Social, and Cultural Rights under the African Charter on Human and Peoples' Rights." *Human Rights Quarterly* 23, no. 2 (May 2001): 327–69.

———. "Back to the Future: The Imperative of Prioritizing for the Protection of Human Rights in Africa." *Journal of African Law* 47, no. 1 (2003): 1–37.

Oduro, Kwame. "Four Years Ago." *Legon Observer*, 1966.

Oglesby, Elizabeth. "Educating Citizens in Postwar Guatemala: Historical Memory, Genocide, and the Culture of Peace." *Radical History Review* 2007, no. 97 (December 21, 2007): 77–98. doi:10.1215/01636545-2006-013.

Ogundipe-Leslie, Molara. "Invite Tyrants to Commit Suicide: Gender Violence, Human Rights and African Women in Contemporary African Nation States." In *Gender Violence and Women's Human Rights in Africa*, edited by Center for Women's Global Leadership, 1–14. Highland Park, NJ: Plowshares Press, 1994.

Ohene, Elizabeth. *Thinking Allowed: A Collection of Articles on Events in Ghana 1978–1981 Through the Eyes of One Woman*. Accra, Ghana: Bluc Savana, 2006.

Ojeifo, Sufuyan, and Lemmy Ughegbe. "No Regrets for the Asaba Massacre of Igbo-Haruna." *Vanguard*, October 10, 2001.

Okafor, Obiora Chinedu, and Shedrack C. Agbakwa. "On Legalism, Popular Agency and 'Voices of Suffering': The Nigerian National Human Rights Commission in Context." *Human Rights Quarterly* 24, no. 3 (2002): 662–720. doi:10.1353/hrq.2002.0038.

Okello, Moses Chrispus, Chris Dolan, Undine Whande, and Nokukhanya Mncwabe. *Where Law Meets Reality: Forging African Transitional Justice*. Nairobi: Pambazuka Press, 2012.

Olick, Jeffrey K. "From Usable Pasts to the Return of the Repressed." Hedgehog Review 9, no. 2 (July 2007): 19–31. http://iasc-culture.org/THR/archives/UsesPast/Olick.pdf.

Oloka-Onyango, J., and Sylvia Tamale. "'The Personal Is Political,' or Why Women's Rights Are Indeed Human Rights: An African Perspective on International Feminism." *Human Rights Quarterly* 17, no. 4 (1995): 691–731.

Olsen, Tricia D., Leigh A. Payne, Andrew G. Reiter, and Eric Wiebelhaus-Brahm. "When Truth Commissions Improve Human Rights." *International Journal of Transitional Justice* 4 (2010): 457–76.

Olusanya, G. O. "The Role of Ex-Servicemen in Nigerian Politics." *Journal of Modern African Studies* 6, no. 2 (August 1, 1968): 221–32.

Omoruyi, Omo. "Refocusing the Oputa Commission (II): The Military." The Omoruyi Papers. Nigeria World. August 9, 2001. http://nigeriaworld.com/feature/publication/omoruyi /080921.html.

Onunaiju, Charles. "Oputa Panel as Obasanjo's Comic Diversion." *Vanguard Daily*, January 11, 2001. http://www.nigerdeltapeoplesworldcongress.org/articles/oputa_panel_as_obas.pdf.

Opoku, Darko K. "Political Dilemmas of Indigenous Capitalist Development in Africa: Ghana under the Provisional National Defence Council." *Africa Today* 55, no. 2 (December 1, 2008): 25–50.

———. *The Politics of Government-Business Relations in Ghana, 1982–2008*. New York: Palgrave Macmillan, 2010.

Oquaye, Mike. "Human Rights and the Transition to Democracy Under the PNDC in Ghana." *Human Rights Quarterly* 17, no. 3 (August 1995): 556–73.

Ortiz, Paul. "Behind the Veil." *Radical History Review* 2007, no. 97 (December 21, 2007): 110–17. doi:10.1215/01636545-2006-016.

Osei, Robert, and Peter Quartey. "The HIPC Initiative and Poverty Reduction in Ghana: An Assessment." Working Paper. WIDER Discussion Papers // World Institute for Development Economics (UNU-WIDER), 2001. https://www.econstor.eu/handle/10419/52965.

Osei-Assibey, Eric. "Nature and Dynamics of Inequalities in Ghana." *Development* 57, no. 3–4 (December 1, 2014): 521–30. doi:10.1057/dev.2015.25.

Our Accra Reporter. "Ashie Nikoi Tells Rally of His Sufferings." *Ashanti Pioneer*, January 20, 1960.

Our Own Reporter. "Drivers Strike Brings Trade to a Standstill." *Ashanti Pioneer*, July 23, 1957.

Our Staff Reporter. "Act Violates UN Charter—Railmen." *Ashanti Pioneer*, August 1, 1959.

Our Staff Writer. "Democracy Is Definitely on Trial in Ghana! Soon All Opposition Will Be Crushed, Says Lagos Paper." *Ashanti Pioneer*, August 2, 1957.

Our Tamale Reporter. "NT Council Against Nkrumah's Head on Coins." *Ashanti Pioneer*, August 1, 1957.

Owusu, Maxwell. "Democracy—A View from the Village." *Journal of Modern African Studies* 30, no. 3 (1992): 369–96.

———. "Domesticating Democracy in Africa." *Comparative Studies in Society and History* 39, no. 1 (1997): 120–52.

———. "The Search for Solvency: Background to the Fall of Ghana's Second Republic, 1969– 1972." *Africa Today* 19, no. 1 (1972): 52–60.

———. Economic Nationalism, Pan-Africanism and the Military: Ghana's National Redemption Council," *Africa Today* 22, no. 1 (1975): 31–50.

Owusu, Robert Yaw. *Kwame Nkrumah's Liberation Thought: A Paradigm for Religious Advocacy in Contemporary Ghana*. Trenton, NJ: Africa World Press, 2006.

Owusu-Nsiah, Charles. "National Reconciliation and the Rule of Law." *Ghanaian Chronicle*, January 31, 2002.

Palmary, Ingrid. "Nationalism and Asylum: Implications for Women." *Agenda*, no. 55 (January 1, 2003): 4–14.

Pandey, Gyanendra. *Remembering Partition: Violence, Nationalism and History in India*. New York: Cambridge University Press, 2001.

Panford, Martin Kwamina. *IMF–World Bank and Labor's Burdens in Africa: Ghana's Experience*. Westport, CT: Praeger Publishers, 2001.

Parpart, Jane L., and Kathleen A. Staudt. *Women and the State in Africa*. Boulder, CO: Lynne Rienner Publishers, 1989.

Paupp, Terrence E. *Redefining Human Rights in the Struggle for Peace and Development*. Cambridge: Cambridge University Press, 2014.

Payne, Leigh A. *Unsettling Accounts: Neither Truth nor Reconciliation in Confessions of State Violence*. Durham, NC: Duke University Press, 2008.

Payne, Leigh A., and Paloma Aguilar. *Revealing New Truths About Spain's Violent Pasts: Perpetrators' Confession and Victim Exhumations*. New York: Palgrave Macmillan, 2016.

Pellow, Deborah. *Ghana: Coping with Uncertainty*. Boulder, CO: Westview Press, 1986.

Perugini, Nicola, and Neve Gordon. *The Human Right to Dominate*. Oxford Studies in Culture and Politics. Oxford: Oxford University Press, 2015.

———. "Is There a Human Right to Kill?" *Nation*, July 2, 2015. https://www.thenation.com/article/is-there-a-human-right-to-kill/.

Peters, Pauline E. "Inequality and Social Conflict Over Land in Africa." *Journal of Agrarian Change* 4, no. 3 (July 2004): 269–314.

Phillips-Fein, Kim. "The 9/11 Commission Report." *Radical History Review* 2007, no. 97 (December 21, 2007): 163–69. doi:10.1215/01636545-2006-022.

Pigou, Piers. "Accessing the Records of the Truth and Reconciliation Commission." In *Paper Wars: Access to Information in South Africa*, edited by Kate Allan, 17–55. Johannesburg: Witswatersrand University Press, 2009.

Pirouet, M. Louise. "Religion in Uganda under Amin." *Journal of Religion in Africa* 11, no. 1 (1980): 13–29.

Pommerolle, Marie-Emmanuelle. "Universal Claims and Selective Memory: A Comparative Perspective on the Culture of Opposition in Kenya." *Africa Today* 53, no. 2 (2006): 75–93.

Portelli, Alessandro. *The Death of Luigi Trastulli and Other Stories: Form and Meaning in Oral History*. Albany: SUNY Press, 1991.

Posel, Deborah. "History as Confession: The Case of the South African Truth and Reconciliation Commission." *Public Culture* 20, no. 1 (Winter 2008): 119–41.

———. "The TRC Report: What Kind of History? What Kind of Truth?" Working paper, Wits History Workshop, Johannesburg: University of Witswatersrand, June 11, 1999. http://wiredspace.wits.ac.za/handle/10539/8046.

Posner, Eric A. *Twilight of Human Rights Law*. Oxford: Oxford University Press, 2014.

Quarm, S.E. *Diplomatic Offensive: An Overview of Ghana's Diplomacy Under Dr. Kwame Nkrumah*. Accra, Ghana: Afram Publications, 1997.

Quinn, Joanna R. "Constraints: The Un-doing of the Ugandan Truth Commission." *Human Rights Quarterly* 26, no. 2 (May 2004): 401–27.

Quist-Arcton, Ofeibea. "Ghana's Kufuor Defends His Government's Record on Transparency, the Economy." AllAfrica. May 25, 2002. http://allafrica.com/stories/200205240737.html?page=3.

Radačić, Ivana. "Human Rights of Women and the Public/Private Divide in International Human Rights Law." *Croatian Yearbook of European Law and Policy* 3, no. 3 (March 18, 2008): 443–68.

Rajagopal, Balakrishnan. "International Law and the Development Encounter: Violence and Resistance at the Margins." In *On Violence, Money, Power, and Culture: Reviewing the Internationalist Legacy,* edited by American Society of International Law, 16–27. Proceedings of the 93rd Annual Meeting of the American Society of International Law. Washington, DC: ASIL, 1999.

———. "The Violence of Development." *Washington Post,* August 9, 2001. https://www .washingtonpost.com/archive/opinions/2001/08/09/the-violence-of-development /1b169574-3992-44ec-bff9-a1e42857f192/?utm_term=.9d8abd83a98a.

Ramphele, Mamphela. "Teach Me How to Be a Man: An Exploration of the Definition of Masculinity." In *Violence and Subjectivity*, edited by Veena Das, Arthur Kleinman, Mamphela Ramphele, and Pamela Reynolds, 102–19. Berkeley: University of California Press, 2000.

Ranger, Terence O. "Towards a Usable African Past." In *African Studies Since 1945: A Tribute to Basil Davidson,* edited by Christopher Fyfe, 17–30. London: Longman Group Limited, 1976.

———. "Personal Reminiscence and the Experience of the People in East Central Africa." *Oral History* 6, no. 1 (1978): 45–78.

Raschid-Sally, L., E. K. Akoto-Danso, E. A. K. Kalitsi, B. D. Ofori, and R. T. Koranteng. "The Resettlement Experience of Ghana Analyzed via Case Studies of the Akosombo and Kpong Dams." Paper presented at Exploring Experiences of Resettlement, 9th Annual Symposium on Poverty Research in Sri Lanka. November 2008. http://www.rlarrdc.org.in/images/The %20Resettlement%20Experience%20of%20Ghana%20-%20Final%20Paper.pdf

Rathbone, Richard. "Law, Politics and Interference." In *Recasting the Past: History Writing and Political Work in Modern Africa,* edited by Derek Peterson and Giacomo Macola, 113–24. Athens: Ohio University Press, 2009.

———. "Native Courts, Local Courts, Chieftaincy and the CPP in Ghana in the 1950s." *Journal of African Cultural Studies* 13, no. 1 (June 2000): 125–39.

Ravenhill, F. J. "Military Rule in Uganda: The Politics of Survival." *African Studies Review* 17, no. 1 (April 1974): 229–60.

Research Directorate, Immigration and Refugee Board, Canada. "Ghana: Update on the Fourth Republic," September 1, 1994. http://www.refworld.org/docid/3ae6a8118.html.

Reynolds, Pamela. *The Ground of All Making: State Violence, the Family, and Political Activists.* Berkeley: University of California Press, 2000.

Rich, Sam. "Africa's Village of Dreams." *Wilson Quarterly* 31, no. 2 (2007): 14–23.

Rimmer, Douglas. "The Crisis in the Ghana Economy." *Journal of Modern African Studies* 4, no. 1 (May 1966): 17–32.

Risse, Thomas, Stephen C. Ropp, and Kathryn Sikkink. *The Persistent Power of Human Rights: From Commitment to Compliance.* Cambridge: Cambridge University Press, 2013.

Robben, Antonius C. G. M. "How Traumatized Societies Remember: The Aftermath of Argentina's Dirty War." *Cultural Critique* 59 (2005): 120–64.

Roberts, Jonathan. "Remembering Korle Bu Hospital: Biomedical Heritage and Colonial Nostalgia in the *Golden Jubilee Souvenir.*" *History in Africa* 38 (January 1, 2011): 193–226.

Roberts, Richard. "History and Memory: The Power of Statist Narratives." *International Journal of African Historical Studies* 33, no. 3 (January 1, 2000): 513–22. doi:10.2307/3097432.

Robertson, Claire. "Comparative Advantage: Women in Trade in Accra, Ghana, and Nairobi, Kenya." In *African Market Women and Economic Power: The Role of Women in African Economic Development*, edited by Bessie House-Midamba and Felix K. Ekechi, 99–119. Contributions in Afro-American and African Studies 174. Westport, CT: Greenwood Press, 1995.

———. "The Death of Makola and Other Tragedies." *Canadian Journal of African Studies / Revue Canadienne des Études Africaines* 17, no. 3 (1983): 469–95.

———. "Economic Women: Women's Rights and Entrepreneurial Women." In *Ghana in Africa and the World: Essays in Honor of Adu Boahen*, 609–20. Trenton, NJ: Africa World Press, 2003.

———. "Response to John Campbell." *Canadian Journal of African Studies / Revue Canadienne des Études Africaines* 19, no. 2 (1985): 431–32. doi:10.2307/484836.

Robinson, Mary. "Advancing Economic, Social, and Cultural Rights: The Way Forward." *Human Rights Quarterly* 26, no. 4 (November 5, 2004): 866–72. doi:10.1353/hrq.2004.0054.

Rodney, Walter. *How Europe underdeveloped Africa*. London: Bogle-L'Ouverture Publication, 1972.

Roper, Steven, and Lilian Barria. "The Use of Truth and Reconciliation Commission in Africa: Does Establishing a Historical Record Lead to Reconciliation." Paper presented at the International Studies Association 48th Annual Convention, Chicago, IL, February 28, 2007.

Ross, Fiona C. "An Acknowledged Failure: Women, Voice, Violence and the South African Truth and Reconciliation Commission." In *Localizing Transitional Justice*, edited by Rosalind Shaw, Lars Waldorf and Pierre Hazan, 69–91. Stanford Studies in Human Rights. Stanford, CA: Stanford University Press, 2010.

———. *Bearing Witness: Women and the Truth and Reconciliation Commission in South Africa*. London: Pluto Press, 2003.

Rothchild, Donald. "Military Regime Performance: An Appraisal of the Ghana Experience, 1972–78." *Comparative Politics* 12, no. 4 (1980): 459–79. doi:10.2307/421836.

Ruff-O'Herne, Jan. "Fifty Years of Silence: Cry of the Raped." In *Listening to the Silences: Women and War,* edited by Helen Durham and Tracey Gurd, 3–8. Vol. 8 of International Humanitarian Law Series. Leiden, The Netherlands: Martinus Nijhoff Publishers, 2005.

Ryan, Selwyn. "The Theory and Practice of African One Partyism: The CPP Re-examined." *Canadian Journal of African Studies / Revue Canadienne des Études Africaines* 4, no. 2 (April 1, 1970): 145–72. doi:10.2307/483858.

Saaka, Yakubu. "Recurrent Themes in Ghanaian Politics: Kwame Nkrumah's Legacy." *Journal of Black Studies* 24, no. 3 (March 1994): 263–80. doi:10.2307/2784582.

Sachs, Jeffrey, John W. McArthur, Guido Schmidt-Traub, Margaret Kruk, Chandrika Bahadur, Michael Faye, and Gordon McCord. "Ending Africa's Poverty Trap." *Brookings Papers on Economic Activity* 35, no. 1 (2004): 117–240. https://www.brookings.edu/wp-content/uploads/2004/01/2004a_bpea_sachs.pdf.

Sagoe, K. Amanfo. "Valuation Acquisition and Compensation for Purposes of Resettlement." In *Volta Resettlement Experience*, edited by Robert Chambers, 58–77. New York: Praeger Publishers, 1970.

Sahadeo, Jeff. "'Without the Past There Is No Future': Archives, History, and Authority in Uzbekistan." In *Archive Stories: Facts, Fictions and the Writing of History*, edited by Antoinette Burton, 45–67. Durham, NC: Duke University Press, 2005.

Sanders, Mark. *Ambiguities of Witnessing: Law and Literature in the Time of a Truth Commission.* Stanford, CA: Stanford University Press, 2007.

———. "Renegotiating Responsibility After Apartheid: Listening to Perpetrator Testimony." *Journal of Gender, Social Policy and the Law* 10, no. 3 (2002): 587–95.

"Saving Amina Lawal: Human Rights Symbolism and the Dangers of Colonialism." *Harvard Law Review* 117, no. 7 (2004): 2365–386. doi:10.2307/4093341.

Saunders, Christopher. "Historians and the South African Truth Commission." *History Compass* 2, no. 1 (January 1, 2004): n.p. doi:10.1111/j.1478-0542.2004.00092.x.

Saunders, Rebecca. "Lost in Translation: Expressions of Human Suffering, the Language of Human Rights and the South African Truth and Reconciliation Commission." *SUR International Journal on Human Rights* 5, no. 9 (December 2008): 50–69. http://www.conectas.org/en/actions /sur-journal/issue/9/1000083-sobre-o-intraduzivel-sofrimento-humano-a-linguagem-de -direitos-humanos-e-a-comissao-de-verdade-e-reconciliacao-da-africa-do-sul.

Schaffer, Kay, and Sidonie. Smith. "Conjunctions: Life Narratives in the Field of Human Rights." *Biography* 27, no. 1 (2004): 1–24.

———. *Human Rights and Narrated Lives: The Ethics of Recognition.* New York: Palgrave Macmillan, 2004.

Scherer, Michael. "Barack Obama's Speech to Africa." *Time*, July 11, 2009. http://swampland .time.com/2009/07/11/barack-obamas-speech-to-africa/.

Schleh, Eugene P. "Post-Service Careers of World War Two Veterans: The Cases of Gold Coast and Uganda." Paper presented at the Annual Meeting of the African Studies Association, vol. 3, New York, November 1967.

Schneider, Leander. "Colonial Legacies and Postcolonial Authoritarianism in Tanzania: Connects and Disconnects." *African Studies Review* 49, no. 1 (2006): 93–118.

Scudder, T. "Development-Induced Relocation and Refugee Studies: 37 Years of Change and Continuity Among Zambia's Gwembe Tonga." *Journal of Refugee Studies* 6, no. 2 (January 1, 1993): 123–52. doi:10.1093/jrs/6.2.123.

Scully, Pamela. "Gender, History and Human Rights." In *Gender and Culture at the Limit of Rights*, edited by Dorothy L. Hodgson, 17–31. Philadelphia: University of Pennsylvania Press, 2011.

Ševčenko, Liz. "Sites of Conscience: Reimagining Reparations." *Change Over Time* 1, no. 1 (Spring 2011): 6–33.

Shaw, Rosalind. "Displacing Violence: Making Pentecostal Memory in Postwar Sierra Leone." *Cultural Anthropology* 22, no. 1 (February 2007): 66–93.

———. "Linking Justice with Reintegration? Ex-combatants and the Sierra Leone Experiment." In *Localizing Transitional Justice: Intervention and Priorities After Mass Violence*, edited by Rosalind Shaw, Lars Waldorf, and Pierre Hazan, 111–34. Stanford, CA: Stanford University Press, 2010.

———. "Memory Frictions: Localizing the Truth and Reconciliation Commission in Sierra Leone." *International Journal of Transitional Justice* 1, no. 2 (July 1, 2007): 183–207. doi:10.1093/ijtj/ijm008.

Shaw, Rosalind, and Lars Waldorf, eds. *Localizing Transitional Justice: Intervention and Priorities After Mass Violence.* Stanford Studies in Human Rights. Stanford, CA: Stanford University Press, 2010.

Shefner, Jon. "Do You Think Democracy Is a Magical Thing? From Basic Needs to Democratization in Informal Politics." In *Out of the Shadows: Political Action and the Informal Economy in Latin America*, edited by Patricia Fernández-Kelly and Jon Shefner, 241–68. University Park: Pennsylvania State University Press, 2006.

Shepherd, George W. "The Price of Progress." *Africa Today* 9, no. 10 (December 1962): 4–14.

Shipley, Jesse Weaver. "The Market Decides If We Are Free." Africa Is a Country. January 16, 2017. http://africasacountry.com/2017/01/the-market-decides-if-we-are-free/.

Shivji, Issa. *The Concept of Human Rights in Africa*. Dakar, Senegal: CODESRIA,1989.

———. "Is Might a Right in International Human Rights? Notes on the Imperial Assault on the Right of People to Self-Determination." In *Taking Stock of Human Rights Situation in Africa*, edited by Sifuni Ernest Mchome. Dar es Salaam: Faculty of Law, University of Dar es Salaam, 2002.

Sikkink, Kathryn. *Evidence for Hope: Making Human Rights Work in the 21st Century*. Princeton, NJ: Princeton University Press, 2017.

———. *The Justice Cascade: How Human Rights Prosecutions Are Changing World Politics*. New York: W. W. Norton, 2011.

Sitze, Adam. *The Impossible Machine: A Genealogy of South Africa's Truth and Reconciliation Commission*. Ann Arbor: University of Michigan Press, 2016.

Skjerdal, Terje. "Mapping the Gap: Finding a *raison d'être* in South Africa's TRC's media hearings." *Ecquid Novi: African Journalism Studies* 21 no. 2 (2000): 175–89.

Slyomovics, Susan. "The Argument from Silence: Morocco's Truth Commission and Women Political Prisoners." *Journal of Middle East Women's Studies* 1, no. 3 (Fall 2005): 73–95.

Smith, Andrew Brodie. "Review of Martin, Ged, Past Futures: The Impossible Necessity of History." H-Canada, H-Review, October 2005. http://www.h-net.org/reviews/showrev.php?id=10920.

Smith, Tammy A. "Remembering and Forgetting a Contentious Past: Voices from the Italo-Yugoslav Frontier." *American Behavioral Scientist* 51, no. 10 (June 2008): 1538–54.

Special Correspondent. "Issue for Our New Constitution (3)." *Legon Observer*, October 14, 1966.

Spengler, Joseph J. "Right to Work: A Backward Glance." *Journal of Economic History* 28, no. 2 (June 1968): 171–96.

Spillius, Alex. "Barack Obama Tells Africa to Stop Blaming Colonialism for Problems." *Telegraph*, July 9, 2009. http://www.telegraph.co.uk/news/worldnews/africaandindian ocean/5778804/Barack-Obama-tells-Africa-to-stop-blaming-colonialism-for-problems .html.

Spivak, Gayatri Chakravorty. "Can the Subaltern Speak?" In *Colonial Discourse and Post-Colonial Theory: A Reader*, edited by Patrick Williams and Laura Chrisman, 66–111. Hertfordshire: Harvester Wheatsheaf, 1994.

Staley, David J. "A History of the Future." *History and Theory*, no. 41 (December 2002): 72–89.

Stanley, Elizabeth. "Evaluating the Truth and Reconciliation Commission." *Journal of Modern African Studies* 39, no. 3 (September 2001): 525–46.

Stern, Steve J., and Scott Strauss. *The Human Rights Paradox: Universality and Its Discontents*. Madison: University of Wisconsin, 2014.

Subotic, Jelena. *Hijacked Justice: Dealing with the Past in the Balkans*. Ithaca, NY: Cornell University Press, 2009.

Suh, Jae-Jung. "Truth and Reconciliation in South Korea." *Critical Asian Studies* 42, no. 4 (December 2010): 503–24. doi:10.1080/14672715.2010.515386.

Summerfield, Derek. "Raising the Dead: War, Reparation, and the Politics Of Memory." *BMJ* 311, no. 7003 (1995): 495–97.

Sutton, Inez. "Law, Chieftaincy and Conflict in Colonial Ghana: The Ada Case." *African Affairs* 83, no. 330 (January 1, 1984): 41–62.

Tetteh, M. N. *Anatomy of Rumour Mongering in Ghana: Factors Contributory to the Overthrow of Dr. Kwame Nkrumah.* Accra, Ghana: Ghana Publicity, 1976.

Theidon, Kimberly. "Histories of Innocence: Postwar Stories in Peru." In *Localizing Transitional Justice: Interventions and Priorities after Mass Violence,* edited by Rosalind Shaw, Lars Waldorf, and Pierre Hazan, 92–110. Stanford, CA: Stanford University Press, 2010.

Thompson, W. Scott. *Ghana's Foreign Policy, 1957–1966; Diplomacy, Ideology, and the New State.* Princeton, NJ: Princeton University Press, 1969.

Torpey, John, ed. *Politics and the Past: On Repairing Historical Injustices.* World Social Change. New York: Rowman and Littlefield Publishers, 2003.

Trachtman, Lester N. "The Labor Movement of Ghana: A Study in Political Unionism." *Economic Development and Cultural Change* 10, no. 2 (January 1962): 183–200.

Trinch, Shonna. "Risky Subjects: Narrative, Literary Testimonio and Legal Testimony." *Dialectical Anthropology* 34, no. 2 (June 1, 2010): 179–204.

Trouillot, Michel-Rolph. *Silencing the Past: Power and the Production of History.* Beacon Press, 1995.

Truth and Reconciliation Commission, Grenada. *"Redeeming the Past, a Time for Healing": Report on Certain Political Events Which Occurred in Grenada 1976–1991.* Grenada: Truth and Reconciliation Commission, 2006.

Tutu, Desmond. *No Future Without Forgiveness.* New York: Doubleday, 1999.

Twining, William. *Human Rights, Southern Voices: Francis Deng, Abdullahi An-Na'im, Yash Ghai and Upendra Baxi.* Cambridge: Cambridge University Press, 2009.

Twumasi, Yaw. "Ghana's Draft Constitutional Proposals." *Transition,* no. 37 (1968): 43–52.

Taalor, Laura K., and Alexander Dukalskis. "Old Truth and New Politics: Does Truth Commission 'Publicness' Impact Democratization?" *Journal of Peace Research* 49, no. 5 (2012): 671–84.

Uche, U. U. "Changes in Ghana Law since the Military Take-Over." *Journal of African Law* 10, no. 2 (1966): 106–11.

Udombana, Nsongurua J. "So Far, so Fair: The Local Remedies Rule in the Jurisprudence of the African Commission on Human and Peoples' Rights." *American Journal of International Law* 97, no. 1 (January 1, 2003): 1–37. doi:10.2307/3087102.

Valji, Nahla. *Gender Justice and Reconciliation.* Dialogue on Globalization. Occasional Paper no. 25. Berlin: Friedrich-Ebert-Stiftung, November 2007. http://library.fes.de/pdf-files/iez/05000.pdf.

——. *Ghana's National Reconciliation Commission: A Comparative Assessment.* Occasional Paper Series. International Center for Transitional Justice, September 2006. http://www.dhnet.org.br/verdade/mundo/gana/cv_15_gana_csvr.pdf

Vaughan, Megan. "Reported Speech and Other Kinds of Testimony." In *African Words, African Voices: Critical Practices in Oral History,* edited by Luise White, Stephan F. Miescher, and David W. Cohen, 53–77. Bloomington: Indiana University Press, 2001.

Vehnamaki, Mika. "Culture and Economic Development in Ghana: The Conventional Wisdom Revisited." *Nordic Journal of African Studies* 8, no. 1 (1999): 57–77.

Vella, Louise. *Translating Transitional Justice: The Solomon Islands Truth and Reconciliation Commission.* SSGM Discussion Paper 2014/2. Canberra: State, Society and Government in Melanesia, Australian National University, 2014. http://bellschool.anu.edu.au/sites/default/files/publications/attachments/2015-12/DP-2014-02-Vella-ONLINE_0.pdf.

Verbuyst, Rafael. "History, Historians and the South African Truth and Reconciliation Commission." *New Contree* 66 (2013): 1–26.

Verdoolaege, Annelies. *Reconciliation Discourse: The Case of the Truth and Reconciliation Commission*. Amsterdam/Philadelphia: John Benjamins Publishing, 2008.

Vertzberger, Yaacov Y. I. "The Antinomies of Collective Political Trauma: A Pre-theory." *Political Psychology* 18, no. 4 (December 1997): 863–76. doi:10.2307/3792214.

Viljoen, Frans. *International Human Rights Law in Africa*. Oxford: Oxford University Press, 2012.

———. "The Special Rapporteur on Prisons and Conditions of Detention in Africa: Achievements and Possibilities." *Human Rights Quarterly* 27, no. 1 (February 1, 2005): 125–71.

Viljoen, Frans, and Lirette Louw. "State Compliance with the Recommendations of the African Commission on Human and Peoples' Rights, 1994–2004." *American Journal of International Law* 101, no. 1 (January 1, 2007): 1–34.

Vora, Jay A., and Erika Vora. "The Effectiveness of South Africa's Truth and Reconciliation Commission: Perceptions of Xhosa, Afrikaner, and English South Africans." *Journal of Black Studies* 34, no. 3 (January 2004): 301–22. doi:10.2307/3180939.

Walker, Alice. *In Search of Our Mothers' Gardens*. New York: Mariner: 2003.

Walker, Charles F. "Teaching Truth Commissions." *Radical History Review* 2007, no. 97 (December 21, 2007): 134–42. doi:10.1215/01636545-2006-019.

Waltz, Susan. "Reclaiming and Rebuilding the History of the Universal Declaration of Human Rights." *Third World Quarterly* 23, no. 3 (June 2002): 437–48.

Watts, Michael. "Petro-violence: Some Thoughts on Community, Extraction, and Political Ecology." Berkeley Workshop on Environmental Politics Working Paper 99-1. Institute of International Studies, University of California, Berkeley, 1999. http://escholarship.org/uc/item/7zh116zd#page-1.

Weah, Aaron. "Hopes and Uncertainties: Liberia's Journey to End Impunity." *International Journal of Transitional Justice* 6, no. 2 (July 1, 2012): 331–43. doi:10.1093/ijtj/ijs007.

Weist, Katherine M. "Development Refugees: Indians, Africans, and the Big Dams." The Elisabeth Colson Lecture, Refugee Studies Center, Department of International Development, University of Oxford, March 9, 1994.

Weld, Kirsten. *Paper Cadavers: The Archives of Dictatorship in Guatemala*. Durham, NC: Duke University Press, 2014.

Werbner, Richard. *Memory and the Postcolony: African Anthropology and the Critique of Power*. London: Zed Books, 1998.

White, Hayden. "Historical Emplotment and the Problem of Truth." In *Probing the Limits of Representation: Nazism and the "Final Solution,"* edited by Saul Friedländer, 37–53. Cambridge, MA: Harvard University Press, 1992.

White, Lucie E., and Jeremy Perelman. *Stones of Hope: How African Activists Reclaim Human Rights to Challenge Global Poverty*. Stanford, CA: Stanford University Press, 2011.

White, Luise. "Telling More: Lies, Secrets, and History." *History and Theory* 39, no. 4 (December 2000): 11–22.

———. *Speaking with Vampires: Rumor and History in Colonial Africa*. Berkeley: University of California Press, 2000.

Whitfield, Lindsay. "'Change for a Better Ghana': Party Competition, Institutionalization and Alternation in Ghana's 2008 Elections." *African Affairs* 108, no. 433 (2009): 621–41.

Whitfield, Lindsay. "Growth without Economic Transformation: Economic Impacts of Ghana's Political Settlement." Working Paper. DIIS Working Paper. Copenhagen, Denmark: Danish Institute for International Studies, DIIS, 2011.

Whitlock, Gillian. "In the Second Person: Narrative Transactions in Stolen Generations Testimony." *Biography* 24, no. 1 (February 1, 2001): 197–214. doi:10.1353/bio.2001.0026.

———. "Review Essay: The Power of Testimony." *Law and Literature* 19, no. 1 (2007): 139–52. doi:10.1525/lal.2007.19.1.139.

Wiebelhaus-Brahm, Eric. *Truth Commissions and Transitional Societies: The Impact on Human Rights and Democracy.* London: Routledge, 2010.

Wiesel, Elie. "A Tribute to Human Rights," in *The Universal Declaration of Human Rights: Fifty Years and Beyond*, edited by Yael Danieli, Elsa Stamatopoulou, and Clarence J. Dias, 3–4. Amityville, New York: Baywood Publishing, 1999.

Wieviorka, Annette, and Jared Stark. "The Witness in History." *Poetics Today* 27, no. 2 (July 1, 2006): 385–97.

Wieviorka, Annette. *The Era of the Witness.* Ithaca, NY: Cornell University Press, 2007.

Wilcox, Luke. "Reshaping Civil Society Through a Truth Commission: Human Rights in Morocco's Process of Political Reform." *International Journal of Transitional Justice* 3, no. 1 (2009): 49–68.

Wilder, Gary. "Practicing Citizenship in Imperial Paris." In *Civil Society and the Political Imagination in Africa*, edited by John L. Comaroff and Jean Comaroff, 44–71. Critical Perspectives. Chicago: University of Chicago Press, 1999.

Williams, Michael W. "Nkrumahism as an Ideological Embodiment of Leftist Thought Within the African World." *Journal of Black Studies* 15, no. 1 (1984): 117–34.

Wilson, Richard. *The Politics of Truth and Reconciliation in South Africa: Legitimizing the Post-apartheid State.* Cambridge: Cambridge University Press, 2001.

Wingo, Ajume. "The Odyssey of Human Rights." *Transition*, no. 102 (January 1, 2010): 120–38. doi:10.2979/TRS.2010.-.102.120.

Wiseberg, Laurie S. "The African Commission on Human and Peoples' Rights." *Issue: A Journal of Opinion* 22, no. 2 (July 1, 1994): 34–41. doi:10.2307/1166731.

Wohlgemuth, Lennart, and Ebrima Sall, eds. *Human Rights, Regionalism and the Dilemmas of Democracy in Africa.* Dakar, Senegal: Council for the Development of Social Science Research in Africa, 2006.

World Economic Forum, the World Bank, and the African Development Bank. *The Africa Competitiveness Report 2011.* Geneva: World Economic Forum, 2011. http://documents.worldbank .org/curated/en/550331468010248107/pdf/628730PUB0Afri00Box0361495B0PUBLIC0 .pdf

Wright, Kwesi. "Criticism of Billy Graham." *Ashanti Pioneer*, January 30, 1960.

Wright, Melissa W. "Epistemological Ignorances and Fighting for the Disappeared : Lessons from Mexico." *Antipode* 49 (2017): 249–69.

Yankah, Kwesi. "Narrative in Times of Crisis: AIDS Stories in Ghana." *Journal of Folklore Research* 41, no. 2/3 (December 2004): 181–98.

Yayoh, Wilson Kwame. "Resurgence of Multi-party Rule in Ghana 1990–2004: A Historical Review." *Transactions of the Historical Society of Ghana* 10 (2006–2007): 125–47.

Yifru, Katema, J. Rudolph Grimes, Ibrahim Abboud, Mongi Slim, Kwame Nkrumah, Louis Lansana Beavogui, Leopold Sedar Senghor, and Alhaji Sir Abubaker Tafawa Balewa. "Africa Speaks to the United Nations: A Symposium of Aspirations and Concerns Voiced by Representative Leaders at the UN." *International Organization* 16, no. 2 (Spring 1962): 303–30. doi:10.2307/2705387.

Yoneyama, Lisa. "Politicizing Justice." *Critical Asian Studies* 42, no. 4 (December 2010): 653–71. doi:10.1080/14672715.2010.515391.

Yoon Chung Ro. "Politics of Memory and Commemoration of the Vietnam War in Korea." *Korean Social Sciences Review* 3, no. 1 (2013): 1–32. http://s-space.snu.ac.kr/handle/10371 /83055/browse?type=subject&order=DESC&rpp=30&value=Transitional+Justice.

Zeleza, Paul Tiyambe. "The Struggle for Human Rights in Africa." *Canadian Journal of African Studies / Revue Canadienne des Études Africaines* 41, no. 3 (2007): 474–506.

INDEX

ACKNOWLEDGMENTS

This work would not have been completed without the support and solidarity of numerous people and communities. My immense gratitude extends to all the family members, mentors, colleagues, and fellow travelers who offered direction, sustenance, and assistance at critical moments in the research and writing process.

Without attempting to name all the individuals who have generously given of their time, expertise and insight, I would like to draw attention to a few organizations whose dedicated staff and leadership enabled me to pursue this project. The University of Ghana's Balme Library, the Public Records and Archives Administration Department of the Ghana National Archives, the Center for Democratic Development–Ghana, and the Human Rights Archive at the Duke University David M. Rubenstein Rare Book and Manuscript Library were critical parts of the process. The editor and editorial team of the University of Pennsylvania Press had faith in this book from the beginning and improved it along the way. Thanks also to Selorm Dogoe who contributed his artwork.

My thanks to Mohammed Awudu, the brilliant graphic artist whose work graces the cover of this book.

I am blessed to have siblings, family and friends who have been sources of divine renewal, creativity, and support throughout the years. I am thankful for the love and patience of Kerim, Nazim, and Kofi. Finally, words cannot express my gratitude to my parents. Their example of love, service and courage has always been my touchstone.

And to the one person who made this book possible, in ways practical and existential, but who is no longer here: your hand is on all that is good about this work. I dearly wish you could share this moment.